HISTORY from THINGS

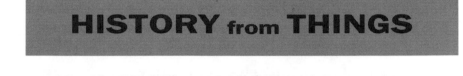

HISTORY from THINGS

Essays on Material Culture

Edited by Steven Lubar and W. David Kingery

SMITHSONIAN INSTITUTION PRESS
WASHINGTON AND LONDON

Copy Editor: Gretchen Smith Mui
Production Editor: Duke Johns
Designer: Kathleen Sims

Library of Congress Cataloging-in-Publication Data
History from things : essays on material culture /
edited by Steven Lubar and W. David Kingery.
     p.   cm.
   Includes bibliographical references.
   ISBN 1-56098-204-7 (alk. paper)
   1. Archaeology and history. 2. Material
culture. I. Lubar, Steven. II. Kingery, W. David.
CC77.H5H59 1993
930.1—dc20   92-20535

British Library Cataloging-in-Publication Data is
available

Contents

Introduction

Steven Lubar and
W. David Kingery

We are surrounded by things, and we are surrounded by history. But too seldom do we use the artifacts that make up our environment to understand the past. Too seldom do we try to read objects as we read books—to understand the people and times that created them, used them, and discarded them.

In part, this is because it is not easy to read history from things. They are illegible to those who know how to read only writing. They are mute to those who listen only for pronouncements from the past. But they do speak; they can be read.

But how? Scholars from a wide range of fields have approached reading history from things in a variety of ways. No one field has a monopoly; none has found all the answers. Not only are their methods different; the questions they ask, the objects they ask them of, and the uses to which they put the answers are different, too.

The study of artifacts in relation to past human behavior might serve as a broad definition of archaeology. Everything included under this umbrella could be described as one or another species of archaeology. In practice, however, many archaeologists disengage themselves from the study of belief, the province of cultural anthropology, and even more so from aesthetics, the province of art history. And for the most part archaeologists do not use documents as artifacts unless they are written on clay tablets. The well-developed fields of historical archaeology and industrial archaeology tend to be seen as cooperative efforts between archaeologists dealing with things and historians dealing with documentary evidence.

Similarly, the subject of *History from Things* might be considered a branch of history, differing from the mainstream of that field only in the nature of the evidence. Historians traditionally use documents rather than artifacts in their effort to understand the past. But the artifact-document dichotomy is to a great extent artificial; documents are a species of artifact, and some historians, notably paleographers, make use of the document as artifact. By neglecting all but a narrow class of artifacts, those with writing on them, historians have missed opportunities. Artifacts are remnants of the environment of earlier periods, a portion of the historical experience available for direct observation. Not only do artifacts present new evidence to support historical arguments; they also suggest new arguments and provide a level of rhetorical support to arguments that mere documents cannot begin to approach. Artifacts, especially when used in conjunction with the sorts of history gleaned from documentary sources, widen our view of history as they increase the evidence for historical interpretations.

Art historians, a third group for whom artifacts provide data about history, consider artifacts on an aesthetic level. More than other groups of scholars interested in the past, art historians have insisted on the primacy of the sensory reaction to an artifact, the link the artifact provides with its creator. Only a small minority of art historians have investigated beneath the perceived surfaces of the artifacts, and most have placed the artistic creations of the past in a category separate from less purely aesthetic creations.

In the past decade materials scientists, conservation scientists, and archaeometrists have developed increasingly sophisticated means of studying, measuring, and characterizing artifacts. The availability of added levels of artifact data—such as the capability of carbon-14 dating with milligram samples of material, evaluating internal and surface structures with electron microscopy, and determining chemical analyses of trace elements to parts per billion—provides impressive new opportunities; it also places a heavy burden on archaeologists, historians, and other students of material culture to use these new tools effectively. We still have a long way to go.

The contributors to this volume fall into all these categories as well as others: anthropology, folklore, history of technology, cultural geography, and so forth. They can also be identified by the geographical area—the United States, China, Italy, the Near East—and the time frame— twentieth century, nineteenth century, Renaissance, third millennium B.C.—on which they focus. These are the usual divisions of scholarly symposia, university department organization, professional publications, and both formal and informal professional groupings.

In this volume, however, we have examined not the differences in the groups but the similarities. We have brought together these various peer groups and encouraged interaction by focusing on the artifacts, the material culture, which they all use as primary data for developing inferences about cultural, social, and other types of history.

This volume is based on papers presented at the conference "History from Things: The Use of Objects in Understanding the Past," held at the Smithsonian Institution in April 1989. The goal of that conference was to see whether a group of distinguished scholars in different fields using artifacts in different ways could pierce the boundaries separating them, communicate with one another, and discover common ground. For that purpose a small group met at the Smithsonian for a day and a half in April 1988. It was agreed that establishing a meaningful dialogue would not be easy but was worth attempting. With the encouragement of Arthur Molella, chairman of the department of history of science and technology at the National Museum of American History, Roger Kennedy, director of the National Museum of American History, Robert Hoffman, assistant secretary for research, and Robert McC. Adams, secretary of the Smithsonian Institution, the 1989 meeting was organized. About fifty scholars participated, and a wide peer group was represented. At the meeting we found that material culture did provide a topic through which meaningful communication among different specialists could begin. At the end of the meeting it was agreed that it would be appropriate to publish these working papers and continue interdisciplinary discussion at future meetings.

One purpose of an introduction is to provide an overview that will help the reader organize and comprehend the essays that constitute this volume. Since our whole intention has been to focus on the role of material culture studies as providing a meeting point for scholars from a variety of established disciplines, it hardly seems appropriate to attempt a disciplinary organization. Some contributors discuss theories of artifact interpretation—Jules David Prown, an art historian; Jacques Maquet, an anthropologist; and Rita Wright and C. C. Lamberg-Karlovsky, archaeologists. A group of contributors are concerned with the history of technology: Robert B. Gordon, Steven Lubar, W. David Kingery, Robert W. Bagley, and Rita Wright. Other contributors focus more directly on sociological concerns (Mihaly Csikszentmihalyi) and cultural concerns (Jacques Maquet, Jessica Rawson, Thomas Williamson, Peirce Lewis, Mark P. Leone, Barbara J. Little, Ian W. Brown, and Michael Owen Jones). But theoretical issues, methodological issues, technological issues, and cultural issues are included in virtually every presentation, so these divisions may be more in the eye of the beholder than in the content of what are multifaceted essays. The final essay, by John Dixon Hunt, warns of the inherent danger of ethnocentric interpretations of material culture evidence, and we must be equally wary of discipline-oriented overviews.

Each essay focuses on one or more artifacts that are studied not in their own right but as a means to an end. (Indeed, one omission that prevents this volume from constituting a complete range of approaches to artifact study is the absence of artifacts that have been self-consciously created as art objects and interpreted as art.) In some of these papers an object is analyzed to consider issues important for developing theory or developing method. Other essays use artifactual data to illustrate the application of a theory or method. These studies are applied to understanding human beliefs, behavior, and history in the cultural and social context of the individual, family, community, or organized society.

In the opening essay Jules Prown argues that artifacts provide a way in which the past can be directly reexperienced with our senses and, thus, a way of getting at historical beliefs. The style of objects, particularly utilitarian un-self-conscious creations, reflects not only craft traditions and the individual creator but also the contemporary culture in which they were developed. Seen as cultural creations, both their associations and structure invoke multiple metaphors that serve to materialize belief. A teapot and two sorts of card tables illustrate how analysis of material objects can expose cultural truths. Mihaly Csikszentmihalyi's essay complements Prown's by focusing on why people want and need things to objectify the self, organize the mind, demonstrate power, and symbolize their place in society.

The kinds of selves we choose to build are rooted in a culture that today includes an addiction to things, but that addiction is not always inevitable. Jacques Maquet points out that there are several kinds of meaning inherent in an object. Artifacts are instruments intended to be used, and inferences about this utilitarian purpose are not culture-sensitive. But artifacts also serve as signs, and their meaning as signs usually changes when the audience changes. When objects are used as symbols, as indicators by association, and finally as conventions or referents, their meaning becomes increasingly culture-specific. A full interpretation of objects, understanding what they mean for the people who make and use them, requires knowing beliefs and perceptions that are external to the object itself.

In an entirely different and somewhat unexpected approach, Robert Friedel asks us to consider the implications of the actual material used to make the artifact—the significations of wood, porcelain, gold, plastic, aluminum, and so forth. The reasons for using particular materials and the values attached to different materials are affected by changed technologies and changed perceptions; they provide new insights into understanding material culture. Jessica Rawson introduces the concept that objects have a lineage, an ancestry, that is as essential in understanding their roles in and reflection of society as their current appearance and function. Three-legged Chinese bronze *ding* ritual vessels were first made in the Shang dynasty beginning circa 1700 B.C.; they remained objects of intense preoccupation for both Chiang Kaishek and Mao Zedong four and a half millennia later. In the interim they were continually unburied, rediscovered, and copied. In each of five eras of rediscovery they have accumulated new values and roles in a lineage that can be taken as a paradigm illustrating the need to interpret objects in a historical context.

Robert Gordon directly addresses the issues involved in interpreting artifacts for the history of technology. He takes the artifact as the primary evidence in a field where documentary sources are generally one step removed from actuality and often have questionable motivations. Two basic steps are proposed: first, artifact analysis by archaeometry (the study of internal structure, formal analysis including reproductions and engineering interpretations, surficial marking, and physical properties) and, second, contextual analysis (the study of backward linkages to materials used, human and social components of design and manufacture as well as forward linkages to users and observers). This methodology is applied to a nineteenth-century axe from Connecticut, a nineteenth-century bloomery smelting slag from New York State, and a twentieth-century steam locomotive. Gordon concludes that although archaeometric analysis is essential for a complete investigation, the most significant history results from contextual interpretations.

Four essays are concerned with cultural landscapes as artifact. Thomas Williamson concentrates on the development of garden parks in eighteenth-century England by looking at the "natural" landscape design rather than contemporary written descriptions. This approach allows him to focus on the social function of parkland at a time of social stress in the rural countryside and social change in the ranks of the gentry. He concludes that parks proliferated because they helped define social roles in a changing social system. Studying the artifacts allows one to understand meanings of texts and illuminates the social history embedded in them. Peirce Lewis illustrates his method of reading the landscape as a kind of cultural document by taking us on a tour of a small town in Pennsylvania. This requires first seeing this human manipulation of the environment in its geographical and historical context. As closer views are encompassed, a picture emerges as to what was important to the people who lived there, of the way America was converted from a rural world to an urban one, and how a small town changed from a bustling county center to an empty shell. Ian Brown investigates a Watertown, Massachusetts, cemetery as a cultural landscape in which he traces the burial arrangements of the Coolidge family over six generations. The gravestones and their relationships to one another highlight social relationships not evident in the written record and contribute to a deeper understanding of local history. Mark Leone and Barbara Little use archaeological data along with historical records to study the late seventeenth-century town plan of Annapolis, which they compare as an artifact with a natural history museum created by Charles Peale in Philadelphia. Each of these artifacts reflects a way of categorizing material and a vision of order that are part of a cultural continuum and that, Leone and Little argue, serve as a material culture representation of genealogy—not only the way things are but also how they inevitably came to be that way, evidence of the continuity between past and present.

In the realm of American folklore Michael Jones takes a different approach, focusing on the relationships of artifacts—in this instance, chairs of southeastern Kentucky—to the behavioral characteristics of the producer, the producer's technology, the consumer's perceptions and stipulations, and particularly the interaction of product and producer. The behavioral approach reveals why certain objects were made, what they mean, and why they are made in a particular material form and style.

Three essays use technological artifacts to illustrate the development and application of material culture interpretation in a historical context. Steven Lubar looks at how factory machines reveal culture and how culture reflects machines. How machines are constructed illustrates their role as mediators between managers and workers; their efficiency turns out to be a social construct. Machine design reflects politics, on both a local and a national scale, and the same broad cultural trends as do other artifacts. Machine design also reflects the structure of society and the patterns of technology. Historians must endeavor to investigate the context and conflicting forces that create these patterns. David Kingery makes explicit the requirements of Robert Gordon's backward- and forward-linkage components of an artifact by insisting that artifacts be set into a system of technologies—material selection, design, manufacture, distribution, and use. Artifacts participate in activities where they are associated with social organization, human perception, and human behavior. The interaction among perception, use, and manufacturing technology is illustrated by Italian Renaissance painterly maiolica, which represents a paradigm change in a normally conservative ceramic technology. Kingery suggests that couplings of different lineages are a principal source of technological change. Robert Bagley presents an elegant description of the manufacture of Chinese Zhou bronze casting during the sixth and fifth centuries B.C. Detailed examination of the objects reveals the pattern-block technique, which allowed an efficient division of labor. The process implies a factory system of production in China as early as the fifth century B.C. with a division of labor and a highly organized workshop that are nowhere attested to in documentary sources.

Prehistorians have no documents to shore up their artifact interpretations, and Rita Wright notes this limitation in her discussion of technological style in the framework of a structural analysis. She draws on David Keightley's cognitive archaeology of Shang-dynasty China as a paradigm for discussing the production, use, and inspiration of Harappan pottery. C. C. Lamberg-Karlovsky's saga of the interpretations of a widespread class of soft-stone carved chlorite vessels with an intercultural style decoration illustrates some of the difficulties facing prehistorians. In archaeology different schools have developed that deeply influence the way in which material culture artifacts are interpreted. For these vessels there has been a variety of approaches, including narrative descriptions, archaeometric determinations of provenance, inferences about market networks, and interpretations of their use for rituals of death and burial. As evidences of form and style, associations, chemical composition, provenance, and spatial distribution accumulate, the bounds of interpretations are notably narrowed; materialist conceptions and symbolic appreciations complement each other in the complex meanings of things.

In the final essay John Dixon Hunt's commentary adopts the viewpoint that most material culture studies should reflect, as in historical archaeology, the symbiotic relationship of words and things—a nexus that should be welcomed rather than avoided. He also warns against the problem of invoking ethnocentric interpretations based on our own cultural views. Finally, seeing artifacts as signs, he proposes that their reading requires precisely the same sorts of interpretation and translation necessary for the interpretation of texts and utterances.

The range of artifacts that these contributors have used as exemplars is truly remarkable: teapots, Chippendale tables, Federal card tables, Chinese bronze vessels, seventeenth-century parks, a Pennsylvania town, a New England cemetery, the town plan of Annapolis, Maryland, Peale's natural history museum, southeastern Kentucky chairs, machine tools, Italian Renaissance maiolica, axes, bloomery slags, steam engines, Harappan pottery, and carved stone vessels. Each of these objects illustrates the development or application of theory or method and the ways in which material culture can contribute to our understanding of cultural and social history.

In searching for similarities and differences between the way different peer groups specializing in a variety of geographical areas and time periods function, it may be helpful to investigate just how they interact with artifacts. Attributes such as size, shape, texture, color, designs, weight, volume, and material composition determine the formal characteristics of artifacts. Groups of artifacts with shared characteristics constitute a style or type. Archaeologists have also been concerned with the spatial characteristics of artifacts, the location where they occur, and also the frequency of their appearance. Another important artifact characteristic is the artifact's associations with other objects of particular sorts of activities. A special aspect of the formal description is the internal composition and structure, the realm of the chemist, materials scientist, and archaeometrist. A characteristic that has been mentioned in several of these essays is the artifact's genealogy, or lineage.

Each essayist describes the formal attributes of the artifacts discussed. For some, such as Prown and Friedel, this was the focus of their attention. Prown considered the form of the objects; Friedel suggests that formal analysis be applied to material choices. A few, such as Wright and Lamberg-Karlovsky, elaborated not only form but also spatial relationships, associations, frequency of appearance, and the internal composition and structure as well. It seems that archaeologists' training sensitizes them to the usefulness of evaluating all dimensions of artifact variability in their interpretations. In addition to form, the variability included in most analyses (in seven essays) was the relational associations placing the artifact into the context of related activities and behaviors. Few of the essays incorporated the archaeometric analysis discussed by Gordon, but the determination of internal structure of an object seen at different magnifications is plainly evident in the studies of cultural geography. Perhaps surprisingly, five essays include a focus on the artifact genealogy or lineage, certainly appropriate for a volume about history from things.

Another distinction of artifacts that might have distinguished different approaches is the nature of the artifact's function investigated. Artifacts can play a utilitarian role, but almost all also have some social function related to a society's social organization, and many have some ideological function related to a society's ideology. Categorizing the essays on this basis turned out to be unrewarding. All the authors clearly recognized and comment on the multiple functions of even the most common utilitarian objects. Indeed, the un-self-conscious embedded cultural and social signs provide one of the main rewards of artifact study.

Still another way of characterizing the essays might have been on the basis of the stage of an artifact's life that has become the focus of attention: conception, material selection, design, manufacture, distribution, use, and perception. The advantages, perhaps the necessity, for understanding the overall life cycle is addressed by Gordon and by Kingery. It turns out that these essays are almost equally divided in focus; nine essays address the design of the artifact, seven essays address the use of the artifact, and eight essays address the perceptions of the artifact. In five essays the artifact manufacture is of concern, but in only two or three is it connected with conception, material selection, and distribution. Thus, at least two essays are concerned with each stage of artifact life. The principal dichotomy seems to occur between the authors who are mostly interested in design and manufacture and those who focus on perception and use. The essays reflect a much broader distribution of concern than might have been anticipated.

Finally, one might expect that we can divide these practitioners of material culture study by the sources of their artifactual data: ethnographic field studies, field archaeology, documentary archives, and museum collections. In light of our discussions of the document-artifact dichotomy, it is notable that all the authors except those concerned with folklore and prehistoric archaeology have freely used documentary sources for information about material culture. Other than that, the sources of the artifacts being studied in this particular collection of essays derive equally from ethnographic field studies, field archaeology, and museum collections.

Overall, one is struck by the commonality of the authors' use of artifactual material culture evidence in addressing issues of theory and method or applying material culture data to illustrate theory and develop social and cultural histories. Without much prior intent on the part of the editors, an intriguing variety of objects has been selected for study, and several different measures of the nature of artifact use—the dimensions of artifact variability used, the stage of artifact life examined, the artifact function, and the source of a material culture data—demonstrate a breadth of approach that is quite remarkable. The essays in this volume not only penetrate the boundaries between fields that use material evidence to understand history but also push the boundaries of the field of material culture further than before, in new and interesting directions.

Taken as a whole, the essays indicate that material culture studies do provide meaningful interactions for bringing together different peer groups and piercing boundaries between what superficially seem to be widely disparate disciplines.

This assembly of quite different approaches to the appreciation and use of material culture in developing a better understanding of society and culture leads to a whole that is much more impressive than its separate parts. These studies—from folklore to geography to technology, from prehistory to present-day—demonstrate a set of approaches to material culture that together have the intellectual and emotional content necessary to allow a field of study to develop as, in essence, a peer group of its own.

The Truth of Material Culture: History or Fiction?

Jules David Prown

Material culture is just what it says it is—namely, the manifestations of culture through material productions. And the study of material culture is the study of material to understand culture, to discover the beliefs—the values, ideas, attitudes, and assumptions—of a particular community or society at a given time. The underlying premise is that human-made objects reflect, consciously or unconsciously, directly or indirectly, the beliefs of the individuals who commissioned, fabricated, purchased, or used them and, by extension, the beliefs of the larger society to which these individuals belonged. Material culture is thus an object-based branch of cultural anthropology or cultural history.

What material do we study in material culture? Obviously we study things made by human beings—a hammer, a card table, a plow, a teapot, a microscope, a house, a painting, a city. But we also study natural objects that have been modified by human beings—stones arranged into a wall, a garden, a prepared meal, a tattooed body. We may even study unmodified natural objects, as Cyril Stanley Smith has done, to understand better the relationship between the structure of human-made things and the structure of natural things in the physical universe in which we live.

Objects made or modified by humans are clumped together under the term *artifact*. That word connects two words—*art* and *fact*—reflecting its double Latin root. The word *art* derives from *ars, artis* (skill in joining), and *fact* derives through *factum* (deed or act) from *facere* (to make or to do), emphasizing the utilitarian meaning already implicit in the word *art*; thus, skill or knowledge is applied to the making of a thing. This verbal conjunction introduces an issue that often derails material culture discussions, namely the relationship between artifacts and art. The term *art* refers to objects whose primary initial purpose has been to represent, to memorialize, to induce veneration, elevation or contemplation, to provide access to or influence supernatural forces, to delight the eye, or otherwise to affect human thought or behavior through visual means. Many cultures do not have a special category of objects identified as art. In our culture, art is what we say is art, including ethnographic and technological objects that were not created as art but that have been aestheticized by being placed in museums or other special collections.

There are two ways to view the relationship between art and artifact—inclusive and exclusive. The inclusive approach asserts that just as the word *art* is incorporated in the word *artifact*, so too are all works of art, as fabricated objects, by definition artifacts. Some even hold that the terms are interchangeable. Several years ago the art historian Irving Lavin of the Institute for Advanced Study set forth a series of what he termed "assumptions" about art, leading to a definition of art history.[1] "The first assumption," he wrote, "is that anything man made is a work of art, even the lowliest and most purely functional object." For Lavin, and for an increasing number of art historians, art is equatable with artifacts, the material of material culture.

Several scholars have observed that any artifact—and the inclusive view would mean any work of art as well—is a historical event. This brings me to the first part of this paper's subtitle—history. An artifact is something that happened in the past, but, unlike other historical events, it continues to exist in our own time. Artifacts constitute the only class of historical events that occurred in the past but survive into the present. They can be reexperienced; they are authentic, primary historical material available for firsthand study. Artifacts are historical evidence.

Artifacts, like other historical events, do not just happen; they are the results of causes. There are reasons why an object comes into existence in a particular configuration, is decorated with particular motifs, is made of particular materials, and has a particular color and texture. Peter Gay, in the introduction to his book *Art and Act*, identified three types of historical causation that apply to artifacts just as to other historical events. These he calls craft, culture, and privacy. The first, craft, refers to tradition. Things are done or made in the way they were done or made previously. This is obviously true about artifacts whose artists and craftspeople are trained in art schools or apprenticeships, learn from design books, and learn from other objects. The second type of causation, culture, refers to the mind of contemporary culture—prevailing attitudes, customs, or beliefs that condition the ways in which things are said, done, or made. It refers to the world in which both maker and consumer lived and which affected their values. People are a product of their time and place. The third causal factor, privacy, refers to the individual psychological makeup of the person who made the object; it might be entirely conformist and therefore reflective of contemporary society, or it might be quirky or eccentric, producing an original, novel, or idiosyncratic result.

The objective of a cultural investigation is mind—belief—the belief of individuals and the belief of groups of individuals, of societies. There are surface beliefs, beliefs of which people are aware and which they express in what they say, do, and make, and there are beliefs that are hidden, submerged. If we may return to etymology for a moment, beliefs that are on the surface are *sur-face* or *super-ficial* (on the face). The cultural analyst wants to get at hidden beliefs, at what lies behind surface appearance, behind the mask of the face. What lurks behind the face is our quarry—mind. A culture's most fundamental beliefs are often so widely understood, so generally shared and accepted, that they never need to be stated. They are therefore invisible to outsiders. Indeed, they may be beliefs of which the culture itself is not aware, and some of them may be so hard to face that they are repressed.

Mind, whether individual or cultural, does not reveal itself fully in overt expression; it hides things from others, and it hides things from itself. It can express itself in complex or elliptical ways. Just as some of the secrets of the physical world cannot be observed directly but only through representations—DNA, quarks, black holes—so secrets of the mental world—the world of belief—are manifest only in representations. Dreams are one example of the representations of hidden mind, of the expression of meaning in masked form. The capacity of human beings to process the unnoticed material of daily life into fictions that surface in dreams suggests to me that human beings constantly create fictions unconsciously, using the language of fiction—simile, metonomy, synecdoche, metaphor. I wish to suggest that like dreams artifacts are, in addition to their intended function, unconscious representations of hidden mind, of belief. If so, then artifacts may reveal deeper cultural truth if interpreted as fictions rather than as history. I realize that an analogy between dreams and artifacts as expressions of subconscious mind is not self-evident; indeed, it seems unlikely. Let me develop the case further.

Because underlying cultural assumptions and beliefs are taken for granted or repressed, they are not visible in what a society says, or does, or makes—its self-conscious expressions. They are, however, detectable in the way things are said, or done, or made—that is, in their style. The analysis of style, I believe, is one key to cultural understanding.[2] What do I mean by style? The configuration of a single object is its form. When groups of objects share formal characteristics, those resemblances or resonances constitute style. In the practice of art history, the study of those characteristics is called formal or stylistic analysis. When it is used in practice to discriminate between objects, it is often called connoisseurship. That term is unfortunately maligned because it seems to smack of preciousness and elitism. But in fact connoisseurship is a powerful scholarly tool, permitting rapid distinctions between what is true and what is false. I know of no other field of historical inquiry in which it is possible to achieve such rapid and precise analytical results as connoisseurship, which enables an analyst to say immediately and with assurance that this chair is Philadelphia, 1760–70, made by X, or this chest is Essex County, Massachusetts, probably Ipswich, about 1670, from the workshop of Y, or this table is a forgery, a cultural lie.

Whereas iconography, the analysis of subject matter, serves an art historian well in discerning and tracking linkages of objects across time and space, the analysis of style facilitates the identification of difference, of elements that are specific to a place, a time, a maker. Why is this so? Because form is the great summarizer, the concretion of belief in abstract form. A chair is Philadelphia of the 1760s because it embodies elements of what was believed in Philadelphia in the 1760s, and that formal pattern is what enables an analyst to determine the truth of the chair. It follows logically that formal patterns should also allow an analyst to reverse the process: to consider the beliefs, the patterns of mind, materialized in the chair. Instead of analyzing the concrete formal expressions of belief to determine the authenticity of the chair, the concrete formal expressions of an authentic chair are analyzed to get at belief. When style is shared by clusters of objects in a time and place, it is akin to a cultural daydream expressing unspoken beliefs. Human minds are inhabited by a matrix of feelings, sensations, intuitions, and understandings that are nonverbal or preverbal, and in any given culture many of these are shared, held in common. Perhaps if we had access to a culture's dream world, we could discover and analyze some of these hidden beliefs. In the absence of that, I suggest that some of these beliefs are encapsulated in the form of things, and there they can be discerned and analyzed.

Style is most informative about underlying beliefs when their expression is least self-conscious, and a society is less self-conscious in what it makes, especially such utilitarian objects as houses, furniture, and pots, than in what it says or does, which is necessarily conscious and intentional. Purposive expressions—for example, a diplomatic communique or an advertisement—may be intended to deceive as well as to inform. It is just here that the inclusive approach accepting a close linkage or even identification between art and artifact causes problems. The function of art is to communicate—whether to instruct, record, moralize, influence, or please. In this abstract mode of operation it resembles literature more than it does other physical artifacts. It is self-conscious, intentional expression. An icon of Saint Francis of Assisi or a representation of the Madonna and Child may be intended to arouse religious sentiments, to persuade, or even to convert; a portrait may be intended to flatter. Art may be true or deceptive; in either case it is intentional. Works of art are conscious expressions of belief, fictions composed of a vocabulary of line and color, light and texture, enriched by tropes and metaphors. As cultural evidence, works of art have many of the same liabilities as verbal fictions with their attendant problems of intentionality. The distinction between art and artifact is that artifacts do not lie. That is an exaggerated way to put it, but it makes the point. Card tables and teapots, hammers and telephones—all have specific functional programs that are constants, and the variables of style through which the program is realized are unmediated, unconscious expressions of cultural value and beliefs.

However, it is in what we call art—whether painting, sculpture, literature, theater, dance, music, or other modes of aesthetic expression—that societies have expressly articulated their beliefs. Because material culturalists are interested in objects as expressions of belief and because art is specifically material that is expressive of belief, it would be absurd to exclude art from material culture. Although we may attach special importance to uncovering deep structures of belief that may underlie the conscious, articulated top layer of belief, we cannot simply exclude the most obvious expressions of belief—art, literature, and so forth—from cultural analysis because they are self-conscious. So if an inclusive approach that identifies art and artifact closely is unsatisfactory, so too is an exclusive approach that would pry art completely away from artifacts as unsuitable for material culture analysis.

For those of us who think that as material culturists we are "doing history" with objects, it is a sobering corrective to realize that in one sense history consistently uses small truths to build large untruths. History can never completely retrieve the past with all its rich complexity, not only of events but of emotions and sensations and spirit. We retrieve only the facts of what transpired; we do not retrieve the feel, the affective totality, of what it was like to be alive in the past. History is necessarily false; it has to be. On the other hand, literature can weave small fictions into profound and true insights regarding the human condition. It can recreate the experience of deeply felt moments and move us profoundly. It can trace inexorable patterns of cause and effect in fiction and concentrate the largest universal truths into myth.[3]

I suggest, then, that deep structural meanings of artifacts can be sprung loose by going beyond cataloguing them as historical facts to analyzing them as fictions, specifically artistic fictions. While hierarchically art is a subcategory of artifact, analytically it is useful to treat artifacts as if they were works of art. Viewing all objects as fictions reduces the distinction between art and artifacts.

As an example, I will analyze a single artifact (fig. 1). This object is 6⅜ inches high, 4¾ inches wide at the widest part of the body, and 7⅞ inches wide from spout tip to handle. It is wider than it is high and could be inscribed within a rectangle. The primary material is pewter, although the handle and lower ring of the finial are of wood. There is a small hole in the top of the lid, and inside the vessel there is a circular arrangement of small holes where the spout joins the body.

The vessel is divided by a horizontal line three-fifths of the way up where the lid rests on the body. The lid and the body also are subdivided

*Fig. 1. Teapot, pewter. Thomas Danforth III (American, c. 1777–c. 1818).
Yale University Art Gallery, Mabel Brady Garvan Collection.*

by horizontal moldings, the lower one exactly midway between the base
and the top of the handle and at a height exactly equal to the total height
of the lid. Viewed from the side the object presents a series of S-curves,
including the handle, the spout, and the outlines of the body, the lid, and
the finial. The spout and the handle rise above the rim. The vessel stands
on a raised base ⅜ inch high.

Seen from the top (fig. 2), the object presents a series of concentric
circles surrounding the finial. The spout, finial, hole, hinge, and handle
are aligned to form an axis through the vessel at its largest dimension.

The object consists of five separate parts—lid, body, handle, spout,
and finial. The lower section of the body is a flattened ball, the upper part

Fig. 2. Detail of pewter teapot by Danforth. Yale University Art Gallery, Mabel Brady Garvan Collection.

a reel. The lid is bell-shaped and surmounted by a finial that echoes in simplified form the shape of the vessel—a flattened ball surmounted by a reel, with a hemisphere above.

Setting aside previous knowledge, it could nonetheless be deduced that this hollow-bodied object is a vessel or container, that the larger opening at the top revealed when the lid is opened is used to put some substance into the vessel, and that the spout is used to redirect that substance into a smaller container. The small holes in the body at the base of the spout suggest that the contained substance is strained in the act of pouring to retain in the vessel particles larger than the holes. The fact that the spout rises above the rim suggests that the substance contained is liquid, since if the spout were below the rim, liquid would overflow when the vessel were full. The use of wood in the handle and in the finial, which is grasped to open the lid, suggests that the liquid may be hot, since wood is not as good a conductor of heat as metal. The fact that an attached rim raises the bottom of the pot off the surface on which it stands also suggests that the contents may be hot.

Manipulating the object suggests the use of the handle and the finial. Opening the lid indicates that the finial makes contact with the handle, and the absence of wear suggests that the handle, and perhaps the finial disk as well, is a replacement. The bell shape of the lid suggests sound, and actual sound results from opening and closing the lid.

When respondents have been asked to express their feelings about this object following extended analysis, they have used such words as "solid," "substantial," "cheerful," "comfortable," "grandmotherly," and "reliable." The object evokes recollections, and the identification of the links between the object and the memories of experience for which it stands as a sign is the key to unlocking the cultural belief embedded in it. If you ask what in the object triggered such words as "solid," "substantial," and "reliable," respondents will note that the object is wider than it is high and that the flattened ball of the lower part gives it a squarish and bottom-weighted appearance, suggesting stability. The responses are based on experience of the phenomenal world. The words "cheerful," "comfortable," and "grandmotherly" reflect more subjective life experiences that also can be located with some precision by asking questions based on the previously deduced evidence. Under what circumstances do we drink warm liquids? When we are cold, warm liquid warms us inside; when we are hot, it causes perspiration that evaporates, cooling the body surface. We drink hot liquids when we are ill—soup or tea—again because they make us feel better, perhaps by promoting perspiration and helping break a fever. When we are ill and incapacitated, warm liquids are often brought to us, and the care of another person is comforting. Hot liquids are also drunk on social occasions. Drinking coffee and tea is marked by a sense of well-being that derives from the stimulation of the drink itself, by the physical act of giving or pouring and receiving, and frequently by conversation. Drinking hot liquids and talking seem to go together.

James Fernandez has written of the importance of metaphor to anthropologists in decoding culture, a process he referred to punningly as "an-trope-ology."[4] Although he was discussing verbal metaphors, several of his discriminations are applicable as well to the understanding of how artifacts function as metaphorical expressions of culture. He distinguishes between two kinds of metaphor—structural metaphors, which conform to the shape of experience and thus resemble actual objects in the physical world, and textual metaphors, which are similar to the feelings of experience. Structural metaphors are based on physical experience of the phenomenal world; textual metaphors are based on the emotive experience of living in that world.

The object, which we can now refer to as a teapot since our analysis of it is complete, invokes multiple textual metaphors—cheerful, comfortable, reliable, grandmotherly, and so forth—metaphors based on the feelings of experience. It also embodies structural metaphors based on the shape of experience. The lid and finial, for example, can be read as a bell metaphor. And the bell shape suggests calling—whether by a dinner bell or ringing from a sick bed—calling for and receiving help or comfort or sustenance. Another structural metaphor, equally obvious, is less easily retrieved, however, perhaps because repressed. If you ask the respondent (or the analyst asks him- or herself) to identify the Ur-experience, the earliest human experience of ingesting warm liquids, the immediate response is as a baby feeding from a mother's breast. Structural analogies between the shape of the lower section of the body of the vessel and the female breast now become evident. And when the object is viewed from above, with the finial at the center like a nipple, the object is even more breastlike (fig. 2). The teapot is revealed, unexpectedly, as a structural metaphor for the female breast.

Fernandez defines a metaphor as a sign, a combination of image and idea located between a signal and a symbol, between perception and conception. A signal invokes a simple perception that orients some kind of action or interaction. A picture of a teapot could function literally as a signal hanging outside a tea room beckoning the tourist to enter; at a tea party the teapot itself serves as a signal for pouring and serving. At the other end of the scale, a symbol triggers a conception whose meaning is fully realized. A common denominator linking the various circumstances cited earlier in which warm liquids are ingested is that all involve an act of giving and receiving, which is, in its largest social sense, the act of charity.[5] A teapot, fully conceptualized in meaning, could become a symbol of the act of giving, of charity. One can envision a page in an emblem book with an image of a teapot, a symbol of charity, and an accompanying moralizing text.

Located between signal, a simple perception, and symbol, a fully realized conception, the teapot by itself stands as a sign, a metaphor both structural and textual. It embodies deeply felt but unconceptualized meanings relating to giving and receiving, to such things as maternal love and care, oral gratification, satisfaction of hunger and thirst, comforting internal warmth when cold or ill, and conviviality. And it is thus as a sign or metaphor that the teapot works as evidence of cultural belief.

If artifacts express culture metaphorically, what kinds of insight can they afford us? What, for example, does the teapot tell us about belief? The object has given us a clue that the drinking of tea, and perhaps the entire ceremony of tea drinking, may be related metaphorically to the fundamental human act of giving and receiving and has the potential of being a symbol of generosity or charity, of *caritas*. The humanness as well as the humaneness of the act is suggested in this teapot by the fact that the liquid is encased in an organic, breastlike form. But, as we well know, a teapot can be precisely the opposite in form (fig. 3); it can deny the humanly anatomical or personal aspect of giving, or charity, and by using purely inorganic, intellectual, geometric forms deny personal involvement and emphasize the cerebral character of the act. In so doing it conveys something about the different character of a different culture.[6]

The fundamental structural linkage of warm liquids, breast feeding, and charity—the human metaphor—suggested to us by our study of a single teapot is now understood to be a formal potential for all vessels used to pour out hot liquids. The extent to which it is generated, tolerated, or rejected by a culture is an index of one aspect of that culture's belief. Objects are evidence, and material culture enables us to interpret the culture that produced them in subjective, affective ways unachievable through written records alone. They did not write much about breasts in the late eighteenth century, and even less about the linkage between breasts and charity, but the metaphorical language of teapots conveys a livelier and perhaps truer picture. What we have perceived in the teapot are indicators of beliefs about giving and receiving, generosity, charity, and definitions of the self in relation to others. Can one go on to describe with greater precision the terrain of cultural belief expressed by artifacts? The most persistent metaphors in objects of which I have become aware relate to such fundamental human experiences as mortality and death; love, sexuality, and gender roles; privacy (seeing and being seen) and communication; power or control and acceptance; fear and danger; and, as here, giving and receiving.

Metaphors, Fernandez says, locate beliefs in what he calls the "quality space" of a culture.[7] Among several formulations he noted as to how metaphors locate belief is one that accords closely with the polarities of belief I have encountered in my analysis of American artifacts, that articulated by

Fig. 3. Teapot, silver. Loring Bailey (American, 1740–1814). Hood Museum of Art, Dartmouth College, Hanover, N.H. Gift of Frank L. Harrington, Class of 1924.

W. T. Jones as seven "axes of bias."[8] These "axes" are lines of predisposition, along the calibration of which beliefs are situated. They are static-dynamic, order-disorder, discreteness-continuity, process-spontaneity, sharp-soft, outer-inner, and other world–this world. (The first term in each opposition cited applies more to the neoclassical Bailey teapot, the second to the Danforth teapot, but in varying degrees). I wonder whether it would not be possible to graph these points, an admittedly subjective exercise, to arrive at abstractions of artifacts that would constitute a type of cultural fingerprint.

It should be understood that the analysis of artifacts as fictions to discover otherwise unexpressed cultural beliefs does not so much answer questions as raise them. Artifacts make us aware affectively of attitudes and values; they provide only limited amounts of data. In the language of semiotics, they are artistic signs articulating a climate of belief; they are often poor informational signs. But the questions they pose are authentic ones, arising from the primary evidence of the artifact rather than being imposed by the investigator.

If artifacts materialize belief, then it follows that when a society undergoes a traumatic change, that change should manifest itself artifactually. Perhaps the most clearly defined moment of social change in our country occurred at the time of transition from colony to nation; that is the change signalled in the configuration of these two teapots.[9] We can corroborate the connection by looking at two stylistically similar expressions in a different type of object. A pre-Revolution New York Chippendale or rococo card table (fig. 4) is irregular, organic, curvilinear, jutting into and penetrated by ambient space, heavy, and decorated with carved leafage, shells, claw and ball feet, and rope gadrooning. It has wells for counters, recesses at the corners for candlesticks, a drawer to hold cards and counters, and a baize cover to protect the surface, make it easier to pick up cards, and keep them from sliding. A post-Revolution Federal or classical revival card table (fig. 5) is regular, geometrical, self-contained, light in weight and structure, and decorated on its smooth veneered surfaces with inlaid images of flowers and eagles. It has three fixed and one fly leg; two sides have legs in the center, and two sides are open. Questions arise. Did women in dresses tend to sit at the open sides and men in trousers take the sides with the center legs, which they could straddle? If so, if two men and two women played, the player across the table was always of the opposite sex. In the games played, was the opposing player a partner or an adversary, or was each player out for him- or herself? A player at a Chippendale table (fig. 4) is drawn into closer physical proximity to the other players, in part because the sides, although bowed in the center, are recessed from the corners. The sensation of closeness is especially pervasive if one is forced to circle one's legs around the solid protruding cabriole leg in the center of three of the four sides, becoming literally wrapped up with the table. The other players are near, their faces loom large, their voices are close, their aromas are pervasive, as is the warmth and smell of the candles at either elbow. There is a sense of intimacy, of coziness, reinforced by the warmth of the nearby candles, the soft baize covering, and a sheltered trove of private wealth in a well—a kind of security, like food in a bowl or money in one's pocket.

We are aware of the reality of physical substances—the sturdiness

Fig. 4. Card table (American, New York, 1760–70). Yale University Art Gallery, Mabel Brady Garvan Collection.

and weight of the table, the solidity of elements carved of mahogany that replicate organic elements in the natural world, such as rope carvings, leafage, shells, and claws clutching balls. We are comforted by the real, natural environment of substantial, tangible things. The functionalism of the table is reassuring. Places are carved out for candlesticks, counters, even players. The sinuous curves of solid organic forms that surround the player suggest not only the natural world but also the complexity of human relations within that world. Deviousness might be a natural and not unfriendly part of the game—it is a fact of life, like sinuous curves in

Fig. 5. Card table (American, Massachusetts, 1785–1815). Yale University Art Gallery, Mabel Brady Garvan Collection.

nature. The table suggests a culture in which value is placed on and pleasure derived from substantial things—the realities of the world and of life as well as warm, complex, intimate human relations.

The Federal card table (fig. 5) seems to substitute the mental for the physical, fragility for substantiality, intellectual geometry for organic complexity, aloofness for intimacy. Forms are slender and orderly; surfaces are sheer and planar; clarity and regularity replace complexity and sinuousness. The decorative elements on Federal card tables tend not to be real things but pictures of things—inlay—abstract images rather than the things themselves. Projecting sides often serve to keep each player at a slight distance from the table. The players are thus farther away from each other. Objects on the table surface are less secure, less rooted, set on a flat, all-purpose surface rather than nestled into designed concavities. The entire enterprise is cooler, more distant, more abstract, and in a sense more tentative, less friendly. It is almost as if at the Chippendale table one tries to win real property from intimates, to put their goods in your pocket, while at the Federal table one attempts to win intellectual supremacy over adversaries and perhaps money in a more abstract form.

An investigation now could go in many directions; a particularly promising one would be a study to see whether the actual games played during the pre-Revolution and post-Revolution periods changed and how these changes, if any, related to relations between men and women, ideas about independence and authority, private and corporate entrepreneurship, generosity and greed, hostility and friendship, and a host of other attitudes, values, and beliefs imbedded in the artifacts and acted out in the games people played.

Obviously not all belief can be retrieved. An artifact is embedded in its culture and embodies some of that culture's beliefs. We are deeply embedded in another culture, and our understandings are colored by its beliefs. One great advantage of the study of material culture is the extent to which it provides a way to overcome the problem of cultural perspective by establishing the broadest possible base of commonality. A society we would study had its set of beliefs, its culture, while we who would seek to understand that culture are the products not only of a different cultural environment but of a complex of cultural environments. Each of us is pervaded by the beliefs of our own particular groups—nationality, place of residence, class, religion, politics, occupation, gender, age, race, ethnicity, and so forth. We all have biases of which we are not aware, convictions that we accept as unquestioningly as the air we breathe. The issue that haunts all cultural studies is whether it is possible for us to step outside our own cultural givens, our own time and place, and interpret the evidence of another culture objectively—that is, in terms of the individuals and society who produced it rather than in our own terms. If not—if we are irredeemably biased by our own unconscious beliefs, if we are hopelessly culture-bound to our own time and place—then all efforts to inter-pret other cultures should be avoided since our interpretations will inevita-bly be distorted.

The problem is a problem of mind. We are trying to understand another culture whose patterns of belief, whose mind, is different from our own. Our own beliefs, our mindset, biases our view. It would be ideal, and this is not as silly as it sounds, if we could approach that other culture mindlessly, at least while we gather our data. This is the great promise of material culture: By undertaking cultural interpretation through arti-facts, we engage the other culture in the first instance not with our minds, the seat of our cultural biases, but with our senses. Figuratively speaking, we put ourselves inside the bodies of the individuals who made or used these objects; we see with their eyes and touch with their hands. To identify with people from the past or from other places empathetically through the senses is clearly a different way of engaging them than ab-stractly through the reading of written words. Instead of our minds mak-ing intellectual contact with their minds, our senses make affective contact with their sensory experience.

Certainly it is true that sense perceptions filtered through the brain may also be culturally conditioned. But although commonality of sense perception cannot be proven either empirically or philosophically, certain conclusions can be drawn on the basis of the shared neuro-physiological apparatus of all human beings, which is not culturally specific and has evolved only slowly over time, and also from the inescapable common-alities of life as lived. All humans undergo a passage from birth, through nurturing and aging, to death. En route they experience the realities of the physical world: gravity, a sense of up and down, an awareness of night and day, of straight, curved, and crooked, of enclosure and exclu-sion. Through the channels of the senses they taste sweet, sour, and bitter; smell the acrid and the fragrant; hear sounds loud and quiet; perceive through touch the difference between rough and smooth, hot and cold, wet and dry; and see colors and shapes. They know hunger and thirst, illness and health, pain, sexual passion, bodily functions, loss and discovery, laughter and real tears. The human body constantly pro-vides a sense of scale. It all adds up to a tremendous body of experience that is common and transcultural. This experience is transformed into belief that finds material expression in artifacts, the analysis of which—material culture—provides privileged paths of access for us to an understanding of other peoples and other cultures, of other times and other places.

NOTES

Part of this essay is derived from a paper given at a conference on North American material culture research, sponsored by the Institute of Social and Economic Research, Memorial University of Newfoundland, and Winterthur Museum, St. John's, Newfoundland, June 1986, and published in *Living in a Material World: Canadian and American Approaches to Material Culture*, edited by Gerald L. Pocius (St. John's: Institute of Social and Economic Research, Memorial University of Newfoundland, 1991).

1. "The Art of Art History," *Art News*, October 1983.

2. For more on this, see my "Style as Evidence," *Winterthur Portfolio* 15, no. 3 (Autumn 1980): 197–210.

3. Henry Glassie resolved this paradox by viewing history as myth, as art, in his article "Meaningful Things and Appropriate Myths: The Artifact's Place in American Studies," *Prospects* 3 (1977):1–49, reprinted in Robert Blair St. George, *Material Life in America, 1600–1860* (Northeastern University Press: Boston, 1988).

4. James Fernandez, "The Mission of Metaphor in Expressive Culture," *Current Anthropology* 15, no. 2 (June 1974):119–45.

5. The Roman legend of Cimon and Pero, known as the legend of Roman charity, tells of the daughter who visits her elderly father starving in prison. She nourishes him by feeding him from her own breast.

6. Although the Danforth teapot is in the Queen Anne style, it may well be as late in date as the Bailey teapot. One would expect that contemporaneous teapots would be similar in form, and the formal opposition of these two pots would seem to undercut the claim that difference in form conveys difference in cultural character. Apparent anomolies that arise in material culture study pose questions—What is the explanation for the formal difference of contemporary objects?—and it is precisely such questions that stimulate further investigation, new thinking, and enlarged understandings. Pursuit of the question was beyond the scope of the present paper because of time constraints, but what is involved here is a difference in technologies required by the difference in materials (the Danforth pot is pewter; the Bailey pot is silver) relating to significant differences in stylistic persistence between rural Connecticut (Danforth) and the ur-

ban Boston region (Bailey). Retention of a colonial style half a century later might well suggest a hypothesis about post-Revolution Connecticut, a particular part of Connecticut, or a particular clientele that would need to be tested more widely.

7. I am not comfortable with the spatial or topographical model for imaging cultural belief, but neither is Fernandez.

8. W. T. Jones, *The Romantic Syndrome* (Martinus Nijhoff: The Hague, 1961).

9. This section develops ideas introduced in "Style as Evidence," 200ff.

Why We Need Things

Mihaly Csikszentmihalyi

I t goes without saying that one consequence of our evolution as cultural beings has been an increasing dependence on objects for survival and comfort. Compared with the hunter-gatherers, described by Marshall Sahlins, who were horrified by the idea of having to accept gifts because it meant having to carry one more blanket or kettle along on their nomadic journeys, we are slowly being buried under towering mounds of artifacts. Recently it has been calculated that every American will own more than four hundred electronic appliances during his or her lifetime (Massimini 1989).

This proliferation of artifacts would not be a problem were it not for the fact that objects compete with humans for scarce resources in the same ecosystem. Forests are being destroyed to provide lumber, wood, and pulp; metals and oil are consumed to build and propel vehicles. The potential energy contained in our environment is dissipated as we convert it into objects, which rapidly become obsolete; thus we accelerate the processes of entropy that degrade the planet.

The survival of humankind depends on finding a modus vivendi not only with the physical world—viruses, bacteria, the animal kingdom, and one another—but also with the objects that we are incessantly producing. Some of these are obviously dangerous, such as the innumerable missiles, bombs, assault rifles, and automobiles that currently are the leading causes of death for people under forty years of age. Others are dangerous only indirectly, such as the plastic containers that are slowly shrouding our beaches, the aerosol cans that are destroying the ozone layer, and the computer on which I am writing these lines, whose chips were etched with acids that are polluting the water table in Silicon Valley.

In some respects artifacts are like new species that reproduce themselves alongside biological ones. Looking at an illustrated history of musical instruments or weapons or vehicles, it is easy to imagine that one sees the record of an evolutionary process tending toward greater and greater complexity of function. We like to think that because objects are human-made they must be under our control. However, this is not necessarily the case. An object with a specific form and function inevitably suggests the next incarnation of that object, which then almost certainly will come about. For instance, the first crude stone missile begat the spear, which begat the arrow and then the bolt, the bullet, and so on to Star Wars. Human volition seems to have less to do with this development than do the potentialities inherent in the objects themselves.

Every artifact is the product of human intentionality, but that intentionality itself is conditioned by the existence of previous objects. When General Motors decides to build a new line of cars, its decision is contingent on what models are already available. When the Pentagon commissions a new submarine, this act is not the expression of some abstract human purpose but the reaction to the existence of other submarines. Whenever someone buys a new food processor, that person is not expressing an essential human need but acting in terms of a consciousness shaped by appliances. Thus artifacts are sometimes symbiotic with humans, but at other times the relationship is parasitic, and the survival of the object is at the expense of its human host (Csikszentmihalyi 1988).

Given this interdependence between our survival and that of the artifacts we produce, it seems useful to look a little more closely at the relationship we have with objects. If we do not achieve a better under-standing of things, we may find ourselves entirely in their thrall. The point I wish to emphasize is that our dependence on objects is not only physical but also, more important, psychological. Most of the things we make these days do not make life better in any material sense but instead serve to stabilize and order the mind.

OBJECTS AND THE ORGANIZATION OF EXPERIENCE

It is difficult to understand our psychological dependence on objects as long as we hold to the belief that human beings are naturally in control of what happens in their minds. This cozy anthropocentric illusion is a useful prejudice in navigating through the shoals of life, but it does not bear up well under closer examination. The fact is that our hold over mental processes is extremely precarious even in the best of times (Csikszentmihalyi 1978, 1982).

Contrary to what we ordinarily believe, consciousness is not a stable, self-regulating entity. When left to itself, deprived of organized sensory input, the mind begins to wander and is soon prey to unbridled hallucina-tions. Most people require an external order to keep randomness from invading their mind. It is very difficult to keep ideas straight without the assistance of a sensory template that gives them boundaries and direction. When people have nothing to do, they generally begin to fret, become depressed, and become anxious; unless they turn on the television or find some other activity that will direct their attention, their moods progres-sively deteriorate. That is why people report their worst moods on Sunday mornings, when, deprived of a cultural script, they flounder in the quag-mire of freedom. The mind was not designed to be self-regulating or to function well when idling (Csikszentmihalyi and LeFevre 1989; Kubey and Csikszentmihalyi 1990).

Nor is it easy for the mind unaided to keep order in the temporal progression of events. It is difficult to remember the quality and texture of past experiences and keep in mind one's plans and hopes for the future. Without external props even our personal identity fades and goes out of focus; the self is a fragile construction of the mind. One must conclude that a state of psychic entropy is the normal state of consciousness—at least for organisms, like us, who have stepped beyond the guidelines of

their genetic programming and have become conscious of themselves. Yet
we experience this psychic entropy as something unpleasant and therefore
keep searching for ways to reestablish a purposeful order in its stead.

This is where objects can be helpful. As Arendt observed:

> The things of the world have the function of stabilizing human life,
> and their objectivity lies in the fact that . . . men, their ever-changing
> nature notwithstanding, can retrieve their sameness, that is, their iden-
> tity, by being related to the same chair and the same table. In other
> words, against the subjectivity of men stands the objectivity of the
> man-made world. . . . Without a world between men and nature,
> there is eternal movement, but no objectivity. (Arendt 1958: 137)

Artifacts help objectify the self in at least three major ways. They do so
first by demonstrating the owner's power, vital erotic energy, and place in
the social hierarchy. Second, objects reveal the continuity of the self
through time, by providing foci of involvement in the present, mementos
and souvenirs of the past, and signposts to future goals. Third, objects
give concrete evidence of one's place in a social network as symbols (literally, the joining together) of valued relationships. In these three ways
things stabilize our sense of who we are; they give a permanent shape to
our views of ourselves that otherwise would quickly dissolve in the flux of
consciousness.

Objects of Power

From earliest times people have taken pains to choose and own things that
encapsulate their personal power. For men this power tends to be synonymous with traditional virile virtues such as strength and endurance. Native American braves carried around their necks medicine bundles holding the claws of the bear they defeated in combat or other objects of
momentous significance that reflected the owner's ability to control physical and sacred energy. Evans-Pritchard noted that for the Nuer pasto-
ralists of the Sudan power was concentrated in the spear:

> A man's fighting spear (*mut*) is constantly in his hand, forming almost
> part of him . . . and he is never tired of sharpening or polishing it,
> for a Nuer is very proud of his spear. . . . In a sense it is animate, for
> it is an extension and external symbol . . . which stands for the

strength, vitality and virtue of the person. It is a projection of the
self. (Evans-Pritchard 1956:233)

Power is still symbolized by kinetic objects, although today it is expressed
through cars, boats, tools, sports equipment, and household appliances.
It is also invested in objects that have a great mass, such as houses or
imposing furniture. But symbols of status have become extremely complex, and now one can show superiority by collecting art (or almost anything else that is rare) or by owning things that are tasteful, ancient, or
just ahead of the times.

The power of women has traditionally been expressed through objects symbolizing equally stereotyped feminine qualities, such as seductive-
ness, fertility, and nurturance. Dresses, ornaments, jewelry, furs, silver,
china, domestic appliances, and fine furniture witness to a woman's ability to control energy (often meaning the psychic energy of men) and hence
the importance of her self.

It has been argued that the desire or compulsion to display one's
identity may have been a stronger impetus in the development of technology than the search for survival and comfort. Discussing the introduction
of the first metal objects at the end of the Neolithic period, Renfrew
writes:

> In several areas of the world it has been noted, in the case of metallur-
> gical innovations in particular, that the development of bronze and
> other metals as useful commodities was a much later phenomenon
> than their first utilization as new and attractive materials, employed
> in contexts of display. . . . In most cases early metallurgy appears to
> have been practiced primarily because the products had novel proper-
> ties that made them attractive to use as symbols and as personal
> adornments, in a manner that, by focusing attention, could attract or
> enhance prestige. (Renfrew 1986:144, 146)

Objects still serve the same self-enhancing purpose. In describing the
eating utensils used by traditional upper-class families of the New England
towns he studied, Warner (1953:120) writes: "They give objective expression to the inner feeling of the person involved about themselves, help to
reinforce the person's opinion about himself, and increase his sense of
security." Because our sense of self is vague and insecure and because it
depends on the reflection we get from others' reactions to it, we shall

continue to rely on displaying objects having qualities others prize so as to get a solid and positive sense of who we are through the mediation of the things we own.

Objects and the Continuity of the Self

For most people the home is not just a utilitarian shelter but a repository of things whose familiarity and concreteness help organize the consciousness of their owner, directing it into well-worn grooves. The home contains a symbolic ecology that represents both continuity and change in the life course and thus gives permanence to our elusive selves, as we learned in a study of the meanings that household objects had for a representative sample of American families (Csikszentmihalyi and Rochberg-Halton, 1981).

A wealthy attorney whose home was full of rare art and expensive furniture, when asked what was the most special object he owned, invited the interviewer down to the basement den and took out of a trunk an old trombone. He used to play this instrument in college, he explained, when life was fresh and spontaneous. Now he feels weighed down with cares, and whenever he is depressed he goes to the den to play a few tunes, and some of his worries disappear for a time. So the trombone helps both focus attention, reducing entropy in consciousness, and vividly brings back old memories and experiences, thus adding a sense of depth and wholeness to the self of its owner. For this man the expensive collection of art and furniture served as power objects, as signs of his status and achievements. But the most meaningful symbol of his private self was the trombone, which alone had the power to put him back in touch with himself.

The selves of young people and old, of men and women, are usually expressed through different objects. In our study we found that the most important household object for young people is the stereo set and, quite a bit further down the line, the television set, followed by some musical instrument such as a guitar or a trumpet. All these are things that produce ordered stimulation, either auditory or visual, and hence help the mind stay on track. Music is especially important in adolescence as a modulator of moods: Whenever these threaten to engulf a teenager's consciousness, turning on a tape helps focus and objectify emotions; the music and the lyrics reflect the formless yearnings of the listener and give them substance and legitimacy.

For adults, furniture, paintings, sculpture, and books serve as the main repositories of meanings about the self. These objects embody the values and tastes as well as the accomplishments of the owner. For older people photographs are the things most often mentioned as special. Pictures serve as icons of the past, concrete reminders of a life that otherwise would run the risk of getting lost in the labyrinths of memory.

The objects people see as special in their home point to different directions in time, revealing different aspects of the self that are important, depending on the person's age. Teenagers, for instance, are interested almost exclusively in objects that embody their current concerns, things with which they can interact here and now. The present self holds center stage, and action is its main mode of expression.

Their parents are almost evenly divided between the past, present, and future. Some of the objects they own are cherished because they bring back earlier aspects of the self: examples are a youthful diary, a well-used hiking boot, or the attorney's trombone mentioned earlier. Some of the objects are things being used right now and thus express the current stage of the self's development—a musical instrument, perhaps, or some plants. And some things are important because they stand for what the owner hopes to accomplish in the future—a French grammar, which is a reminder of an imminent and long-anticipated European vacation, or a kit for assembling a rooftop solar energy collector, which urges the owner to act out his or her environmental concerns in the future.

For the grandparents the temporal balance shifts again; the past self is most prominently evoked by the symbolic ecology of the home. Instead of action, contemplation is the preferred way of relating to things that represent former actions and events. But an emphasis on the past does not mean a complete absorption in it; in our study 97 percent of the oldest generation of respondents also mentioned objects that were special because they pointed to the present or to the future.

In addition to differences due to progression along the life course, one finds many patterns that distinguish one gender from the other. As one would expect, the selves of men are much more often expressed through active instrumental objects such as television sets, stereos, power tools, sports equipment, vehicles, and cameras. Women, on the other hand, mention significantly more often things that express a concern for nurturance and conservation—houseplants, plates, glass, photographs, textiles, and sculptures. It is remarkable how even in this day and age gender stereotypes still flourish in the objects men and women choose to represent their identities with.

Objects and Relationships.

Next to giving permanence to the self, the most frequent symbolic use of household objects is to give permanence to the relationships that define the individual in the social network. In this sense things stand for the ties that link a person to others. Of the youngest respondents 71 percent mentioned objects that were special because they reminded the owner of his or her family; in the parental generation the proportion was 85 percent; and in the grandparents' generation, 86 percent.

A woman feels a special attachment to the chair in which she sat to nurse her babies; a man looks with pleasure at the seascape hanging on the living-room wall, which he bought during his Mexican honeymoon; photographs chronicle the growth of children and grandchildren. But it is not only the immediate family whose presence shines forth from special objects. Relatives of all kinds are recalled by the objects filling up the home. There is the quilt sewn by Aunt Elly, the bed in which Grandmother was born, porcelain cups from Great-grandmother's family, and the Bible inscribed by even more distant ancestors.

Friendships also are commemorated by objects in at least one-fourth of the homes. The objects that most often recall friends are paintings, furniture, and sculptures (including plastic figurines). One-fifth of the homes contain objects that embody some ideal of the owner, and the objects that most lend themselves to this are books, which generally signify values such as wisdom, creativity, and courage; plants, which usually refer to such values as nurturance, care, and love for life, and musical instruments. Ethnic origins are most often objectified by plateware, sculpture, and paintings; religious identity, by books and sculpture.

Families whose members have strong positive feelings for one another and for their home possess many objects that are cherished because they symbolize common ties. In the ten "warmest" households in our study, seven husbands mentioned special objects that referred to their wives, whereas only one of ten husbands in the "coolest" families mentioned a symbol having to do with his wife. In warm homes adults have more symbols relating to their own parents, their children, and their own childhood.

In a stable culture, where relationships continue uninterrupted from cradle to grave, there may not be a need to secure one's position in the web of kinship through material symbols. But in our mobile American society things play an important role in reminding us of who we are with respect to whom we belong. One young woman we interviewed answered our questions about things with disdain, professing that she was not "a goddam materialist," that objects did not matter to her, that she cared only for human relationships. It turned out, however, that she had no family and no friends. In general, if the home had few things that evoked meaning, its owner tended to be socially isolated.

Our addiction to materialism is in large part due to a paradoxical need to transform the precariousness of consciousness into the solidity of things. The body is not large, beautiful, and permanent enough to satisfy our sense of self. We need objects to magnify our power, enhance our beauty, and extend our memory into the future.

In looking at these functions, it seems clear that power objects are not only the most dangerous but also the most expensive with respect to scarce resources and labor. When things are necessary to prove dominance and superiority, human costs start to escalate very quickly. It is striking to note in comparison how inexpensive things that stand for kinship and relatedness tend to be. Tokens of remembrance, respect, and love typically have trivial intrinsic value, and the labor invested in them is usually voluntary. Thus, the kind of selves individuals choose to build have great consequences for the material culture and for the natural environment that must be despoiled in order to create it. In times past it was said that the saints wore their selfhood as a light cloak on their shoulders. Now that each of us on this planet carries the burden of the equivalent of 4,000 pounds of TNT, we can see the wisdom of that image.

The addiction to objects is of course best cured by learning to discipline consciousness. If one develops control over the processes of the mind, the need to keep thoughts and feelings in shape by leaning on things decreases. This is the main advantage of a genuinely rich symbolic culture: It gives people poetry, songs, crafts, prayers, and rituals that keep psychic entropy at bay. A Brahmin can afford to live in an empty home, because he does not need objects to keep his mind on course. In our culture mathematicians, musicians, and others adept at the use of symbols are also partially freed from reliance on an objectified consciousness. We very much need to learn more about how this inner control can be achieved. Then objects can again be used primarily as instruments rather than as projections of our selves, which, like the servants created by the sorcerer's apprentice, threaten to drown their masters with relentless zeal.

REFERENCES

Arendt, Hannah. 1958. *The Human Condition*. Chicago: University of Chicago Press.

Csikszentmihalyi, Mihaly. 1978. "Attention and the Wholistic Approach to Behavior." In *The Stream of Consciousness*, edited by K. S. Pope and J. L. Singer, 335–358. New York: Plenum.

———. 1982. "Towards a Psychology of Optimal Experience." In *Review of Personality and Social Psychology*, vol. 2, edited by L. Wheeler. Beverly Hills, Calif.: Sage.

———. 1988. "The Ways of Genes and Memes." *Reality Club Review* 1, no. 1: 107–108.

Csikszentmihalyi, Mihaly, and Judith LeFevre. 1989. "Optimal Experience in Work and Leisure." *Journal of Personality and Social Psychology* 56, no. 5: 815–822.

Csikszentmihalyi, Mihaly, and Eugene Rochberg-Halton. 1981. *The Meaning of Things: Domestic Symbols and the Self.* New York: Cambridge University Press.

Evans-Pritchard, E. E. 1940, 1956. *The Nuer: A Description of the Modes of Livelihood and Political Institutions of a Nilotic People.* New York: Oxford University Press.

Kubey, Robert W., and Mihaly Csikszentmihalyi. 1990. *Television and the Quality of Life*. Hillsdale, N.J.: Laurence Erlbaum.

Massimini, Fausto. 1989. "Psychological Evolution." Paper presented at the Evangelical Lutheran Church of America meeting "Fear 2000 and Beyond," St. Charles, Ill., March 30–April 2.

Renfrew, Colin. 1986. "Varna and the Emergence of Wealth in Prehistoric Europe." In *The Social Life of Things*, edited by A. Appadurai, 141–168. New York: Cambridge University Press.

Warner, W. Lloyd. 1953. *American Life: Dream and Reality*. Chicago: The University of Chicago Press.

Objects as Instruments, Objects as Signs

Jacques Maquet

Reading objects as instruments and reading objects as signs require two different perspectives. In the former the observer considers the object and draws inferences from its design and its situation in the social and physical environment. In the latter the observer considers the meanings ascribed to the object.

Although they are made in a certain society—and thus are made according to the cultural patterns of that society—objects as instruments may be understood independently from their cultural determinations. An artifact made of a sharp blade and a handle, a knife, is a cutting instrument in any culture. Its use can be inferred from its design and materials. A machine made of four wheels driven by an internal-combustion engine, an automobile, is an instrument for land transportation in any contemporary society, whatever its culture.

On the other hand, the meaning of an object—what it stands for—is cultural when it is recognized as part of the collective reality built by a group of people. But in most cases it is not culture-specific; it is grounded in common human experiences.

Suppose that in a certain society knives are weapons that only hunters have the right to possess. The knife would then be a sign for hunting, a highly regarded occupation. An outsider will probably discover the meaning of the knife because to signify an occupation by a characteristic implement is fairly common. Let us say that in another society the knife is recognized as a symbol of masculinity; this symbolic meaning is based on the phallic shape of the knife. Again, this cultural symbolism is also grounded in the human experience.

In many Third World countries traveling by car means that one belongs to the privileged minority of government officials. In affluent postindustrial societies certain types and makes of car stand for and thus confer social prestige. These are meanings by association. The automobile, through its size and self-propulsion, stands also for technical power. This is a symbolic meaning.

The only meanings that are culture-specific and require decoding are referents. As for the words of a language, the relationship between referents and their signifieds is arbitrary and founded only on a convention, an agreement, explicit or implicit, among the speakers of the language (Maquet 1986:93–96).

In reading objects, awareness of the distinction between objects as instruments and objects as signs is important for reaching critical knowledge—the best cognitive value that can be obtained in a particular situation. We shall attempt to demonstrate the usefulness of this distinction in considering a few cases.

INSTRUMENTS

In his paper "Machine Politics: The Political Construction of Technological Artifacts" (in this volume), Steven Lubar discusses the stop-motion spinning frames from Lowell, Massachusetts. These machines were instruments for drawing and twisting fibers into yarn and automatically halting the motion when a thread broke. Any observer taking the trouble to study the machine could infer its use from its structure and operation.

Lubar goes one step further in his deductive reasoning: The stop-motion device in the machine made it possible for one worker to attend more than one machine. Thus textile manufacturers could stretch out labor in their industry.

To be convincing, an inferred conclusion must necessarily follow from the premise. Here, the premise is the object. From the spinning frame we can indeed state that its only use is to produce fabrics: It could not make anything else. The further inference—that the stop-motion device makes it possible to stretch out labor—is a conclusion that states only a possibility. We do not know if, in fact, labor has been stretched out, although it is probable. Indeed, one can not see why manufacturers would have adopted the stop-motion device if it did not stretch out labor. This is an example of what we have called elsewhere "the soft logic of partial conditioning: if A, then probably B" (Maquet 1986:193). This soft logic has to be supplemented by other evidence than that provided by the reading of the object.

The bridges on Long Island parkways is another case mentioned by Lubar. The instrumental use of bridges on a parkway is to permit traffic to go under them. The Long Island bridges have a clearance of less than 12 feet, thus making it impossible for 12-foot-high vehicles, among them buses, to pass under. This is, of course, a necessary logical conclusion. Lubar further states that the bridges were too low for buses because the builder wanted to keep poor people away from the Long Island beaches. Again this conclusion goes beyond what the instrumentality of the bridge can tell us: It has to be documented by the usual sources of history, the written records.

Let us take another case where inferences from objects can take us a long way in our knowledge of the economic system and the political structure of the society in which the artifacts were made. After the British punitive expedition of 1897, many bronze objects from Benin were brought to London. By analyzing the plaques and figurines in the round, one can see that they had been made by the lost wax procedure. This technique of production requires highly skilled artisans, whereas carving masks and figurines in soft wood could be done by any farmer using simple tools: knife, adze, and gouge. It requires also copper, which in that part of Africa had to be imported.

From these conditions necessary for the production of Benin artifacts—professional artisans and imported copper—we may infer that Benin was economically producing an important surplus from an origin other than agriculture, which does not yield high returns in West Africa. In the physical environment of Benin the only other resources fitting to a preindustrial technology were ivory, precious timber, pelts, and gold, which had to be exported by long-distance trade. A societal surplus of such extent and complexity makes it useful to develop a group that can appropriate (by coercion, if necessary), accumulate, manage, and exchange collective resources, employ professionals, and provide them with casting equipment and raw material: the rulers (Maquet 1986:195). Essential economic and political features of the Benin society can be inferred in this manner from the Benin spoils brought to London at the end of the nineteenth century.

These Benin bronzes can tell us more if we consider their formal characteristics. Some are sparingly ornamented and have idealized faces whereas other ones are heavily ornate and have stylized faces and heavy collars. From this formal change it may be inferred that the copper supply increased at a certain time and made it possible for the casters to use more metal. This improved availability of copper made possible and probable a change in style.

In fact this is what happened. Through written sources we learn that during the seventeenth century copper transportation switched from camel caravans across the Sahara desert to sea ships and that indeed a larger quantity of copper became available to the king of Benin (Maquet 1972a:137).

The Benin case confirms that reading objects by means of inferences is a valid and fruitful method if we accept its limitation: In most cases its conclusions are simply probable, not necessary. When making positive inferences (if A, then B), we establish relationships that are rarely of necessity and usually of probability. "If Benin-type bronzes, then professional artisans" is one of these rare necessary inferences. "If surplus, then rulers" is a probable inference. If the units of production of a society produce more than they consume, there is a surplus; this situation is conducive to the emergence of a ruling group or individual, but this emergence may not happen.

It should be noted that if we reverse the relationship, we make negative inferences (if no B, then no A), and these are of necessity—"If no professional artisans, then no Benin-type bronzes"; "If no surplus, no rulers." This process of exclusion, while bringing only a negative knowledge, has the merit of pointing out that there is a significant relationship between the two phenomena, A and B.

In this section we have considered objects as instruments: artifacts designed to do something, such as cutting a solid substance, transporting people and commodities on land, making yarn, and casting bronze. When reading an object as an instrument, the observer considers how it does what it was designed to do and how it affects the physical and social environment.

The hoe, traditionally used in central Africa for cultivating, scratches the topsoil, whereas the plow breaks up the soil more deeply. As in most of the arable land in central Africa, the humus layer is thin, and plowing bares sterile layers and facilitates erosion (Maquet 1972b:17). The cultural significations of hoe and plow are not relevant to their instrumentality.

The objects discussed in this section have so far been tools or machines. What about objects, such as the Benin figurines, which are neither tools nor machines. Are they instruments too?

They are in the sense that they have an instrumentality, a use that is inherent to them. The Benin figurines were made to be looked at; they had an intrinsic visual instrumentality. Yet their significance as signs was dominant. Similarly, knives and cars are predominantly instruments, although they also convey meanings.

IMAGES AND INDICATORS

In this section we begin our discussion of objects as signs. We understand a sign (or signifier) to be something that stands for something else (its signified).

The 1851 Greek Revival steam engine located in Charleston, South Carolina, that Lubar mentions in his article offers a good example of a machine as a sign. That steam engine was an instrument and also, because of its decoration based on the Greek column motif, a sign. In the context of the mid-nineteenth-century South, the architecture of classical Greece stood for a configuration of political ideas and social values that were deemed to be characteristic of the ancient Greek republics, republicanism. The column motif in the machine stood for Greek architecture.

In this chain of signification the first link—the column motif stands for Greek architecture—is based on visual isomorphism: The decorative column is an image of an actual column supporting the pediment of a Greek temple. The second link—Greek architecture stands for republicanism—is based on metonymy: Classical architecture is a part and an indicator of the Greek civilization, which includes republicanism.

When considering the steam engine as an instrument, an observer studies only the engine and not what it meant for the people at the time it was manufactured and was operating. When considering the engine as a sign, the observer's attention is focused on the group that conferred to the engine its signification.

It is the consensus of a group, not the designer or maufacturer, that establishes cultural meaning. In this case it seems that the designer attempted "to fit the new technology into the accepted forms of everyday life" in order to be able to locate the engine in Charleston, "a city opposed to industry in general and steam engines in particular but one that looked kindly on the sort of republicanism represented by the Greek Revival," as Lubar puts it (this vol.: 200–201). Manufacturers and designers certainly have the intention to suggest meanings—and they do it through publicity—but it is the consensus of the concerned audience that matters.

More than a century later, the concerned audience is different: museum visitors for whom the engine stands for a quaint and obsolete technology and not republicanism. Meanings are not inherent to the object (as instrumentality is) or ascribed by the designer (as the meaning of a message is ascribed by the sender): They are given by the group of people to whom the object is relevant. This is why meanings may change, and usually do, when audiences change.

The groups that confer meanings may be as large as a nation or even larger. For the contemporary world audience two buildings, the White House and the Kremlin, stand for the governments of the United States and Russia, and the Eiffel Tower stands for Paris. The groups may be as small, informal, and fleeting as tourists visiting the Taj Mahal or as specialized and scholarly as the archaeologists who study Borobudur.

From this come two conclusions concerning historical research in which human-made things are used as primary sources. First, because artifacts have cultural meanings, the latter have to be elicited from the groups—some stable, some ephemeral—that conferred meanings to objects. It would be a fallacy to think that the meaning is somehow included in the object and has to be retrieved from it. In this respect the object is not a substitute for the more traditional sources of history, the written records.

Second, to search for "the correct signification" of the object in the intention of the makers or in the interpretation of one group over the others would be another fallacy. The intention of the designer and those who have commissioned the design does not determine the meaning of the object. They may try to promote favorable associations of the product with positive cultural values by advertising and public relations; there is no reason to privilege these meanings as the right ones simply because they were intended. And there is no reason to privilege one group over the others. Meanings have to be put in the perspectives of the groups that have expressed them; all are correct in these perspectives.

SIGNS, REFERMENTS, AND SYMBOLS

Images by similarity (e.g., decorative columns) and indicators by association (e.g., the White House) are the two subclasses of signs we have discussed so far. Two other ones are useful to distinguish: referents by convention and symbols by participation.

Referents are signs arbitrarily selected to stand for what they represent, like the words of a language. The only foundation for the relationship between a referent and its signified is an explicit or implicit social convention. Medieval Christian painters and their contemporaries who beheld their works were aware of the convention that associated blue with the Virgin Mary. So, in paintings where there was no image of Mary, the painter could use a blue shape to evoke her presence. Blue was the conventional referent of Mary. The relationship between the color blue and Mary was arbitrary, and one had to know the code.

Some objects are referents. In Rwanda, drums of a certain shape stood for the king, as did a certain kind of stool among the Ashanti and a throne in the United Kingdom. More frequently, a referential form is engraved or added to an object, such as a cross or crescent, pentagram or trident, swastika or eight-spoked wheel. These formal features have to be learned.

Sharply contrasting with referents are symbols. They are not arbitrary signs and are not based on a group's convention. A symbol stands for its signified because it participates in the nature of the signified. The symbol corresponds in the strong sense of partial identity with what it symbolizes.

Lubar gives the example of three nineteenth-century locomotives—one British, one French, and one American. Their designs have to meet the same technical requirements, yet they are different: "English locomotives of the turn of the century look like a substantial building—very solid, very establishment; French locomotives are of a rational, extremely efficient design that shows off all their scientific improvements; and American locomotives are practical, easy to repair, only superficially decorated" (this vol.: 202). Lubar interprets the differences as "reflecting local beliefs and traditions, as well as environmental and economic conditions."

I would like to offer another conceptualization with respect to symbolism. The design of the British locomotive symbolizes the value of solidity; it corresponds to it by creating it. The visual forms stand for solidity and make the locomotive strong; the symbol (the English locomotive) is equivalent to the quality of solidity. The design of the French locomotive symbolizes the value of rationality. Here again the difference between the sign and the signified is blurred: The design stands for rationality and is rational. The design of the American locomotive symbolizes the value of practicality. Again, it can be said that it is practical. There is a continuity from the machine to the quality—in fact, an identity: The locomotive is practical; the practicality is embodied in the locomotive.

For historians and other social scientists the symbolic approach is different from the ones discussed so far. Here observers may rely on their own mental apprehension of the locomotive designs. Whether the English, French, and American engineers wanted to symbolize the national values of solidity, rationality, and practicality in their designs does not matter. What matters is that we perceive these national values.

Similarly, we do not have to approach symbolic meanings necessarily through the views of the cultural insiders as we have to do for referents and indicators. Of course, it is important to know how they perceive symbols and how they verbalize their perceptions, but this is not the first step of the research. The first step is to use our own apprehensive powers.

The approach to the object as symbol has in common with the approach to the object as instrument that the encounter between observer and object is direct, with a minimum of cultural mediation. Like instrumentality, symbolism is intercultural. It can be perceived across cultural boundaries. For instruments the reason is that the forms necessary for their operation, the stuff they are made of, and the impact on the environment depend on their physical nature; for symbolic objects the reason is that most of the meanings ascribed to them are grounded in the human condition as experienced by all of us. Instruments and symbols are located, as it were, on a subcultural level.

GESTALT AND ANALYSIS

It has just been stated that in reading objects as symbols observers can and should perceive meanings by looking at the objects. This sounds like subjectivism. It has also been stated that they would do so by a global apprehension. This sounds like intuitionism. How can these capital sins of research be reconciled with the pursuit of critical knowledge?

Global apprehension, in which a visual object is perceived as a whole gestalt, is characteristic of the mental mode we use in tasks requiring a comprehensive attention (Maquet 1986:25–33, 161–162). Perceiving in an object the whole meaning that it has for the beholder requires that mental mode. When looking at the French locomotive, the meaning of rationality emerges from a global, not an analytical, attention. It is thus appropriate to use it in reading symbolic meanings. This is not intuitionism. Here we understand intuitionism as the indiscriminate use of a global mode of perception when an analytic one is appropriate.

A subject, observing and interpreting, is a part of any research process. Cognitive validity is obtained not by pretending that the subject has no impact on the observation but by replicating observations by several scholars. After the first observer reports understanding the three locomotives as symbolizing solidity, rationality, and practicability, another may look comprehensively at the same machines and perceive the same or other symbolic meanings. This is a way to control subjectivism at the gestalt stage of object reading.

The second stage is analytic, the usual mode of cognitive discourse. What are the features in the French locomotive that suggest rationality? Efficient design and display of scientific improvements, mentioned by Lubar (who does not discuss this case in our framework), are among the features accounting for the locomotive's rationality. At the analytic stage, types of proof and reasoning accepted in scholarly and scientific inquiry for testing hypotheses are used.

The third stage is to collect other symbolic meanings that are and have been perceived in the object, particularly by cultural insiders, the members of the society to which the object belongs. Symbols are polysemic signs; we expect that the same material support—the locomotive—will trigger different meanings in the minds of those who have had different individual and collective experiences. The interplay of personal, cultural, and human symbolic meanings perceived in the same object is an illuminating field of study. It also provides another control of the cognitive value of the observer's own perceptions.

This short—too short—epistemic digression is not out of place, we hope. Global apprehension of a phenomenon, although occasionally used in scholarly endeavors, is kept underground. When used with controls (for example, replicability, analysis, and comparison) where the discursive procedures do not work, it is legitimate. We have indicated here the lines according to which an argument could be developed for justifying the use of the observer's global perception in scholarly research (for a further discussion, see Maquet 1986:243–251).

INSIDERS' INTERPRETATIONS

To use human-made objects as sources for history and other social sciences, we have to "read them," a metaphor for interpreting them. Incidentally, this metaphor could be misleading because it suggests that objects are texts. Texts, except poetry, are to be read analytically. Yet we will continue to use this metaphor, which has gained large acceptance.

In this essay we have distinguished five ways to read objects: as instruments, as symbols, as images, as indicators, and as referents (they are ranked here from the less culture-specific interpretation to the one entirely dependent on a particular culture). In other words, written sources for historians and interviews for anthropologists become increasingly significant when we move from instruments to referents.

Most artifacts can be analyzed as instruments without having recourse to the culture to which they belong. From the object alone the observer can infer its use (if it is to be worn on the face, it is a mask) but not its function (to be the receptacle of a spirit, a prop for entertainment, or a means of social control). The function is culture-specific.

A meaning of the object as polysemous symbol may be perceived by the observer. Other outsiders and the insiders may perceive other symbolic meanings in the object. To study the range of meanings, historians and anthropologists must resort to written or spoken sources.

Because images are objects standing for other things by visual similarity, cultural outsiders can perceive what an image stands for (for example, a woman, a man). But without further cultural information, they do not know whether the woman represents Juno or Aphrodite, the man Zeus or Apollo.

Indicators—signs by association or metonymy—are culture-specific. To perceive Greek architecture as standing for republicanism, observers have to know that this association was made by nineteenth-century Americans involved in the Greek Revival.

Because referents are arbitrary signs, there is no possible understanding of what they stand for without learning the conventional code.

For historians and social scientists, who are always concerned with socially constructed realities, it is essential to know what objects mean for the people who make them and use them. Their reading of objects always has to be supplemented by what people say and write about them. Objects can illuminate words; they cannot replace them.

REFERENCES

Maquet, Jacques. 1972a. *Civilizations of Black Africa*. New York: Oxford University Press.
———. 1972b. *Africanity: The Cultural Unity of Black Africa*. New York: Oxford University Press.
———. 1986. *The Aesthetic Experience: An Anthropologist Looks at the Visual Arts*. New Haven and London: Yale University Press.

Some Matters of Substance

Robert Friedel

I n the second book of his *Physics*, Aristotle
sets out the central concerns for students of
the physical world, by which he means not
only the world of nature but also that shaped by
humans—the world of artifacts, if you will. At
the center of these concerns is the recognition
that there are two aspects to all things: matter
and form. He chides earlier philosophers for being too much concerned with matter at the expense of understanding the form or essence of a
thing. As befits Plato's star pupil, Aristotle
urges us to pay more attention to form or design.
Later in the *Physics*, Aristotle delineates his
well-known four causes of things, in which the
design, the maker, and the purpose of a thing
are all part. But, and this is my central point,
his first cause and his first element for compre-

hending a thing is the *material* cause—the matter or stuff that makes up a thing.

I want to suggest that our understanding of history from things also should begin with the materials that go into our artifacts. The essays in this volume are characterized by an overwhelming concern with form and design rather than substance. I have no quarrel with this, but it is ironic that studies of material culture should so neglect the actual materials that go into creating culture. The fallacy of this can perhaps be briefly illustrated by reference to the same object so thoroughly discussed by Jules Prown in his paper—the teapot. If one looks at not one teapot but at several, each of them made of a different material, it quickly becomes apparent that not only the form but also the substance of the pot conveys messages to us. A tin pot, with its straight, angled spout and its severe lines—responses not so much to particular choices by the maker but to requirements of the material itself—tells us a story very different from that of a teapot of fine china. A fragile glass pot, globular not so much because it expresses maternal feelings but because it is made by a blower who knows how to minimize labor and the chances of mishap, makes a statement different from that of a pot of pewter. The form tells us *what* the object is—that it is a teapot and not, for instance, a coffeepot. This is obviously important, but it is only when we take into consideration the materials of each object that we can begin to appreciate the real history of each. The material itself conveys messages, metaphorical and otherwise, about the objects and their place in a culture.

SOME PRINCIPLES FOR UNDERSTANDING PAST THINGS

It is not my intention to examine these messages closely but rather to make the case that these material messages should be part of our interpretation of things of the past. The appreciation of the significance of materials for our understanding of past things begins with some straightforward principles.

Everything Is Made from Something

This is my starting point. The astonishing simplicity and apparent triviality of this statement make it actually quite provocative. I stumbled across this truth while working on the Smithsonian Institution exhibit "A Material World." Anyone who has worked on large, complicated exhibits, especially ones begun by someone else, will appreciate this scene: A number of us were gathered over lunch and beginning to ask whether this exhibit made any sense, whether it had a theme. A number of statements were proposed, but somehow none of them seemed to the point or sufficiently comprehensive. That's when I came up with this statement: Everything is made from something. No one could put a hole in this statement, nor could they claim it was not encompassing. I detected, however, the lingering (if unspoken) thought that no one knew what it meant.

There Are Reasons for Using Particular Materials in a Thing

The making of anything requires that choices be made about the stuff that goes into it. There are a number of grounds for these choices, of which the following seem to be the most important:

Function. The stuff that goes into something must be appropriate for whatever purpose the thing is to serve. Fired clay is suitable for a coffee cup; tissue paper is not.

Availability. Obviously, my choice of materials is shaped by what I can obtain. This physical availability is also joined by intellectual availability—to choose a substance, I have to know of its existence, how to get it and make it useful, and what properties it possesses that are of interest to me. If I have kaolin ("China" clay) at hand, I can make a porcelain cup if I know how to use it. If I know how to make styrofoam, I can even make a plastic cup.

Economy. In most instances my choice of materials is very much affected by what I want to pay for it. This is true literally, of course, but also more figuratively, because the cost of a material may go beyond its price and include the effort I go through to find it or to work it and my future plans for the object. If I want a cup to keep for awhile, I make different economic decisions than if I want one that I can dispose of after a single use.

Style. When I make or choose a thing, I may have certain design criteria that go beyond function. I may have expectations about what something should look like, how heavy it is, what sorts of lines it has, and so forth. These considerations affect my choice of stuff. In some cases, indeed, the stuff itself is part of a particular style. A Windsor chair made out of something other than wood is not a Windsor chair. A coffee cup made of porcelain can have stylistic pretensions not open to styrofoam.

Tradition. Aside from stylistic or aesthetic concerns, I may associate certain materials with certain objects simply on the basis of familiarity or tradition. I might depart from traditional stuff in an object, but if I do so consciously then it is clear that tradition has still played a role in my choices. If I want a cup for serving Christmas punch, tradition might guide me to choose glass, but if I want one for serving tea to my grandmother, out comes the porcelain.

These Reasons Are Subject to Change As Circumstances Change

It should be readily evident that the choices made about stuff are affected by a number of external factors that may change the whole universe of material choices. The most obvious of these factors seem to be these:

Geography. Where I am affects the availability and economy of many materials, and in some cases affects the functioning of the material. Similarly, what I know about my surroundings and its endowments will affect my material choices. In eastern North America I may use wood in ways undreamt of in the desert Southwest.

Technology. We are all familiar with the ability of new or improved techniques to change the status of a material. The classic example of this is the radical change in the place of steel in the second half of the nineteenth century with the introduction of Bessemer, open hearth, and other processes for its manufacture.

Science. I do not want to distinguish too firmly here science from technology, for the distinction is not important to my argument and can get messy and arbitrary. I simply want to call attention to the fact that new knowledge about the world can make a great difference in the perception of available stuff. The metal aluminum, for example, was a scientific discovery before it became a commodity. The role of science in producing completely novel stuff in the twentieth century is an important story itself.

Fashion. Standards of style and taste change over time, and these changes can affect choices about stuff. In our own century certain aesthetic trends can be directly linked to certain kinds of materials, especially novel ones. The Art Deco use of chrome and aluminum springs to mind as one example; the ins and outs of fashion in plastics is another.

Competition. This factor is arguably not distinct from questions of economy or availability, but it should be emphasized that the status of a material and choices made about it are constantly affected by other materials. The choices of entrepreneurs, the development of transportation and distribution networks, and the exploitation of novel processes can enhance one material's position at the expense of another.

Different Values Are Attached to Different Stuffs

There is something about the word "values" that makes a scholar want to run and hide, for few notions are more slippery. But it is actually the question of the relationship between materials and values that is at the heart of this subject. We cannot know the way in which different stuff makes the past different from the present without getting some sense of how values are attached to stuff and how and why these values change. There are some fairly clear sources for many of these values.

Scarcity. Scarcity in itself is not a source of inherent value, although sometimes people behave as if it were. Nonetheless, the value of a material, monetary or other, is directly affected by its supply. The value of precious metals is the most obvious example here, although a little thought will suggest others.

Aesthetic. Some materials are thought to be more beautiful than others, although this aesthetic value rarely exists outside the context of form or design. A lump of unshaped gold may be seen to possess more aesthetic value than a lump of iron, although it is only when it is properly worked that we can appreciate the beauty of one material more than another. Like all values, of course, beauty is in the eye of the beholder, and we must be careful to attach any generalizations about a material and its value—aesthetic or other—to a particular context.

Functional. It might seem redundant to speak of functional values of a material, but in fact the perceived function of a material is very much culturally determined. Under one set of circumstances a material may have a function readily accepted by society but may lose or change this function under different conditions. A particularly apt example of this is the history of radium. When radium was first discovered by the Curies at the turn of the century, it (or, more precisely, its salts) was a precious commodity, valued for radiotherapy and for its luminescence, as on watch dials. It was hailed as one of the wonder substances of the twentieth century. Today it is no more than a detested residue of uranium production—a hazardous waste, if you will. The emergence of more easily controlled and produced radioisotopes and a realization of the material's inherent health hazards have changed its functional value profoundly.

Associative. For a variety of reasons people come to make associations between a material and various feelings, concerns, and attitudes. These associations are rarely stated, but they are quite significant to our understanding of the past and its influence on the present. The rich associations of gold, for example, hardly need to be described, but we should remind ourselves that these associations are cultural artifacts, not inherent linkages. We readily find these associations scattered throughout our language and literature. Think only of the references to a "golden age," "iron men," "paper tigers," and the like.

These Values Are Not Inherent in the Material but Are Determined by Circumstances

This principle should be quite apparent from the preceeding examples, but it still needs to be made explicit. By making it so, the nature of the real historical problem becomes more evident—that is, understanding the relationship between the values attached to stuff and the values and circumstances of the larger culture.

The Values Attached to Materials Affect the Values Attached to Things, but They Are Not the Same

This too is a straightforward proposition that is useful to make explicit. It is in fact often much easier to determine the value that people place on things rather than on stuff. If one is careful, it may be possible to infer some of the stuff values from the thing values.

Starting with these principles and premises, what then are the directions implied for the student of the past? With respect to the study of individual objects, there are many avenues that a closer look at materials will open up—investigations of how the values, attachments, functions, and significance of different artifacts are bound up in the materials of which they are made. This careful attention to materials opens up a broader set of problems, however. This can be briefly illustrated in the context of one more proposition, this one more an observation or thesis than a premise.

Over the last two centuries the stuff of things has changed far more radically and profoundly than in any other period of history. One can identify the beginnings of this transformation in the period of early industrialization, and its acceleration can be identified closely with changes in

science and the application of scientific knowledge and methods that accompanied spreading industrialization in the nineteenth century. The result is that by the middle third of the twentieth century a conception of the
material world and its possibilities very different from any in the past had
emerged. Understanding the nature and causes of this emergence and its
significance for how the present differs from the past is a key historical
issue.

PATTERNS AND ANALYTICAL PATHS

As we look more closely at these changes of two centuries, some important
patterns emerge, patterns that allow us to give some shape to our story.
And as we examine these patterns, certain elements of analysis also
emerge—analytical paths, if you will   that promise to make the real
meaning of our story clearer.

Material Changes

A number of authors have remarked on the great changes in materials and
material capabilities in modern history. Perhaps the classic statement is
that of Lewis Mumford (adapting the scheme of Patrick Geddes), who
described in his *Technics and Civilization* three stages of modern technical development. In these stages, materials as well as mechanical and
organizational changes were prominent. "Eotechnic" culture was one in
which "natural" materials such as wood, wool, and clay were central to
human activities. This was followed in the industrial period by a "paleotechnic" culture, in which coal and iron were dominant features of civilization. This in turn, Mumford tells us, was followed by the emergence of a
new order, the "neotechnic," which harnessed the wonders of science to
use new forms of energy, such as electricity, and new materials, such as
aluminum and plastics.

Mumford's outline was mirrored somewhat in the "Material World"
exhibition, in which reference was made to a sequence of three material
"epochs" in American history—natural, manufactured, and artificial. All
such ways of describing material changes are somewhat arbitrary and
unsatisfactory, but they do at least put the emphasis on the dynamic of an
important shift in material life—from a world of a relatively small number of substances, many of them little removed from recognizable natural

forms, to one in which the variety of materials seems literally endless, bounded only by human imagination and as yet unreached natural limits.

Although the general process of this shift has been recognized, scholars have actually done a poor job of explaining its fundamental causes and consequences.

Technical Changes

Other kinds of changes that are clearly an important part of the story involve not the introduction of new or different materials but rather the adoption of new techniques for producing and manipulating stuff. New technologies have given us quantities of stuff, varieties of form and substance, abilities of manipulation that were undreamed of in the preindustrial world. These things have to be accounted for to explain how past stuff is different from present stuff.

Perceptual Changes

At the same time that scientific and technical advances changed the way old materials were produced and used and introduced new ones into life and commerce, equally radical changes occurred in how people thought about materials, particularly in how they thought about novel materials. I refer to this as a change in the "ideology" of materials, admitting that I use that term a bit loosely here.

I perceive three stages that this ideology goes through in the nineteenth century: (1) bounty and stasis; (2) ingenuity and change; and (3) science and novelty.

The first stage is the traditional perception of materials and the material world—a kind of "pre-Darwinian" perception, one characterized by a belief in the essentially unchanging mix of materials available in the world. The second stage is a transitional one, peculiar to the mid-nineteenth century and of relatively short duration. It is a view that recognizes the possibility of new materials but sees them as unusual or extraordinary. The third stage best characterizes current thinking about materials; it emerges in the last decades of the nineteenth century, and we would call it "modern." I would describe this modern view as one that sees the development and adoption of new materials as an ordinary and expected aspect of technological progress.

For the first stage I have found some writings that, while certainly not typical, reflect fully what I believe is the traditional image of the material world as an unchangeable, God-given world of specific substances. The materials of this world are not subjects for innovation, technology, and change. In its most extreme form, this point of view becomes a kind of material theology, in which the distribution and form of natural materials are looked on as evidence of the wisdom and foresight of the Creator, not conditions to be improved on.

The second stage, ingenuity and change, is a transitional one, characterized by the growing perception of the possibilities of important material innovation tempered by perceived limits to human knowledge and nature's possibilities. The individuals in the mid-nineteenth century who discovered new forms of steel, new ways of using rubber, and new metals such as aluminum and chromium stand as representatives of this new kind of thought. It is the thinking of ambitious, creative artisans who chafe at the idea that the material world is static but who are still, in the manner of artisans, respectful of nature's own ways of doing things.

The last stage, science and novelty, is a familiar mode of thought for us. The men and women who created the plastics, the fibers, and even the isotopes that gave the lie to the notion that there is nothing new under the sun were clearly guided by an ideology of novelty that knew no visible bounds. True, the laws of nature were not to be broken, but, as the episode of the superconductor reminds us, we hardly know what limits these laws place on us in the realm of stuff.

Only when historians turn their attention to materials and the kinds of changes outlined here does the challenge begin. The extent and significance of material changes since the end of the eighteenth century can be appreciated only with respect to the differences they made in people's lives. This is undoubtedly the most difficult question to answer: How does one determine and describe the context of changes in material life? After all, one of the constants in this story is the silence of the actors; people do not generally talk about the meaning of stuff. The meanings and values they attach both to artifacts and to materials are implicit, perhaps even often unconscious. Likewise, our documentary records about possessions and their significance are scanty and unreliable. This is particularly true in the realm of "small things forgotten," to use James Deetz's phrase lifted from a seventeenth-century inventory.

And yet it is of these small things—the kitchen pots, the parlor chairs, the office desks, the window blinds—that our material world is made. To sense their meaning, all I can think to do is understand their making, their acquisition, their use, and even their disposal, all in terms of real people.

On a recent visit to Old Sturbridge Village in Massachusetts, I made a point of taking a close look at the house of Emerson Bixby, a blacksmith in central Massachusetts who lived in this house during most of the first half of the nineteenth century. There, in this painstakingly researched, documented, and reconstructed setting, I could begin to see where our search might lead us. In the kitchen, wood tables, chairs, and bowls on the bare wood floor were conspicuously joined by red earthenware and a couple of iron pots. A few pieces of tinware were conspicuous, not because of their value to the Bixbys but because they remind the modern visitor of the limited role of metal in that world compared to our own. The materials of the Bixbys' working life were simple ones, ones that they or their near neighbors could manipulate to their own ends. The limits of these materials were not limits to them but rather opportunities for them to shape the substance of their own lives.

In moving from the working world to that of living—of leisure, companionship, and family—one can see the forces opening up and complicating the Bixbys' material world. In the sitting room, also, plain wood dominated, with the accent now provided by piles of imported ceramics in the open cupboard, almost the only color in a generally unornamented household. The so-called best room was dominated by the wood bedstead, but on it was a large coverlet, hinting perhaps at the great role to be played by upholstery in other, more comfortable dwellings of this and later times. There is no clock or other complex mechanism in the Bixbys' house. The materials of their family life are still very restricted, but in the reach for comfort and status they become just a bit more exotic and complicated. The porcelain with its colorful glaze is beyond the ken of the working world, and it hints of a dependence on an extended arena of extraction, production, and commerce.

The clearest message conveyed to the modern visitor by the stuff of the Bixbys is the limits of their material world and the hints of surpassing those limits in the generations to come. We are left with a profound appreciation for how the transcending of these limits makes our own world so different from the past. We will find few more important messages from our exploration of history from things.

The Ancestry of Chinese Bronze Vessels

Jessica Rawson

mong the many things that people both treasure and take for granted few have been as
enduring as Chinese bronze ritual vessels,
especially the round basin with two handles,
standing on three legs, known as a *ding*. An example of these massive three-legged *ding* is the
Da Yu *ding*, now in the Shanghai Museum, cast
around 1000 B.C. (fig. 1). First cast as ritual
food vessels more than 1,500 years B.C., bronzes
of the same form are still made today as incense
burners for small household or temple altars.
Twentieth-century woodblock prints often de-
pict altars on which stand small rounded tripods. These vessels and their more distinguished
counterparts, which embellish the palaces of the
emperors (fig. 2), are direct descendants of
these ancient bronzes. This continuity of form
across three thousand years is noteworthy. In

Fig. 1. The Da Yu ding, early Western Zhou, eleventh century B.C., height 56.5 cm., Shanghai Museum. After Shanghai bowuguan zang qingtongqi, Shanghai 1964, vol. 1, pl. 29. © British Museum.

Fig. 2. Incense burner in the form of ancient ding *with an elaborate cover, in a courtyard of the Gugong (the Forbidden City), Beijing, Qing dynasty, eighteenth to nineteenth century, after* Cijin Cheng Gongdian, *Beijing 1982, p. 125.* © British Museum.

Europe and North America only sculptures in the classical tradition can match this survival.[1]

This paper will discuss the longevity of Chinese bronze vessels. The survival of ancient bronzes preserved in museums is easy to explain. Many thousands of vessels were made in the centuries during Shang and Zhou rule (ca. 1500–221 B.C.), and as important ritual utensils they were often buried rather than melted down. Because the vessels were cast in bronze, their walls were comparatively thick, and when buried they usually have not corroded badly. So there are plenty of bronzes available to excavators.

However, the continuity of the bronze shapes across three or four thousand years cannot be accounted for just by the survival of ritual vessels from the Bronze Age down to the present day, either above or below ground. An almost continuous interest in bronzes was generated and sustained by constant rediscovery of ancient pieces. In the centuries that followed their burial, ritual bronzes were rediscovered, exciting interest and even awe. These rediscoveries fall into five main phases: the Han to Tang dynasties (206 B.C.–A.D. 750); the late Tang and Song periods (800–1279); the Yuan and the Ming dynasties (1280–1644); the Qing dynasty (1644–1911); and the twentieth century. As bronzes were retrieved, they inspired the making of copies, which thus kept the ancient shapes alive.

In theory it is possible for a particular bronze or even many particular bronzes to have been rediscovered, say in the first century B.C., to have survived above ground, and to have been valued in all five phases. In fact this has not happened. Bronzes were buried in the Shang or Zhou periods and were then rediscovered in the Han period (206 B.C.–A.D. 220) or perhaps later in the Song dynasty (A.D. 960–1279). They were then lost again, either because collections were dispersed in times of political upheaval or because attitudes changed, altering the evaluation of bronzes within society.[2] The act of rediscovery has been crucial to the role of the bronzes in these later episodes. Even in the twentieth century, a recently rediscovered bronze has a different although not always greater value in our eyes than one handed down through several generations.[3] Once rediscovered, bronzes have enjoyed new existences in new contexts. Thus, it is possible to consider the original existence of the bronzes and the five later phases as six separate episodes in the history of bronzes.

In looking at the episodes here, attention will not be directed at the moment of manufacture or at sequences of different copies, which followed one another over three thousand years. For an understanding of the survival of bronze forms, especially the *ding*, these often small changes in vessel shape or decoration are relatively insignificant. The role or status of bronzes in particular societies was what mattered. Although later generations did not always, indeed if ever, understand the former roles correctly, the bronzes were subsequently treasured for their supposed ancient functions or values in former societies. This paper will briefly outline the significance of Chinese ritual vessels as they were used in the Shang and Zhou periods (ca. 1500–221 B.C.) and will then describe some features of the five later episodes. It is my contention that it is impossible to use the bronzes to understand early Chinese history unless we recognize that they have accumulated new values and roles over the later episodes of their history.[4]

EPISODE 1: CA. 1500–221 B.C.

This section will outline the principal features of ancient Chinese bronzes, especially the *ding*, which were to be relevant to their later evaluation.

From the beginning of the history of the *ding* to the present day, bronze has remained the material of choice. In early times it was a scarce and valuable material and was used for weapons. The fact that this scarce weapon material was chosen for ritual vessels demonstrates their high value to society.[5]

The vessels were essential in the sense that they were the most conspicuous elements in rituals that paid respect to ancestors, rituals that we today call sacrifices. Food and wine were offered at formal banquets to ancestors to ensure their good will. The shapes in which the bronzes were cast were taken from earlier Neolithic ceramic containers. The *ding* itself was an ancient Neolithic shape, consisting of a basin, which was held over a fire, supported by three legs.

Bronzes of all types, but especially ritual vessels, were indissolubly linked with authority and power. Only men of high status—the king, his nobles, and his officials—were able to obtain ritual bronzes. How access to ritual bronzes was controlled we do not know. It seems safe to assume that foundries vital for weapon casting were under royal control. We know from inscriptions in bronzes of the eleventh century and later that the king would occasionally make grants of bronze or cowries to his subjects and that the bronze was then used to cast a vessel, while the cowries might be used as a form of payment for the bronze vessels. Access to vessels was thus an index of a person's relationship with the king and hence of that person's influence within the state.

In the Shang and early Zhou periods the ancestors to whom the sacrifices in the vessels were directed were seen almost certainly in the same hierarchical terms by which the living were already ordered. The ancestors of the king were undoubtedly thought to be more influential than those of a lesser noble. As the manufacture of bronzes developed, the hierarchy in society was expressed in the quality of the bronzes; the vessels of the royal family exceeded those of lesser individuals in their design and casting, their size, and their number. After the mid-eighth century B.C., when China was divided into several competing states, ritual bronzes were used to display the might and wealth of their owners and impress their rivals.

Thus, *ding* and other ritual vessels were made of one of the most valuable materials available in ancient China; they were cast in shapes used for food and wine long before the advent of bronze; they were owned primarily by kings and high nobles; and their size and quality of casting indicated their owner's status within the social hierarchy. In addition *ding* acquired at least two other characteristics that were to contribute to their later value: They became vehicles for long commemorative inscriptions, and they came to be used to indicate the precise ranks of their owners.

Inscriptions in bronze vessels were popular during the reign of the Zhou, who came to power in the middle of the eleventh century B.C. after defeating the long-established Shang. The Zhou borrowed from the Shang the custom of casting these inscriptions but greatly extended the practice, perhaps because political upheavals made new honors and gifts necessary to buy loyalty and those so honored wished to publicize their rewards.

The inscriptions were cast in intaglio, usually inside the bronze vessels, where they would be covered by food and wine, not on the outside, where they could be seen by those participating in the rituals in a temple. From this we may suppose that the inscriptions were intended to be read not only by living and future generations but also perhaps by the dead to whom the food and wine were offered.

The impressive inscription in the Da Yu *ding* records a series of gifts from the king to one Yu. The description of the gift is preceded by a long eulogy on the achievements of the early Zhou kings. Yu thus publicly associated himself with the Zhou royal family, claiming status for himself by this association.[6] The eulogies in these inscriptions are the forerunners of later texts justifying kingly rule on the grounds of the virtue of the kings.

People of later generations were in no doubt as to the purpose of the inscriptions. A famous account appears in the *Li Ji*, a ritual text compiled during the Han period, possibly in the second century B.C.:

> The inscriber discourses about and extols the virtues and goodness of his ancestors, their merits and their zeal, their services and their toils, the congratulations and rewards given to them, their fame recognized by all under Heaven; and in the discussion of these things on spiritual vessels he makes himself famous. (Legge 1885: part 4, 251)

In addition to their use as vehicles for inscriptions, *ding* became increasingly important during the Zhou period to indicate status and possibly even precise rank. As with the inscriptions, this was a role acquired separately from the *ding*'s function as a cooking vessel. At first groups of dissimilar *ding* were buried in tombs. From about 850 B.C. on, sets of *ding* identical in shape and decoration though diminishing in size were used.[7] Burials alone might not have enabled us or indeed earlier generations of Chinese scholars to understand the function of these groups of identical tripods. However, texts dating from before the end of this first period, around the third century B.C., describe the function of sets of *ding*. In a commentary on a text entitled the *Gong Yang Zhuan*, the scholar He Xiu stated, "In ritual offerings the Son of Heaven used nine *ding* tripods, the feudal lords seven, the senior officials five, and the *shi* knights three." During the Han period (206 B.C.–A.D. 220), this commentary was studied fully by rival groups of scholars, one group voicing the view that the numbers were inconsistent with accounts in another text, the *Zhou Li*, and that the emperor must have used twelve *ding* (see Li Xueqin 1985:461).

These texts were probably fundamental in keeping alive, long after the rituals of the Zhou had vanished, some understanding of the roles of Zhou *ding*. The Han may have drawn the wrong conclusions from the texts they inherited. However, they certainly believed that *ding* had been used to indicate rank. In the Han period the Zhou rituals declined, although they did not disappear. This much is evident in the position of sets of ritual vessels in relation to other bronzes in Han period tombs. At tombs at Mancheng, in which the minor prince Liu Sheng was buried with his consort Dou Wan, each in a jade suit, during the middle of the second century B.C., relatively plain ritual vessels were used, while the wine flasks (*hu*) for feasting were extremely ornate, having inlay and gilding (*Mancheng Han mu* 1980: vol. 2, pls. 5 and 6). Thus, although the Han knew that *ding* had been linked to status in some way, this was no longer so evidently the case in their own times.

EPISODE 2: HAN DYNASTY TO EARLY TANG DYNASTY
(206 B.C.–A.D. 750)

A new episode began as this decline took place, for the drop in the status of the *ding* reflected religious changes. Two major new beliefs overshadowed the earlier sacrifices to the ancestors: (1) a belief in abodes of gods and sources of immortality to which humans might gain access and (2) attention to miraculous phenomena, known as *xiangrui*, which indicated the will of heaven (Wu Hung 1984). In this second major episode the *ding* relevant to this discussion were not newly cast but were ancient *ding* rediscovered. These discoveries were treated as examples of such miracles.

The best known occasion when a *ding* was rediscovered occurred in 113 B.C., as recorded by the Han court historian, Sima Qian, in his history the *Shi Ji*, composed in the first century B.C. (Barnard 1973: 493). A long passage describes the discovery, which was then reported to the Emperor Wu (140–87 B.C.), who went to meet the *ding* as it was brought to the capital. At this moment a yellow cloud appeared and also a deer, which the emperor himself shot and offered in sacrifice. All these phenomena were of the *xiangrui* type. Then the emperor sought from his ministers an interpretation of the discovery of the *ding* and associated events with respect to his current problems with floods and droughts. But in fact the interpretation that followed, as reported in the official histories, gave the emperor little direct counsel or even hope. Instead the officials set out the role of *ding* in a legendary past and their consequent significance in the Han period:

> It is known that in antiquity when the Eminent Emperor flourished there was one divine *ding*—"one" signified "Unity": Heaven, Earth, and the Myriad Beings were interwoven. Huang Di made the three precious *ding* representing Heaven, Earth and Humanity. Yu accumulated metals from the Nine Pastors and cast the Nine *ding* with which offerings were cooked in sacrifice to Shang Di, the Spirits and the Gods. Whenever a sage comes on the scene, the *ding* appear. They were transmitted to Xia and then to Shang. When the virtue of Zhou

declined and the Altars of Song, descendants of Shang, were lost, the *ding* fell into the waters where they were covered and lost to sight. (translation after Barnard 1973:474)

The passage shows an awareness of the considerable antiquity of *ding* and their use for sacrifices. The description of their casting and possession by the legendary sage emperors was extrapolated from the ancient kings' possession of fine bronzes. References to the nine *ding* cast by Yu seems to be based on their use by the Zhou as indicators of rank. A new extension of this role is given in the account of their possession by legitimate rulers and their loss once the rulers had erred, thus indicating that they had lost the approval of heaven. In this way *ding* were made to signal the virtue of rulers, a virtue that in ancient times they had advertised in their inscriptions. In the interim the philosophers of the sixth and fifth century had extended the early Zhou concept of a just ruler. Thus, ancient characteristics of *ding* used as ritual vessels had been altered to support a new role in which discovery of *ding* signaled the will of heaven.[8]

Much information on the use of ritual vessels was already available to Han scholars in the major classical works on ritual, such as the *Zhou Li* [*The Rituals of Zhou*] mentioned earlier. These texts were supplemented during the Han period by documents now known as the Han apocrypha, or *chanwei* texts, purportedly works that had been omitted from the classics in error and that should be consulted to supply deficiencies in the main texts (Seidel 1981, 1983). A number of the *chanwei* texts were concerned with the connection between omens and the social order.

From these pseudohistorical accounts, which emphasized *ding* as emblems of legitimacy, grew a long-lasting preoccupation with the miraculous appearance of *ding* as evidence of heaven's approval of the rulers and their deeds. The centuries of divided rule following the collapse of the Han dynasty in A.D. 220 are rich in accounts of the miraculous appearance of *ding*.[9] Indeed at this time the concept of a body of talismans, including charts and texts, which a ruler had to possess if he was to be regarded as legitimate, flourished under the auspices of religious Daoism (Seidel 1983). During this time vessels were collected on behalf of the rulers, and judging by comments in the dynastic histories this tradition must have persisted into the Tang period (A.D. 618–906). Ledderose has shown how these objects and documents, originally collected for their talismanic significance, were the foundations of major imperial collections of art works (Ledderose 1978–79).

EPISODE 3: LATE TANG AND SONG PERIODS (A.D. 800–1279)

From the middle of the eighth century a change in attitudes heralded the third major episode in the history of bronze vessels. In the political upheavals and doubts that followed the An Lushan rebellion of 755, new philosophies were framed in opposition to Buddhism, which was dominant in the early Tang period. Han Yu (768–824), famous for his polemics against Buddhism and his support of traditional ancient philosophies, is recognized as the precursor of the revival of Confucian thought, known as neo-Confucianism (Fung Yu-lan 1983: vol. 2, 408–413). A revival of Confucian thought implied, of course, a concern with the political and social structures of the period of Confucius—that is, the late Zhou period—regarded by Han Yu's successors as a golden age.

Over the succeeding centuries a concern with the texts and ideas of the late Zhou period was fuelled by the political problems faced by the late Tang rulers and the period of disunity that followed the collapse of the Tang, known as the Five Dynasties (907–947). After the great expansion of the early Tang, China was in retreat. This political situation intensified the introspection of political leaders, especially the reformers. Both the innovators, such as Wang Anshi (1021–1086), who cited the *Zhou Li*, in support of his wide-ranging economic proposals, and his opponents among the conservatives, such as Ouyang Xiu (1007–1072) and Sima Guang (1018–1086), took as axiomatic that an understanding of the past was fundamental to good government (Fung Yu-lan 1983: vol. 2, 424–566).

Collections of calligraphy, paintings, and bronzes and the study of those bronzes and their inscriptions must be seen in this context. Through their study of ancient texts on ritual and history, scholars were aware of both the standing of bronzes in the Zhou period and their regard in later times. In the collections of the Song and the catalogues that comment on them, we find serious study of the Zhou period to learn how the rites were practiced and how the bronzes were used in those rites as well as evidence of the belief that collections conferred legitimacy on their owners. In other words, the scholars of the day were conscious of both the ancient roles of bronzes and their talismanic significance under the Han and in subsequent centuries.

The greatest Song collection was that of the Emperor Huizong (r. 1101–1125), intended no doubt to match or surpass that of the Tang Emperor Taizong (626–649). Possession of a collection was probably seen as reinforcing Song claims to have received the mandate of heaven, despite setbacks on their northern borders and invasions by the Liao and later the Jin dynasty.[10] Within this collection the high value of ancient bronzes and associated texts on the rites is demonstrated by their location in the central building of the Hall of Precious Harmony (*Bao he dian*), in which the palace connection was stored (Ledderose 1985:45). The bronzes were illustrated and described in their own catalogue, the *Xuan he bo gu tu lu*. This catalogue followed the earlier pioneering catalogue, *Kao gu tu*, by the neo-Confucian scholar Lü Dalin, compiled in 1092.

The *Kao gu tu* also records bronzes in the hands of officials, for now not only the imperial collections but also those of a growing scholar-official class were of significance. Like the palace collections, these smaller collections reinforced the standing of their owners. The scholar-officials sought and valued this support of their status because they were recruited from a wider social spectrum than before and were therefore dependent on their own credentials rather than those of their families. In this they differed from earlier officials of the Tang, who had been recruited from a landed hereditary aristocracy. Here the talismanic qualities of the bronzes had been extended. The words of the collector Zhao Mingcheng to his wife as they fled before the invading Jin in the early twelfth century evoke the value of both ancient bronzes and contemporary ones, used presumably for ritual, to their owners at this time:

"Follow the crowd. If you can't do otherwise, abandon the household goods first, then the clothes, then the books and scrolls, then the old bronzes, but carry the sacrificial vessels for the ancestral temple your self; live or die with them; don't give them up." (Owen 1986:90)

As were the actual vessels, the inscriptions, which were known from rubbings, were highly prized. The almost irrational value that their owners placed on such rubbings can be seen in the comments of Zhao Mingcheng's wife, Li Qingzhao, as she struggled in vain to hold the collection together during her flight to the south. As Li describes how she progressively lost the collection of texts, rubbings, and calligraphy, she comments: "I still have a few volumes from three or so sets, none complete, and some very ordinary pieces of calligraphy, but I still treasure them as if I were protecting my own head—how foolish I am" (Owen 1986:95).

While Li Qingzhao's writings display a keen awareness of the joys and evils of possessiveness, they and those of other scholars reveal that the desire to possess talismans with quasi-magical properties was being replaced by a greater attention to the content of inscriptions, now seen as giving access to the ideas and lessons that the past could offer the present. So Dong You (fl. 1126), whose *Guang chuan shu ba* is one of the principal Song works on inscriptions on bronze and stone, wrote in the preface:

> When knowledgeable men met with my ancestor, they carefully exam-
> ined his collection. In order to distinguish between true and false,
> they considered the provenances of [pieces]. In the case of calligraphy
> and painting they examined the colophons. Where historical facts were
> concerned, they checked the evidence exhaustively, so that [the pieces
> in their collection] might support understanding, so that their expres-
> sions of the rites and of law could provide models for the world.[11]

Collections of vessels were equally instructive. Because the aims of the neo-Confucians were to restore the practices of the past in order to reform the present, the rites of the past and the role of vessels in them were of intense interest. To the Song period we owe the establishment of the names of most of the different vessel types and the first steps toward an under-standing of their functions. This avenue of study was fuelled by the wish to use the vessels in the rites of the Song period. Ancient vessels were indeed collected to be reused or act as models for new castings. The *Song shi* states:

> As soon as the Office for Ceremonial was established a decree went
> forth that ancient vessels should be sought for throughout the empire,
> in order the more effectively to control the shapes of the ritual ves-
> sels. (translated by Watson 1973:2)

The search for ancient vessels on which to base new ones introduced a new factor that was to remain relevant to the present day. In addition to reusing ancient bronzes, copies were made to place on altars. The princi-pal types were basins used for incense sticks. These were modelled either on the *ding* (fig. 3), on a basin without legs, known as a *gui*, or occasion-ally on a cylindrical vessel on small legs, known as a *zhi* or *lian*. Tall flasks, modelled on wine vessels (*hu*), were used as flower vessels (fig. 4). Thus despite all Song scholarship, the uses of the ancient vessels were generally ignored.

The introduction of copies, however, intensified questions of authen-ticity, a problem already fraught with questions for the study of inscrip-tions. Obviously if both bronzes and rubbings of their inscriptions were to

Fig. 3. Bronze altar vessel in the shape of an ancient ding, *fourteenth to fifteenth century* A.D., *height 16.8 cm. © British Museum.*

be used as sources of true information about the past and as supports for the status of both the emperor and his most influential subjects, it was essential that the valued pieces should be genuine.

EPISODE 4: THE YUAN AND MING DYNASTIES (1280–1644)

During the Yuan and Ming periods serious collecting and study of bronzes were relatively unimportant for the court. This situation alone differentiates the periods from the preceding Song and succeeding Qing dynasties and defines this time as a new episode. Large collections must have remained in the hands of the emperors or of their highest officials, but there are few texts that describe them.[12] Among these few is the listing of ancient bronzes in the hands of the prime minister, Yan Song, impeached in 1562,

Fig. 4. Bronze altar vessel for flowers in the shape of an ancient wine vessel (hu), thirteenth to fourteenth century A.D., *height 28 cm. © British Museum.*

which makes it evident that bronzes were still collected (Zhou Shilian 1727). It seems reasonable to conclude that politics of the day made little call on the study of the rites or their utensils, and thus the imperatives that had stimulated discussion of the bronzes under the Song were absent. Further, because the centers of power were either in the north at Beijing or in the southeast near Shanghai, areas not rich in ancient bronzes, material for collecting and study was less abundant than it had been in the northern Song period, for example, when the ancient centers in Henan and Shaanxi provinces had been within reach of the capital at Kaifeng.

However, if in these centuries the court does not seem to have led the way in the informed collecting of bronzes or inscriptions, the steady growth of a large wealthy class that aspired to prestige and status provided a ready market for bronzes. Here we see at work an extension of the use of collections of calligraphy and antiquities, among which were numbered bronzes, jades, and certain types of ceramics, to provide legitimacy in supporting position and status. The ranking of such antiquities was set out in texts such as the *Zi tao xuan za hui* (*Miscellanea from the Purple Peach Studio*), by the scholar and connoisseur Li Rihua (1565–1635) (Li and Watt 1987:15).

The ancient talismanic qualities of the bronzes are here at work again. Just as during the Song dynasty such collections had reinforced the status of a new and growing scholar class, which had required legitimacy as it replaced the traditional official class drawn from the landed aristocracy, so this newer class based on wealth needed to find support and did so by assuming the trappings of the earlier scholar-officials. Clunas has documented the growth of a literature on taste required to instruct people of this new class in their choice of appropriate objects with which to surround themselves.[13]

Because the supply of ancient bronzes and jades and indeed fine paintings and calligraphy was inadequate to meet a growing demand, fakes of all kinds filled the vacuum. Bronzes that reproduced ancient vessels, other than those used on altars, were probably made as fakes. The bronze animal shown in figure 5 is based on a bronze of the fourth century B.C. reproduced in the *Bo gu tu lu*.[14] Such inlaid bronzes were particularly sought after, both because gold and silver were luxuries of the time and because this taste was supported by mistaken beliefs that the most ancient bronzes of all had been inlaid in gold and silver.

While the gullible and astute alike probably acquired fakes, collectors were now conscious of the problem posed by these copies. Thus from

Fig. 5. Inlaid bronze vessel in the shape of an ancient animal-shaped wine container, probably made as a fake, Ming dynasty, fifteenth to sixteenth century A.D., length 26 cm. © British Museum.

the Yuan period and the publication of writings on connoisseurship, such as the *Ge gu yao lun*, the issue of how genuine and fake bronzes could be distinguished was active (David 1971).

EPISODE 5: THE QING DYNASTY (1644–1911)

The Qing dynasty marks the transition from the ancient views of Chinese bronzes to those we in the twentieth century now hold. In these centuries the collection and study of ancient bronzes and their inscriptions were revived, supported by attitudes to ancient bronzes with which we are now familiar. At the same time the size of the collections and the intensity of the studies set a model that has provided standards for modern collections both in the Far East and the West.

As in the Song period, the study of ancient bronzes was instigated by political upheaval that produced the fall of the Ming dynasty and the conquest of China by foreign rulers, the Manchus. In the first place the Manchus themselves prized the proper performance of ritual to assert their legitimacy in a foreign country and claim continuity with China's past (Greiner 1985). At the same time their opponents also sought the support of history in their questioning of Manchu rule.

The first work on a collection of rubbings of bronze and stone inscriptions since the late Song dynasty was produced by Gu Yanwu (1613–1682), founder of the Han xue school. This school aimed to revive values that had been clearly shown to be lost by the fall of the Ming. Yet again political purity and legitimacy were linked to a correct understanding of the past to be gained through a study of ancient bronzes and inscriptions. Although the precise views of the Han xue school differed from those of the Song neo-Confucians and the Han scholars who sought political lessons from the past, they belonged none the less to the same tradition.

Later scholars, notably Ruan Yuan (1764–1849), made direct use of Song period studies. Among his works on bronzes was an edition of the Song compilation of inscriptions *Li dai zhong ding yi qi kuan zhi*, by Xue Shanggong. By the late eighteenth century, when Ruan Yuan became an official, study of the past was no longer used simply to bolster the opposition; it was an essential element in the life of all scholar-officials and the emperors themselves.

Collections were again amassed. With their increased size came ever larger catalogues. The climax of this endeavour is the *Xi Qing gu jian* and its many supplements, which listed the collection of the Qianlong emperor (1736–1795). These volumes were matched only by those of the emperor's painting and calligraphy collections. Indeed the bronzes were probably valued equally with these works. We regard the imperial collections as collections of art works, but as with the earlier collections the Qianlong collection and those of the scholars of his day were much more than this. They gave enlightened officials insights into the values and achievements of the past and so made it possible for them to fulfill their own roles in the present. We should understand the catalogues and the many indices to these catalogues not as convenient aids for the art historian but as essential tools for politicians and historians wishing to make full use of their heritage.

As in the Ming period, bronzes both ancient and contemporary were displayed in elegant settings to express the status and education of their owners. Bronzes were indeed made on a large scale, both for altars and as playthings. However, because genuine bronzes were actively studied and recognized, there seems to have been less anxiety about forgeries than in the Ming period.

EPISODE 6: THE TWENTIETH CENTURY

Although the retrieval and study of bronzes in the twentieth century cannot be fully considered here, it is worth mentioning one or two salient points, for any discussion today is clearly dependent on much earlier attitudes to bronzes.

The precaution that the troops of Chiang Kaishek took to secure the palace collections for the Nationalists has been recognized by several writers as continuing the perception that possession of the most important works of art and antiquities gives legitimacy to political rulers (Ledderose 1978–79:33; Murray 1986:47, n. 18). Talismanic values of bronzes are thus far from dead. Indeed, it seems likely that ancient Chinese attitudes toward the discovery of relics in the ground, originating in the Han period, still affect their views of antiquities now being excavated. All antiquities are possessions of the state, and their interpretation remains a matter of intense preoccupation, for they are believed to throw light on a past that is still relevant: In Mao Zedong's famous words, "Let the past serve the present." Antiquity, today represented by archaeological finds, is studied for lessons to support present-day social and political policies.

In China, Qing traditions of collecting and scholarship have been maintained, with special emphasis on the study of inscriptions. Studies of characters and indices of inscriptions far outnumber Chinese art history studies of bronzes. They are thus valued in the Song tradition as documents of the past rather than as works of art.

Before the twentieth century ancient Chinese bronzes were little known or regarded in the West. Chinese ceramics had a much larger role because they had been imported to Europe since the seventeenth century for use and display. An understanding of bronzes came about as the nature of Chinese art collecting was understood. A key event in this development was the display of Chinese art in 1935–36 in London in the famous exhibition at the Royal Academy. At that time bronzes and paintings from the imperial collections were included in the exhibition to give status by association to the other objects displayed. This use of the Chinese imperial collections to legitimize European interest in Chinese art shows that even the European pursuit of Chinese bronzes owes much to their previous histories.

In this brief description of the separate episodes in the history of the evaluation of ancient Chinese vessels, I have attempted to show that at each stage the value attached to bronzes was influenced by the values of previous generations. The Han period regarded the discovery of an ancient *ding* as evidence of heavenly approval of a virtuous emperor. Virtuous and nonvirtuous kings alike had owned bronzes. But inscriptions in ancient vessels and later texts still known today had stressed the notion that heaven rewarded only the virtuous. So possession of *ding* came to be regarded as evidence of virtuousness.

If we are to understand how the Han came to formulate their views about the functions of ancient bronzes, we have to look back at their ancient roles. Similarly later collecting was fostered by both a recognition of the ancient functions and contributions of the vessels and by a transformation of Han attitudes. In each major episode described, scholars assimilated earlier views and often altered the accumulated understanding that they inherited. Even today our collections and studies of ancient bronzes are fed by many of the attitudes described above.

The bronzes are in our museums not because we recognize in them a major artistic endeavor nor because we see them as things from which Shang and Zhou history can be read. They are there because we have inherited an interest in them generated in the distant past and sustained by Qing scholars. If, therefore, we want to understand them and the histories that produced them, we first must assess the later episodes that brought them into our collections. We have to strip off layers of preconceived expectations as if they were layers of onion skin.

The peculiar strength of the concern with ritual bronzes throughout later history derives from the intimate connection assumed to exist between them and the political systems of their day. In the first place their casting was an expression of political power, as was their later possession. The political dimension is an insistent thread that runs through the whole of the afterlife of the bronzes, even today.

In addition, the ancient Chinese food vessels were later copied to make incense burners, thus creating not just a new episode but in effect a new kind of object with a life of its own.[15] In introducing such copies or variations we open the discussion yet wider, for such incense burners took over not only ancient shapes but also ancient associations. Such layers or sequences of associations come with almost every type of artifact, be they high art or merely a mundane teapot.

Ancient Chinese bronzes are special cases. But the episodes in their lives and the new lives that they generated are matched in parallel ways all over the world among all peoples. All objects have an ancestry that is as important to an understanding of their roles as are their current appearance and functions. If we do not know its ancestry, we cannot read the history from a thing.

NOTES

1. For the survival and copying of classical sculpture, see Haskell and Penny (1981) and Bobor and Rubenstein (1986).

2. For a note on the times when Chinese paintings were alienated from the imperial collections, see Ledderose (1978–79:41).

3. Bronzes known today that have been in the former imperial collections have a distinct cachet (Lawton 1987–88).

4. Western classical sculpture has had similarly varied roles and values over the centuries. Bobor and Rubenstein (1986) note that the identification in the Middle Ages of the equestrian portrait of Marcus Aurelius as Constantine the Great ensured that it survived destruction and was available to become the model for equestrian statues commemorating great men and rulers in the Renaissance and later.

5. In later times silver and gold were much prized, but because bronze was the metal traditionally used for ancient ritual vessels, it continued to be used for later copies. Copies also were made in ceramics, glazed green to imitate the color of the bronzes.

6. Inscribed vessels were clearly treasured family documents to be preserved rather than buried in tombs. Indeed, large inscribed *ding* are rarely if ever retrieved from graves. They have been found either in sacrificial pits or in hoards, interred under ground when marauding tribes from the north and west drove the Zhou from their capital near Xi'an in 771 B.C.

7. Yu Weichao and Gao Ming (1978) discuss the origin of the use of sets of *ding* and *gui* to indicate rank.

8. The stories current in the Han dynasty had originated in the late Zhou period. Accounts of the conflicts of the time are enlivened with descriptions of

attempts by rulers of the petty states into which China was then divided to take the nine tripods from Zhou and so acquire legitimacy for a new dynasty. The most celebrated account of the search for the nine *ding* concerns the first emperor of the Qin dynasty, who unified China in 221 B.C. He is reputed, of course, to have persistently sought the *ding*, whose possession would confirm his legitimacy. Whatever the truth of these descriptions, Han accounts, especially those in the *Shi Ji*, say that he failed, for one of the *ding* eluded him. This description clearly implies that from the perspective of the Han rulers, Qin Shi Huangdi was not to be regarded as a legitimate ruler. Because the Han had seized power in the confusion that followed the collapse of Qin rule, it was in their interest to stress the failures of Qin.

9. Barnard (1973:491–510) concentrates on records in the dynastic histories.

10. Murray (1986) discusses the Emperor Gaozong's use of the imperial collection and gifts of calligraphy as instruments of dynastic revival after the loss of the northern capital in 1126.

11. For references to Dong You's work and other similar texts, see Rudolph (1962).

12. A recently reported tomb in Sichuan province illustrates an unusual example of the burial of ancient bronzes in a Ming period tomb (*Wenwu* 1989.7:43–47).

13. Some of Clunas's work on texts on taste is found in Clunas (1988).

14. Although new works on bronzes were not written during the Ming dynasty, the existing texts and catalogues were reprinted many times (Poor 1965).

15. Kopytoff (1988) sets out his ideas about the life of an object.

REFERENCES

Barnard, Noel. 1973. "Records of Discoveries of Bronze Vessels in Literary Sources and Some Pertinent Remarks on Aspects of Chinese Historiography." *Journal of the Institute of Chinese Studies of the Chinese University of Hong Kong* 6, no. 2:455–546.

Bobor, Phillis Pray, and Ruth Rubenstein. 1986. *Renaissance Artists and Antique Sculpture*. London and Oxford: Harvey Millar Publishers and Oxford University Press.

Clunas, Craig. 1986. "The Cost of Living and the Cost of Collecting." Paper presented to the Oriental Ceramic Society, Hong Kong.

————. 1988. *Chinese Furniture*. London: Victoria and Albert Museum, Far Eastern Series.

David, Percival, trans. and ed. 1971. *Chinese Connoisseurship: The Ke Ku Yao Lun, The Essential Criteria of Antiquities*. London: Faber and Faber.

Greiner, Peter. 1985. "Das Hofzeremoniel der Mandschu-Dynastie." In *Palast-Museum Peking: Schätze aus der Verbotenen Stadt*, edited by Lothar Ledderose, 56–69. Berlin: Berliner Festspiele, Insel Verlag.

Fung Yu-lan. 1983. *A History of Chinese Philosophy*. Translated from the Chinese by Derk Bodde. Princeton, N.J.: Princeton University Press.

Hakell, Francis, and Nicholas Penny. 1981. *Taste and the Antique: The Lure of Classical Sculpture, 1500–1900*. New Haven and London: Yale University Press.

Kaltenmark, Max. 1960. "Ling-pao: Note sur un terme du Taoïsm Religieux." In *Mélanges publiés par l'institut des hautes études chinoises*, vol. 2, 559–588. Paris: Presses Universitaires de France.

Kopytoff, Igor. 1988. "The Cultural Biography of Things: Commoditization As a Process." In *The Social Life of Things: Commodities in Cultural Perspective*, edited by Arjun Appadurai, 64–91. Cambridge, England: Cambridge University Press.

Lawton, Thomas. 1987–88. "An Imperial Legacy Revisited." *Asian Art* 1, no. 1:51–79.

Ledderose, Lothar. 1970. *Die Siegelschrift (Chuan-Shu) in der Ch'ing-Zeit: Ein Beitrag zur Geschichte der Chinesischen Schriftkunst*. Wiesbaden: Franz Steiner Verlag GMBH.

————. 1978–79. "Some Observations on the Imperial Art Collections in China." *Transactions of the Oriental Ceramic Society* 43:33–46.

Ledderose, Lothar, ed. 1985. *Palast-museum Peking: Schätze aus der Verbotenen Stadt*. Berlin: Berliner Festspiele, Insel Verlag.

Legge, James. 1885. *The Sacred Books of the East, The Texts of Confucianism, Parts III–IV, The Li Ki*. Oxford, England: The Clarendon Press.

Li Chu-Tsing and James Watt. 1987. *The Scholars Studio: Artistic Life in the Late Ming Period*. New York: The Asia House Gallery, in association with Thames and Hudson.

Li Xueqin. 1985. *Eastern Zhou and Qin Civilization*. New Haven, Conn., and London: Yale University Press, 1985.

Mancheng Han mu fajue baogao. 1980. Beijing: Wenwu Chubanshe.

Murray, Julia K. 1986. "The Role of Art in the Southern Sung Dynastic Revival." *Bulletin of Sung and Yuan Studies* 18:41–59.

Owen, Stephen. 1986. *Remembrances: The Experience of the Past in Chinese Literature*. Cambridge, Mass., and London: Harvard University Press.

Poor, Robert. 1965. "Notes on the Sung Dynasty Archaeological Catalogs." *Archives of the Chinese Art History Society* 19:33–44.

Rudolph, R.C. 1962. "Preliminary Notes on Sung Archaeology." *Journal of Asian Studies* 22:169–177.

Ryckmans, Pierre. 1986. *The Chinese Attitude Towards the Past*. The Forty-Seventh George Ernest Morrison Lecture in Ethnology. Canberra: The Australian National University.

Seidel, Anna. 1981. "Kokuhō, Note à propos du terme 'Trésor National' en Chine et au Japon." *Bulletin de l'École Français d'Extreme-Orient* 69: 230–261.

———. 1983. "Imperial Treasures and Taoist Sacraments: Taoist Roots in the Apocrypha." In *Tantric and Taoist Studies in Honour of R. A. Stein*, vol. 2, edited by Michel Strickmann, 291–371. Brussels: Institut Belge des Hautes Études Chinoises.

Watson, William. 1973. "On Some Categories of Archaism." *Ars Orientalis* 9: 1–13.

Wu Hung. 1984. "A Sanpan Shan Chariot Ornament and the Xiangrui Design in Western Han Art." *Archives of Asian Art* 37:38–59.

Yu Weichao and Gao Ming. 1978, 1979. "Zhou dai yong ding zhidu." *Beijing Daxue Xuebao*, 1978, no. 1:84–98; 1978, no. 2:84–97; 1979, no. 1:83–96.

Zhou Shilian. 1727. *Tian shui bing shan lu*. Zhi bu zu zhai congshu.

The Interpretation of Artifacts in the History of Technology

Robert B. Gordon

Artifacts can be useful source material in the history of technology when they are convincingly interpreted. They are particularly important when the documentary record is incomplete or when technological processes cannot be adequately described with words. Nonliterate peoples have carried out complex technological processes with such skill and sophistication that duplicating them has proved to be a challenging task for modern practitioners; making Damascus steel is an example (Bronson 1986). The metallurgical complexity of smelting and working bronze, silver, and gold by the Inca of Peru in the early sixteenth century and the adaptation of iron-smelting technology in the African Iron Age to resources considered unusable in modern metallurgy are examples from archaeology showing that nonliterate peoples often had a good understanding of the technological processes they used (Lechtman 1984; Rutledge and Gordon 1987; Killick 1990).

With few exceptions, practitioners of technology in historic times did not leave written records of their experiences. They usually had neither leisure nor incentive to write because literary skills did not lead to advancement in one's work as an artificer or mechanician. Writing about one's own work has rarely been a part of the culture of artificers in either industrial or nonindustrial societies, and individuals who have written about their work experiences are likely to have been exceptional people. Gale observed of the iron puddlers he knew in the 1920s that "a new man in the trade started to learn in earnest, the hard way, by doing, not talking and he developed a taciturnity which lasted all his life" (Gale 1963–64). We have few accounts of work experiences such as McGeown's (1967) description of an open-hearth steel-melting shop of the early twentieth century that are useful to historians of technology; often, reminiscences of work experiences were written to reconstruct the record of past experiences or advance a cause or political philosophy. An example of this type of industrial history is Davis's (1922) account of iron puddling. (Davis was secretary of labor from 1921 to 1930 and subsequently U.S. senator from Pennsylvania).

Even when authors wanted to describe technological processes and the work of artisans, they encountered the limitations of language. Technology, particularly mechanical technology, involves a large component of nonverbal thinking that is not easily recorded in words or even by drawings (Ferguson 1977). (The instructions for assembling many toys and household appliances illustrate this problem.) Artisans who operate technological devices such as furnaces and machines respond to many clues about their equipment that are neither verbal nor numerical and reach decisions that they are often unable to explain to people who have not shared their work experience. We cannot then expect that the work of these artisans could have been accurately recorded even by the best-intentioned observer. The difficulty of transferring technology by written descriptions and instructions has been explored by Harris (1976).

Another difficulty that arises in using the documentary record of technology is that much of it was written for purposes other than objective description. The reports of industrial spies and accounts written for census reports are the most likely to be objective, but they rarely delve into the work experiences of the artisans and often fail to convey essential information about the practical but essential details of how processes were carried out. Reports of official inspectors were often intended to influence policy and may therefore have used selective reporting. (An example are the reports of the British commissioners sent to study manufacturing technology in the United States in 1853 and 1854. These reports are reproduced and discussed by Rosenberg [1969]. Some of the reporting seems to have been written with a view to influencing government decisions in armaments contracting.)

Primary sources for industrial technology that appears to be objective were sometimes written by people who wished to advance a particular technical process or method without explicitly saying so. Colonel Talcott's account of mechanization at the Springfield Armory, in Springfield, Massachusetts, often quoted as evidence of the deskilling of factory work, purports to be an explanation of how armorers' skills were no longer as important in 1845 as they once were; in fact Talcott's objective was to reduce wage rates, and he chose to advance this cause by asserting that machinery could do what once required skilled armorers to carry out (Gordon 1988a).

Artifacts, products of the hands of artisans of the past, are a direct link with our technological heritage. They are useful to historians to the extent that we can uncover the information they contain.

PRINCIPLES OF INTERPRETATION

There are two basic steps to be taken in the interpretation of artifacts of technology. The first is the analysis of the intrinsic characteristics of an artifact by archaeometry; the second is analysis of the context of the artifact.

Archaeometry

Many intrinsic characteristics of an artifact can be discovered in the archaeometric laboratory. Best known are the chemical methods, used most widely in prehistoric archaeology, for dating and determining provenance through trace element analysis. An example of the use of such techniques in industrial archaeology is the identification of the function of crucibles excavated at the site of Eli Whitney's armory in Hamden, Connecticut. Microprobe analysis of drops of metal within the slag adhering to the crucibles showed that some were brass and others were low-silicon cast iron, evidence that the casting of both brass and iron suitable for subsequent malleabilizing was carried on at the armory (Cooper et al. 1982).

Other archaeometric techniques that were less common in prehistoric archaeology but that can be particularly useful in dealing with technological artifacts from historic times are examination of internal structure, analysis of form in relation to function, and study of superficial markings.

INTERNAL STRUCTURE. The internal structure of an artifact records information about how it was made and used. The pattern-welded swords of early medieval Europe are examples of artifacts in which the internal structure is easily visible. The pattern records the successive steps in constructing the blade by welding iron and steel strips together followed by forging. By reproducing the structure in modern experiments, we can determine how nearly the pattern defines a unique manufacturing procedure; this will then show how closely the reproduction of the blade also reproduces the process by which the original was made.

An early example of the use of microstructure in archaeometry is Mathewson's (1915) study of bronze artifacts from Machu Picchu, Peru, by metallography. Mathewson was able to show how Inca artisans used cold forging, annealing, hot working, and casting to make a wide range of bronze tools and decorative items.

ANALYSIS OF FORM. Analysis with respect to engineering principles can often reveal the function of an artifact or show how it worked, as in Price's (1974) study of the fragments of a bronze mechanism found in a shipwreck off the island of Antikythera, near Crete. The artifact was dated to about 80 B.C. from inscriptions on it, and radiography revealed a complex gear train containing some thirty components within it. Working from the size, number of teeth, and arrangement of parts, Price was able to show that the mechanism functioned as a mechanical computer useful in the preparation of calendars. Since, however, today's engineering principles were not known or, if known, not used in the same form in the past, analysis such as Price's will not necessarily reveal the reasoning used by the designers or builders of an artifact whose function we have been able to identify.

Reproductions of artifacts can be useful in determining how technical procedures were carried out in the past. Forty (1983, 1986) has used replicas of early navigational instruments to discover their capabilities and the skills needed to use them. He found, for example, that the astrolabe is useless for navigation at sea, that the errors inherent in the cross-staff are comparable to the divergence in the positions reported by early maritime explorers for many important headlands, and that a major improvement in accuracy over that attained with a cross-staff was realized with the backstaff. His results put to rest numerous speculations about navigational technology that accumulated over many years of desk-bound, indoor scholarship.

An example of engineering analysis involving a sequence of machines is Cooper's (1981–82, 1984) investigation of the production line set up in 1801 for making ship's blocks at the Portsmouth, England, naval dock-yard. A number of the machines survive in museum collections, where they are out of context. From traces of the machines' placement on the floor of the blockmill building (which is still standing although turned to other uses) and calculation of each machine's production capacity, Cooper was able to show how they functioned together to make what was probably the first mechanized industrial production line.

Another type of engineering analysis useful in industrial archaeology is the study of the dimensions of mechanisms that are supposed to have been mass-produced to be interchangeable. Hoke (1990), for example, measured the dimensions of surviving examples of wood clock parts to show that the level of precision attained by Eli Terry and others in making these parts in the first decades of the nineteenth century was fully adequate for production of woodworks clocks with interchangeable parts. Collections of military firearms are another useful source of specimens illustrating the development of interchangeable manufacture in the United States because they provide multiple examples of standardized mechanisms made from the early nineteenth century onward. Dimensional measurements on lock parts from military small arms have been used to demonstrate the growth of handwork skills in armory practice through the first half of the nineteenth century. They also show the importance of these skills in a period in which documentary records have been interpreted as showing the replacement of the skill of the artificer's hand and eye by the precision of machine tools (Gordon 1988a).

SURFICIAL MARKINGS. Use-wear analysis, the study of surficial markings, has proven to be a useful technique in the study of bone and stone tools. Marks left on the surface of stone or mineral artifacts record information about how the artifact was both made and used (Hayden 1979). The technique has been extended by making silicone impressions of interior surfaces that can then be turned inside out and examined with the scanning electron microscope (Gwinnett and Gorlick 1979). Use-wear markings may also be present on metal artifacts and can yield information similar to that found on stone and bone (Gordon 1985, 1987).

Different types of cutting tools used to shape wood or metal leave distinctive markings that may be used to learn about the tool. Many artifacts suitable for such analysis bear on the history of technology, but only a few have been studied. Battison (1966) was one of the first to apply analysis of surficial markings to problems in industrial archaeology; he used an examination of the lock mechanism of a musket made at Eli Whitney's armory to show that the accepted history of the introduction of milling was wrong. Foley (Foley et al. 1983) has shown how surficial markings can be used to find the method of fitting the wheel to the pan in wheel-lock mechanisms used for gun ignition. Metal forming as well as metal matching leaves characteristic marks; forming marks left on a partially completed axe are discussed later. Sometimes analysis of surficial markings can be combined with examination of an artifact's interior structure to reveal details of its construction, as in Vandiver's (1988) study of the manufacture of Neolithic storage vessels, in which she shows the differences in technology developed in the Near East and in China for forming large ceramic pots.

PHYSICAL PROPERTIES. One component of a society's attainment of technological maturity is its capacity to make materials that will reliably serve in their intended application. Most often the strength properties are the most important, and consequently we may want to know the mechanical properties of historic materials, either to evaluate how well they were made or to know how far they can be trusted when a historic building or other structure is still in service. Inferences about strength can sometimes be made from composition and microstructure, but usually the only reliable way to get this information is to do mechanical tests on specimens of the material of interest (Gordon 1988b).

Context

The techniques of archaeometry are capable of producing much data about a given artifact, but by themselves these data are usually of limited interest; their value is realized by examining the context of the artifact. The context of a technological artifact is made up of components that can be divided into two groups described in terms borrowed from economics. The *backward-linkage* components of context relate to the artifact's origin; the *forward-linkage* components relate to the uses to which the artifact is put.

BACKWARD-LINKAGE COMPONENTS. The natural resources used to make an artifact are the first of the backward linkages. One of the most successful applications of archaeometric techniques has been determining the origins of materials used to make artifacts through chemical analysis, which identifies elements characteristic of particular sources. For example, it has been possible to trace the metal in some artifacts made in southern Africa during the Iron Age to a particular mine because it is the only one in the region that has ore with a high titanium content (Gordon and van der Merwe 1984).

The human resources used in making an artifact are of as much interest in the history of technology as the material ones, but the archaeometric techniques for discovering these are not as well developed. The human resources include the skills of the artisans and the social structures that have to be in place to allow artisans to exercise their skills. Experimental archaeology, in which one attempts to make a replica of an artifact, has been one effective technique for discovering skills needed by artisans. Replication can reveal the technical difficulties that have to be overcome in making the artifact and place bounds on the techniques that may have been used in the past. Showing that a particular technique found by experimental archaeology was the one actually used is a more difficult task.

Comparison of the properties of an artifact with the properties needed for it to function in its intended application is another way to learn about the skills of the artificers who made the artifact because a close match between properties and function is evidence of superior skill. A number of bronze-edge tools found in the vicinity of Machu Picchu appear to have been deliberately work-hardened at their working edges while the body of the tool was left softer (Mathewson 1915). This would produce both a hard working edge and a tough supporting structure, a desirable combination of properties in a tool intended for heavy work. If confirmed by more examples, this procedure could be taken as evidence of the capacity of the Inca artificers who made these tools to match properties to function and control properties through appropriate working technology.

The social structures that must have been in place to allow an artifact to be made are the most difficult of the backward-linkage components of context to discover from artifactual evidence alone. When documents, anthropological data, or oral history are available for comparison, artifacts can give new insights into the social structures within which a technology was carried on. Killick (1990), for example, has used all these sources to reconstruct the social context of iron making in Malawi as practiced into the early twentieth century. Another example is deducing the relationships that must have existed between artificers and inspectors in a factory where a gauging system was used to control the uniformity of the product made. Analysis of the dimensional uniformity of surviving products and the level of judgment needed to operate the gauges will show how much discretion was exercised by artisans and inspectors. This technique has been used to investigate the relationships among artisans, managers, and officers at the Springfield Armory (Cooper et al. 1993).

FORWARD-LINKAGE COMPONENTS. The first forward-linkage component of context is the interaction between an artifact and those who use it after it is made. When the use that an artifact is intended for can be identified, aspects of the work procedures required of those who use it for this purpose can be deduced from study of the artifact or experimentation with a replica of it. Analysis of the operation of a machine used in production, for example, may show that, because of the lack of mechanical feed for the work, steady repetitious labor was needed as successive pieces of stock were fed into it rapidly and always the same way, as in operating a stamping press. Alternatively, a production machine lacking mechanical feed for the work or tools may require the full exercise of the dexterity and the judgment skills of the operator to carry out a succession of operations controlled by hand. Patrick Malone and his colleagues at the Slater Mill Historic Site in Pawtucket, Rhode Island, found that running the spool lathe displayed at the Wilkinson Mill fully challenged the operator's physical and mental abilities.

The second forward-linkage component of context is the interaction between an artifact and observers, people who are not direct participants in the use of the artifact. The observers may be willingly present, as when a group of casual visitors gathers to watch a blacksmith at work, or they may be unwilling, as when smoke and fume from smelting operations drift into a neighboring community. One source of evidence that the designers of an artifact considered observers important is the incorporation of elements in the artifact not needed for its function. The design of early British canal and railway structures in the classical style was evidently intended to gain acceptance of these new modes of transportation by a society that accorded high status to the monuments of the classical world. The elaborate decorative elements incorporated in machinery made in the United States in the mid-nineteenth century have been interpreted as intended to influence people who did not fully comprehend the technology but were in a position to influence the allocation of financial resources among various industrial ventures (Kasson 1976).

To the components of context related to interactions of users and observers with a technological artifact, students today add another forward linkage—the effect on the environment of making and using an artifact. Archaeometric techniques have been used successfully to find evidence of the environmental effects associated with past technologies, but as yet not much has been done with retrospective technological assessment.

EXAMPLES OF INTERPRETATION

The importance of context in interpreting technological artifacts will be illustrated by three examples of artifacts from technology: a partially completed axe, a piece of slag, and a steam locomotive.

The Collins Axe

A partially completed axe from the Collins Company of Collinsville, Connecticut, made about 1866, is shown in figure 1. The body, or poll, of the axe has been formed but not finished, and the steel that will be welded to the poll to make the bit has been put in place. Welding, forging to final shape, grinding, and polishing remain to be done; the axe is about half completed. Archaeometric techniques were used to find out what materials were used and how this artifact was made. The poll of the axe was made of wrought iron of good quality, and steel was used for the bit. The small concentration of nonmetallic inclusions in the bit shows that cast steel was used, and at this time it would have been made by the crucible process. (We lack a reliable way of determining whether the steel was made in Sheffield, England, or in the United States, where in 1866 the crucible steel process was just being learned.) The surficial markings on the axe poll and bit are of special interest because they show that there was sliding motion in a single direction between the surface of the poll and the die in which it was formed; in contrast, the bit is covered with hammer indentations. This means that the poll was not made by either of the

Fig. 1. A partially completed axe placed in the Metallurgical Museum of Yale College before 1866 by the Collins Company of Collinsville, Connecticut. The Collins Company was in the forefront of manufacturing and metallurgical innovation at this time and wanted to make its accomplishments available for study. The poll (body) of the axe is made of wrought iron, and the surficial markings on it show that it was formed with machinery that substituted punches and roller dies for traditional methods of forging. The bit, made of high-carbon cast steel, is ready to be welded to the poll. The total length of the specimen is 140 millimeters. Yale University. Photograph by William Sacco.

conventional axe-making processes—hammering with hand tools or forging under a tilt hammer—that were used to make the bit.

The significance of the archaeometric observations emerges from the context of the axe. The Collins Company was established in 1826 to make axes by using power from the Farmington River in place of hand labor. The company soon achieved a reputation for superior products sold on a worldwide market. The village of Collinsville has been studied by industrial archaeologists and architectural historians as an example of a community on a water privilege that remained a single-company town for more than 130 years.

In its first decades the Collins Company attracted a number of innovative mechanicians, among whom E. K. Root became the best known. The only record of Root's work at the Collins Company is a few incomplete patent documents. Root is thought to have devised machinery that eliminated most of the arduous labor of hand forging and the physically debilitating task of grinding axes. Artifacts can supplement the documentary record and give us a better picture of the work process that evolved through the mechanization of axe making. The patent documents suggest the principal features of Root's machinery: First, the poll was made by punching a hole through a solid piece of iron instead of by folding and welding together two iron plates; second, the poll was shaped by passing it through roller dies and then shaving it to size instead of forging followed by grinding.

The most interesting backward-linkage component of context for the partially completed axe in figure 1 is the interpretation of the surficial markings on the poll. These show that the poll was formed in dies mounted on rolls and, hence, that Root's roll-forming process suggested by the fragmentary patent documents was actually realized in machinery built and used at the Collins Company. Examination of the axe poll adds important detail to our understanding of the mechanization achieved at the Collins works. Interpretation based on the documents alone fostered the belief that Root's machines were self-acting to such a degree that their introduction led to a reduction in the skills needed in axe making. Reconstruction of the successive steps of the forming process with the aid of the artifact shows that this is an oversimplification, that dexterity and judgment skills comparable to those needed in forging were required to make axe polls with the forming machines. The big difference that use of this machinery made to the artisans was a reduction in the physical labor and noise levels in their work environment. The company gained the benefits of increased productivity (Gordon 1983).

The backward-linkage component of context involving material resources is of interest because at the time the axe sample was made the technique of making crucible steel was just being learned in the United States. The Collins Company, along with most other edge-tool makers, had relied on steel imported from Sheffield and began to make its own steel only in 1864. Artifacts from the Collins works show that in 1866 the workers were still learning the process, but the quality of the steel in the various axe bits examined, including that in figure 1, shows that they had succeeded in making good quality steel by 1866 (Gordon and Tweedale 1990).

Bloom-Smelting Slag

Slag from iron smelting holds little intrinsic interest for most people, but it is usually the most abundant artifact at old smelting sites and is, consequently, an important record of the metallurgical skills of people in the past. Much of the technological information that slag carries is in its structure and can be studied by eye or with an optical microscope using methods whose origins are discussed by Smith (1988). Figure 2 shows a sample collected at the site of the Valley Forge bloomery operated at Elizabethtown in the Adirondack region of New York in the nineteenth century. In bloomery smelting, the oldest means of making iron, iron ore is reduced to solid metal with a charcoal fire in a hearth small enough to be manipulated by one artificer. Bloomery smelting in the United States has been described as a backward or primitive technology used before more sophisticated methods of making iron were learned. This idea may have originated with Swank (1892) who, in his classic *History of the Manufacture of Iron in All Ages*, includes a chapter entitled "Primitive Characteristics of the Southern Iron Industry." Bloomery forges serving local needs were common in the southern states at that time. Analysis of slag samples such as that shown in figure 2 leads to a different interpretation.

Bloomery smelting was practiced in the eastern Adirondack region of New York, where pure ore, water power, and abundant forest resources were available, from about 1800 until the early years of the twentieth century (Allen et al. 1990). The bloomery design was a shallow, rectangular hearth made of cast-iron plates cooled with water. The air blast, supplied by a water-powered blower, was preheated by passing it through pipes placed over the hearth before being directed into the fire. One to upward of a dozen or more hearths were placed in one forge building. The method of smelting can be deduced from the slag samples and the historical descriptions of the hearth design. Smelting began with spreading ore on the hot charcoal in the hearth. The iron mineral (magnetite) reacted with the gangue (earthy matter) in the ore to form liquid slag, which ran to the bottom of the hearth. The remaining magnetite was reduced to metal. As the iron formed, a pool of liquid slag had to be kept on top of the metal to protect it from oxidation by the air blast. The smelter manipulated the additions of ore so as to build a lip on the edge of the iron to retain the pool of slag. Additional slag formed during smelting was tapped onto the

Fig. 2. Top (a) and bottom (b) surfaces of a piece of bloomery slag collected from the site of the Valley Forge in Elizabethtown, Essex County, New York. This bloomery forge operated between 1845 and 1873, making wrought iron by the direct reduction of ore. Analysis of the microstructure of the slag and reconstruction of the technology used at Valley Forge show that the process was run with very high efficiency and that this slag sample was tapped from the hearth during the process and run onto the floor in front of the forge hearth. Because ore placed on the forge shop floor in readiness for use became imbedded in the slag (see the bottom surface), we are able to determine the way in which the ore was prepared for smelting. The plate of slag is 20 millimeters thick. Yale University. Photograph by William Sacco.

floor directly in front of the hearth. After it had solidified, it was broken up and carted away.

The slag in figure 2 was formed this way, and its rough surface reproduces the texture of the floor of the forge just in front of the hearth. The composition and microstructure of this slag shows that the Adirondack bloomery process was designed to run rapidly with minimum loss of iron to the slag and, because of the rapid rate of smelting, minimum use of fuel. Rapid reaction was achieved through the use of finely pulverized ore particles (which expose a large surface to the reducing gases in the furnace atmosphere); loss of iron to the slag was minimized by the speed of the process and by making the zone in the hearth in which the ore was reduced very thin, as well as by mechanically removing most of the slag-forming gangue from the ore before smelting.

The design of the Adirondack bloomery to run rapidly and with minimum loss of iron to the slag and, through the use of preheated air blast and finely pulverized ore, with minimum fuel was a choice made within the technical requirements of smelting to adapt the process to its context—production of high-purity metal for a specialized, competitive market with the minimal use of the scarce resources of skilled labor, fuel, and high-grade ore. Compared with other methods of making iron in the United States, the Adirondack bloomery required only a small capital investment. Furthermore, since each hearth was an independent unit of production, it could be easily shut down and left idle or started up as market conditions changed. It was well adapted to the market for premium-grade iron in the late nineteenth century, which was subject to large, rapid fluctuations in price because of variations in the demand for crucible steel (for which bloomery iron was the preferred starting material) and the supply of iron from Scandinavia, which was in direct competition with the Adirondack product.

One important lesson learned from the various attempts to stage bloomery smelts in the field and the laboratory is that the work requires a high level of skill. Most attempts to reproduce the process have either failed to make metal or have produced low-quality metal with an expenditure of fuel and labor far beyond that used by experienced smelters. One consequence of operating the Adirondack bloomeries so as to achieve a high rate of smelting was that there was little room for error by the smelter. This inference drawn from the artifacts is supported by observers' reports that many workers never achieved proficiency and that good smelters were valued employees at the Adirondack forges. Further inferences about the character of the work can be drawn from the material evidence. The smelter was dependent on an organization of other workers to supply ore and fuel of the requisite quality and had to cooperate with the shingler (the operator of the forge hammer that converted the iron made in the forge into sound metal). However, smelting was essentially an individual operation; each smelter was responsible for one hearth and was paid for the weight and quality of the iron produced at it. His reputation for skill rested with specific, measurable characteristics of his work.

Steam Locomotive

Even for people too young to remember them in regular service, steam locomotives are the primary symbol of railroading. Fascination with this obsolete machinery supports one or more steam-powered tourist railways in almost every state in the country. Although the continued popularity of the steam locomotive arises in part from nostalgia, one need only watch the reaction of children and young people to a locomotive in steam to realize that the characteristics of the locomotive itself and the particular person-machine interaction that takes place among the locomotive, the engine crew, train riders, and the surrounding community are much more complex than simple nostalgia. Thus, the forward-linkage components of context are of special interest in the interpretation of this artifact of technology.

People find the steam locomotive itself interesting because it is complex but comprehensible and because it engages the observer's attention through sounds and smells as well as sight. The diesel-electric locomotive, by contrast, appears as a box on wheels that gives no clue about how it works to an outside observer; even the driver is largely obscured from view. Until the mid-1930s, when they were covered with streamlined shrouds designed by Otto Kuhler, Raymond Loewy, and Henry Dreyfus, the working components and to a large degree the engine crew of American steam locomotives were exposed to view, as shown in figure 3. The intrinsic allure of the mechanism has attracted a number of artists. Charles Sheeler's painting "Rolling Power" (1939) accurately depicts the pistons, valve gear, driving wheels, and other parts of the engine and conveys a sense of purpose, order, function, and power in the mechanism. But a painting cannot substitute for watching the parts in motion. In fact, some aspects of the motion are hard to anticipate from study of the mechanism at rest. Another factor that adds to interest in steam engines is that a locomotive is a "tame" machine—that is, people can stand around

Fig. 3. A view of a 1926 steam locomotive in service on the Valley Railroad in Essex, Connecticut. American steam locomotive design placed nearly all the working parts of both freight and passenger engines in full view of observers until the 1930s, when decorative shrouds were introduced. Note the bell, operated by a pull rope running to the fireman's position on the left side of the cab and the large steam whistle attached to the steam dome and controlled by the engine driver. The crew, like the moving parts of the engine, could be easily observed as the locomotive moved along a station platform; the rituals of oiling the running gear and collecting orders from the station master also were done in full view of passengers waiting for the train's departure. Photograph by Robert B. Gordon.

it and watch it at work without personal inconvenience or danger; a locomotive can move along a crowded station platform quietly and on a prescribed course that is readily visible to observers. In addition to these visual effects, a locomotive makes suggestive sounds. The hum of the steam-turbine dynamo and the pumping of the air compressor suggest life while the machine is at rest; the puffs of exhaust steam tell us how hard the engine is working while it is in motion and suggest animal-like qualities to some observers:

> I love to see one of those huge creatures, with sinews of brass and
> muscles of iron strut forth from his stable and, saluting the train of
> cars with a dozen sonorous puffs from his iron nostrils, fall back
> gently into his harness. There he stands champering and foaming
> upon the iron track, his great heart a furnace of glowing coals, his
> lymphatic blood boiling within his veins, the strength of a thousand
> horses nerving his sinews, he pants to be gone. (Reynolds n.d.:1)

A part of our reaction to an operating steam locomotive is what we see of
the work of the engine driver and fireman, who can be watched from a
station platform or seen at work in adjacent switching yards. They work
as a team. Firing a locomotive may appear at first glance to be simply coal
shoveling, but closer study shows that it is actually highly skilled work.
The fire has to be built so that its intensity can be increased when the
demand for steam increases and cut back when the demand slacks. Because the boiler's capacity to store steam is limited and it takes some time
to increase the boiling rate, the fireman has to anticipate the demands of
the journey to be made; poor firing is exposed if the boiler pressure drops
on upgrades or steam is blown off from the safety valve when the engine is
stopped.

The driver of a steam locomotive needs skill and experience to start a
heavy train without spinning the driver wheels, stop the train smoothly at
the desired location, keep to a schedule, and maneuver the locomotive in
coupling and uncoupling cars. Lack of skill in these operations is immediately apparent to the rest of the train crew, the passengers, and observers
on the station platform. Locomotive driving therefore gives many opportunities for the display of professional accomplishments and personal style.
Emerging from the cab to oil the locomotive mechanism is part of the
ritual of display in engine driving. The locomotive whistle provides another outlet for the display of style since the tone of a steam whistle can be
varied according to how much steam is admitted.

Forward-linkage components of context such as these can be deduced
from examination of a locomotive preserved in a museum, but our appreciation of this artifact of technology is greatly enhanced when we are able
to observe a locomotive in steam and in use. This is a form of experimental
archaeology, in which we learn about the interaction between people and
technology by recreating as accurately as possible the use of an artifact.
Experimental archaeology with the steam locomotive is relatively easy

because its use is still within living memory and both the social and physical structures that it helped create are still part of the fabric of our land.

Artifacts can enrich our understanding of the interaction between people and technology by revealing information that cannot be or was not recorded in documents. Many archaeometric techniques developed to solve problems in classical archaeology can be used in the study of artifacts of technology from historic times, but the significance of the findings derives from an analysis of the components of context of the artifact.

REFERENCES

Allen, R. F., et al. 1990. "An Archaeological Survey of the Bloomery Forges in the Adirondacks." *IA: Journal of the Society for Industrial Archeology* 16:1–20.

Battison, Edwin A. 1966. "Eli Whitney and the Milling Machine." *The Smithsonian Journal of History* 1:9–34.

Bronson, Bennet. 1986. "The Making and Selling of Wootz, a Crucible Steel of India." *Archeomaterials* 1:13–51.

Cooper, Carolyn C. 1981–82. "The Production Line at Portsmouth Block Mill." *Industrial Archaeology Review* 6:28–44.

———, 1984. "The Portsmouth System of Manufacture." *Technology and Culture* 25:182–225.

Cooper, Carolyn C., Robert B. Gordon, Patrick M. Malone, and M. S. Raber. Forthcoming. *A Model Establishment: Springfield Armory and Military Small-Arms Making, 1794–1916.* Oxford University Press: New York.

Cooper, Carolyn C., Robert B. Gordon, and H. V. Merrick. 1982. "Archaeological Evidence of Metallurgical Innovation at the Eli Whitney Armory." *IA: Journal of the Society for Industrial Archeology* 8:1–12.

Davis, James J. 1922. *The Iron Puddler.* Indianapolis: Bobs-Merrill.

Ferguson, Eugene S. 1977. "The Mind's Eye: Nonverbal Thought in Technology." *Science* 197:827–836.

Foley, Vernard, et al. 1983. "Leonardo, the Wheel Lock, and the Milling Machine." *Technology and Culture* 24:399–427.

Forty, Gerald. 1983. "Sources of Latitude Error in English 16th Century Navigation." *Journal of the Institute of Navigation* 36:388–403.

———. 1986. "The Backstaff and the Determination of Latitude at Sea in the 17th Century." *Journal of the Institute of Navigation* 39:259–268.

Gale, W. K. V. 1963–64. "Wrought Iron: A Valediction." *Transactions of the Newcomen Society* 36:8–9.

Gordon, Robert B. 1983. "Material Evidence of the Development of Metal Working Technology at the Collins Axe Factory." *IA: Journal of the Society for Industrial Archeology* 9:19–28.

———. 1985. "Laboratory Evidence of the Use of Metal Tools in Machu Picchu and Environs." *Journal of Archaeological Science* 12:311–327.

———. 1987. "Sixteenth-Century Metalworking Technology Used in the Manufacture of Two German Astrolabes." *Annals of Science* 44:71–84.

———. 1988a. "Who Turned the Mechanical Ideal into Mechanical Reality?" *Technology and Culture* 29:744–788.

———. 1988b. "Strength and Structure of Wrought Iron." *Archeomaterials* 2:109–137.

Gordon, Robert B., and Patrick M. Malone. Forthcoming. *The Texture of Industry*. Oxford: Oxford University Press.

Gordon, Robert B., and Geoffrey Tweedale. 1990. "Pioneering in Steelmaking at the Collins Axe Company, 1826–1924." *Historical Metallurgy* 24:1–11.

Gordon, Robert B., and N. J. van der Merwe. 1984. "Metallographic Study of Iron Artifacts from the Eastern Transvaal, South Africa." *Archaeometry* 26:108–127.

Gwinnett, John A., and L. Gorlick. 1979. "Inlayed Teeth of Ancient Mayans: A Tribological Study Using the SEM." *Scanning Electron Microscopy* 2: 575–580.

Harris, J. R. 1976. "Skills, Coal and British Industry in the Eighteenth Century." *History* 61:167–182.

Hayden, Brian, ed. 1979. *Lithic Use-Wear Analysis*. New York: Academic Press.

Hoke, Donald. 1990. *Ingenious Yankees: The Rise of the American System of Manufactures in the Private Sector*. New York: Columbia University Press.

Kasson, John F. 1976. *Civilizing the Machine*. New York: Grossman.

Killick, David. 1990. "Technology in Its Social Context: Bloomery Iron Smelting at Kasungu, Malawi." Ph.D. diss., Yale University.

Lechtman, Heather. 1984. "Andean Value Systems and the Development of Prehistoric Metallurgy." *Technology and Culture* 25:1–36.

McGeown, Patrick. 1967. *Heat the Furnaces Seven Times More*. London: Hutchinson.

Mathewson, C. H. 1915. "A Metallographic Description of Some Ancient Peruvian Bronzes from Machu Picchu." *American Journal of Science* 240: 525–616.

Price, Derek. 1974. "Gears from the Greeks: The Antikythera Mechanism, A Calendar Computer from ca. 80 B.C." *Transactions of the American Philosophical Society* 64.

Reynolds, Michael. n. d. *Locomotive-Engine Driving*. London: Wm. Clowes.

Rosenberg, Nathan. 1969. *The American System of Manufactures*. Edinburgh: Edinburgh University Press.

Rutledge, J. W., and Robert B. Gordon. 1987. "The Work of Metallurgical Artificers at Machu Picchu." *American Antiquity* 52:578–594.

Smith, Cyril S. 1988. *A History of Metallography*. Cambridge, Mass.: MIT Press.

Swank, James M. 1892. *History of the Manufacture of Iron in All Ages*. Reprint. New York: Burt Franklin.

Vandiver, Pamela. 1988. "The Implications of Variation in Ceramic Technology: The Forming of Neolithic Storage Vessels in China and the Near East." *Archeomaterials* 2:130–174.

Gardens and Society in Eighteenth-Century England

Thomas Williamson

Gardens, like large houses and other elite arti-facts in eighteenth-century England, are usually studied by art historians. They are typically analyzed as a separate area of human activity, and few attempts have been made to examine their development within a wider social and economic context. Traditionally, attention has focused on the role of famous designers, whether gentleman amateurs or professionals, whose works were "copied" by "inferior" artists. Moreover, the development of design is usually read as a linear sequence, with each new style developing directly from another, as successive artists adapted the innovations of those who had gone before (Hadfield 1960:179–241; Hunt and Willis 1975:1–43; Stuart 1979; Jacques 1983). This teleological approach is nothing new. It was already well-developed in the eighteenth century, as shown, for example, in Horace Walpole's "History of the Modern Taste in Gardening," first published in 1771.

Conventional accounts generally start with the rigidly geometric gardens of the seventeenth and early eighteenth centuries. In these the layout of the constituent parts was usually symmetrical, and geometric shapes predominated not only in the patterns of grass, paths, and beds but also in the vertical components—trees and bushes were cut to form spheres, pyramids, and so forth. Gardens of this period were usually surrounded by high walls or hedges, which clearly separated them from the working landscape outside (Turner 1986:44–73). During the period 1720 to 1750 Stephen Switzer, Charles Bridgeman, and William Kent developed a less enclosed, simpler style in which rigid geometry was gradually broken down and the excessive use of topiary rejected. In the period after 1750 this development was taken further by Lancelot ("Capability") Brown, who swept away all geometric elements—indeed, effectively abolished the garden altogether—so that residences of the landed gentry in the later eighteenth century stood isolated in a highly irregular, "natural" landscape of grass and scattered trees, into which might be intruded a serpentine lake. The whole creation was usually surrounded, partially or entirely, by a woodland belt. The origins of this distinctive designed landscape—the landscape park—will be the main concern of this paper.

Conventional accounts of stylistic change in the eighteenth century are inadequate because they make little attempt to explain why the successive styles of landscape design gained popularity. Art historians studying gardens have been interested primarily in innovation and innovators and the philosophical and intellectual concerns of the millieu within which they moved. The evidence has been collected accordingly: The traditional account is based on pictorial representations and contemporary high-culture texts, describing particular gardens or advocating particular styles of design.

Consequently, the sample of gardens that forms the usual basis for discussion is comparatively small and biased toward large or innovative sites. Few attempts have been made to widen the sample—to look at the development of sites en masse, to see the "copies" as being as worthy of attention as the "works of art." As a result, whereas we know quite a lot about when and where innovations occurred, we know much less about the broader chronology of stylistic change. This is an important omission, not least because it means that traditional perspectives have been unable to examine in any systematic way the extent to which different groups in society may have varied in the speed or enthusiasm with which they accepted successive styles. The owners of parks and aesthetic gardens in eighteenth-century England were not a homogenous social and economic group. They ranged from great landowners with estates of ten thousand acres or more to the far more numerous local gentry possessing estates of only a few hundred acres (Williamson and Bellamy 1987:116–129).

Because eighteenth-century designed landscapes are studied primarily as works of art, we learn little in published histories about the ways in which they were consumed and how their use may have influenced their form. We learn even less about how the size and number of designed landscapes changed over time—how their creation was constrained or facilitated by the patterns of land ownership or the layout of features in the preexisting landscape or even how much they cost to establish and maintain. In short, the gardens and parks of eighteenth-century England are conceived in a social and physical vacuum. They are presented as expressions of pure art, created by all-powerful individuals in a landscape as empty of other people and other features as the middle of the Sahara.

THE DOMINANCE OF THE TEXT

Such a situation is more or less inevitable given the limited data on which the history of garden design is based. With no firm facts and figures to go on, explanations for stylistic change can be sought only in high-culture texts. Thus it is that all books on the development of gardens during the first half of the eighteenth century devote considerable space to the opinions of men such as the Earl of Shaftesbury, Alexander Pope, and Joseph Addison (Hadfield 1960:173–197; Turner 1986:20–30). Later in the century William Mason and Horace Walpole wrote retrospectively about the development of garden design, and their views have also been extensively quoted. Such texts explain or justify changes in gardening style with respect to contemporary debates about aesthetics or philosophy, often paying homage to the importance of nature as a guide to landscape design. But the significance of such writings is problematic.

To begin with, although they are usually taken as prescriptive and anterior to changes in design, it is also possible that to varying extents they represent rationalizations of changes occurring for other reasons. Second, even if they did adequately represent the reasons for stylistic change at the level of the famous innovators—and it should be noted that

Bridgeman, Kent, and Brown never wrote down the theory behind their designs—they do not necessarily explain why styles were taken up by wider social groups.

In addition, it is easy to be misled by the apparent familiarity of the terminology of these texts and overemphasize the continuity of philosophical and aesthetic ideas during the eighteenth century. It is easy to assume that when Shaftesbury wrote in 1709, "I shall no longer resist the passion growing within me for things of a natural kind, where neither art nor the conceit or caprice of man has spoiled their genuine order by breaking in upon the primitive state" (Shaftesbury 1709:125), he was advocating something akin to the "natural," irregular style of gardening later practiced by Brown. But this was far from being the case. Indeed, most of Shaftesbury's own garden was highly geometric (Leatherbarrow 1984). "Nature" in this context referred to the perfect geometric order that was the gardener's role to bring out in his designs and cultivation. By the time Mason and Walpole were writing, in the 1770s, other meanings of the word "nature" had become dominant in high-culture discourse.

High-culture texts may show how a small educated group articulated the changes taking place in garden design, but they should not be interpreted either as the sole and direct cause of those changes or as attempts to provide a complete explanation of why alterations were made. Many factors that influenced landowners in their choices about how their grounds should be shaped could not easily be expressed in a form of writing dedicated to the analysis and aesthetics of taste. Individuals could be influenced by a host of mundane and practical considerations, including not only limitations of their finances or the terrain with which they worked but also aesthetic or philosophical predilections rather different from those aired in the dominant discourse. Nostalgia for the old styles, ignorance of and dislike of the new could all affect the appearance of parks and gardens. Moreover, many developments in landscape design were the consequence not of the landowners' decisions but of more general changes in the patterns of landholding, agriculture, and the distribution of wealth.

It follows that to understand the development of landscape design in this period we need to look beyond the kinds of texts usually studied and concentrate on the artifacts themselves within their social, economic, and topographic context. We need to take a limited area, find out all we can about how the size and layout of designed landscapes within it changed over time, and attempt to relate such changes to wider developments. At the University of East Anglia we are currently using a wide range of documentary, archaeological, and cartographic evidence to examine the development of parks and gardens in eighteenth-century Norfolk. This work is still in its early stages, and much that follows must be considered highly provisional. It does, however, indicate some of the advantages of an approach that takes the artifact itself, rather than high-culture texts, as its starting point.

GREAT NAMES: PATRON AND ARTIST

Systematic research of this kind soon reveals that the role of the great names in the design of parks and gardens is rather less straightforward than conventional accounts suggest. For example, there are frequent and significant discrepancies between the plans prepared by famous artists and their executed form. The activities of Lancelot Brown in Norfolk are particularly interesting in this respect. At Langley, in the south of the county, few elements of Brown's design for the park were actually executed. The owners rejected the more expensive features, particularly the lake (the site is on a level clay plateau, and its construction would have involved considerable feats of earth movement), and the eventual pattern of clumps and plantations was rather different from that originally proposed. At Kimberley, where Brown worked on two commissions, in 1762 and 1778, the owners insisted on retaining the unfashionable formal avenue focusing on the house. Many characteristic "Brownian" elements owe as much to the existing fabric of the landscape as they do to Brown himself. The "Brownian" lake, for example, had been in existence since the 1730s.

Brown worked at Melton Constable in 1767 and is often credited with sweeping away the geometric gardens illustrated in Kip and Knyff's *Britannia Illustrata* of 1707 (fig. 1). But the walled gardens were in fact removed by the 1740s. Brown probably gothicized an existing garden building, extended the perimeter belt of trees, and added a lake, but it is clear that the essential form of the park was established long before he arrived. The gardens shown by Kip and Knyff already lay within an irregular "natural" landscape: a medieval deer park.

In all these cases the history of a landscape has been oversimplified by exaggerating the role of the individual genius. This process may have begun in the eighteenth century, when owners were anxious to claim the kudos associated with having their estates landscaped by an eminent de-

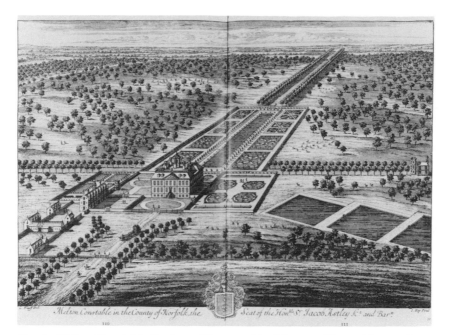

Fig. 1. Melton Constable Park, as illustrated in Johannes Kip and Leonard Knyff's Britannia Illustrata *(1707).*

signer. It has certainly been reinforced by the development of garden history as the study of innovative individuals. In practice even parks planned by a great designer were seldom the product of the imposition of a preconceived scheme on a virgin landscape. The existing features were vitally important, but so too was the role of the owner. The designer did not have a free hand. The landscapes were the result of a series of compromises with the patron's needs, tastes, and resources as well as the nature of the existing terrain.

What was true of landscapes designed by the great names for the leading landowners in the county was even more true of those on smaller estates, which were the work of local designers, estate gardeners, or the owners themselves. William Faden's map of Norfolk, published in 1797 but surveyed between 1790 and 1794, shows 117 parks and gardens extending over fifteen hectares or more; of these no more than 20 were worked on by designers of national importance such as Charles Bridgeman, William Kent, Lancelot Brown, William Emes, or Nathaniel Richmond. All this should encourage us to look at the landscape park not as a fashion slavishly adhered to by members of the landed classes but as something that developed with their full participation and reflected their particular needs.

THE PATTERN OF CHANGE

One major problem with most conventional accounts is their failure to trace the history of the park back before the time of Brown. The impression gained from reading books such as Hadfield's *History of British Gardening* (1960) is that before the mid-eighteenth century the only distinctive landscape associated with the country house was the garden and that parkland was something new, created by a developing enthusiasm for things "natural." Illustrations such as those of Melton Constable clearly demonstrate the problems with such a notion. In reality, areas called "park," consisting of pasture irregularly scattered with timber trees and interspersed with blocks of woodland, had been a feature of the English landscape since the time of the Domesday Book. In the Middle Ages a park had been an enclosure serving as a venison farm and hunting reserve, although with some subsidiary economic functions such as livestock grazing, timber and wood production, and so forth (Rackham 1986:122–129). As late as 1755 Johnson's *Dictionary* still defined a park as "a piece of ground enclosed and stored with wild beasts of chase." But the transition from park as hunting ground to park as pleasure ground and setting for a great house was well underway by this time. The nature of this transition is crucial to any understanding of the evolution of the landscape park. The differences between the two kinds of parks are by no means clear-cut, and parks had important aesthetic functions long before Brown's arrival.

The characteristic features of these ancient landscapes had originally developed for functional rather than aesthetic reasons. In the Middle Ages parks seldom formed the setting for elite residences. Some ran up to the backs of their owners' homes, but many were located miles away, although they usually contained a lodge, which provided temporary accommodation during hunting trips as well as permanent accommodation for the keeper, who maintained the park and its deer (Rackham 1986:148).

In the late medieval period there was a sharp decline in the number of parks in Norfolk, as in other parts of England, partly for economic reasons.

Those that survived tended to be those actually attached to large houses. Melton Constable was typical: The great house was surrounded by a relatively small formal garden, beyond which avenues ran out across a deer park (see fig. 1). Like many other illustrations in *Britannia Illustrata*, the Melton engraving shows that the deer park was considered an appropriate adjunct to a country house in the early years of the eighteenth century. Indeed, the late seventeenth and early eighteenth centuries saw something of a renaissance of the deer park. In Norfolk new deer parks appeared at, among other places, Buckenham Tofts in the 1660s (fig. 2), Houghton Hall in the early 1700s (fig. 3), and Gunton Hall in the 1730s, while existing parks at Felbrigg, Blickling, and elsewhere were extended.

But the function of deer parks was changing. In the course of the seventeenth century they began to be used for more than just hunting. At Hunstanton Hall, for example, the Octagon, an elaborate moated summer house set in the heart of the park, appeared in the 1650s. There also seems to have been a change in the management of parkland timber. Illustrations and estate accounts suggest that parkland trees were no longer being pollarded—that is, repeatedly cut back to the trunk to produce a regular crop of poles that could be used for firewood or other practical uses. Instead, they were allowed to grow into handsome standard trees. Moreover, by the end of the seventeenth century deer were no longer being regularly hunted within parks, although they were still culled.

Already, therefore, in the sixteenth and seventeenth centuries the park's role as an aesthetic landscape was of importance, and this was further encouraged by the savage antipoaching legislation of the early 1720s, the Black Acts, which inter alia removed venison from the commercial market and made it in effect an article of elite gift exchange (Thompson 1975). The distinctly aristocratic aura of deer was thus increased and with it the status of the landscape with which they were intimately associated.

The increased importance of the parkland landscape in Norfolk during the late seventeenth and early eighteenth centuries is reflected in other ways. In a few places landowners found that they could no longer afford the luxury of maintaining a herd of deer. Yet the park beside the house was not disparked—that is, subdivided by hedges or ploughed. Instead, the distinctive landscape was maintained, although now grazed by cattle or sheep. This, at least, appears to be what happened at Hunstanton, Hedenham, Costessey, and perhaps elsewhere. Even more interesting is the appearance during the 1720s and 1730s of entirely new areas of park adjacent to country houses that were never, apparently, stocked with deer,

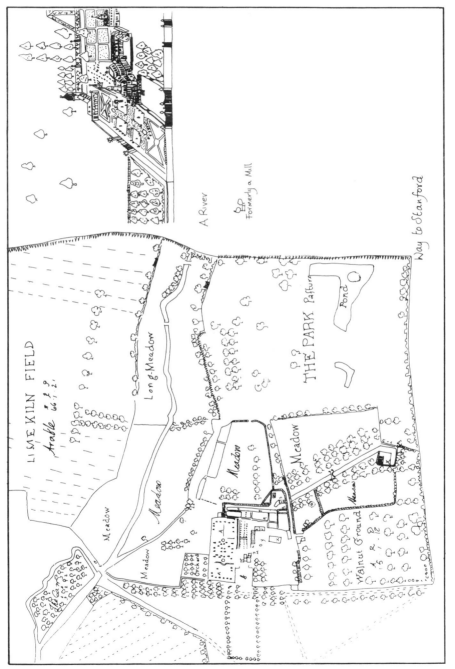

Fig. 2. Buckenham Tofts Park in 1700; plan and elevation from a damaged estate map. Norfolk Record Office.

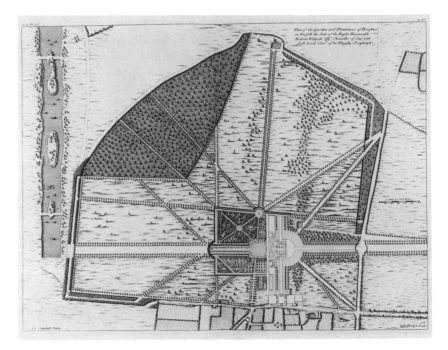

Fig. 3. Houghton Hall gardens and park, as illustrated in Colen Campbell's
Vitruvius Britannicus or the British Architect, *volume 3 (1725).*

as at Merton (shown on an estate map of 1733) and Mannington (in existence by 1742).

Long before Brown's arrival, therefore, many elite residences were
associated with irregular, informal, "natural" landscapes. Yet we must not
exaggerate their number in the first half of the eighteenth century, especially in agriculturally productive areas such as Norfolk. Present research
suggests that in 1750 the county contained no more than twenty-nine parks.
Of these perhaps nine were stocked with deer. With few exceptions parks
were attached only to the houses of the greatest landowners, forming a
powerful visual contrast to the ordered regularity of the gardens beside the
house, although the park too could contain some geometric features, most
notably avenues. The houses of the broad mass of the local gentry, in
contrast, did not have parks, only comparatively small areas of walled
geometric gardens. Beyond the walls lay agricultural land, perhaps crossed
by a single avenue of trees focused on the main elevation of the house.

Elite gardens, those of the greatest landowners, went through a number of stylistic changes in the early decades of the eighteenth century. Gardens of the kind seen at Melton Constable, with elaborate parterres, had by the late 1730s been succeeded by simpler designs. The dominant elements were now plain grass parterres, or plats; hedged or tree-lined gravel walks; and groves or wildernesses—that is, areas of ornamental woodland intersected by hedged paths. By the 1730s these wooded walks in the more stylistically "advanced" gardens often took an irregular, serpentine form.

There were other, more significant changes. At places such as Houghton or Narford the gardens were now more open to the surrounding parkland, being encompassed not by a wall but by a sunken fence or ditch. Moreover, whereas the principal compartments of the greatest gardens in the late seventeenth century had been laid out in a symmetrical plan, on either side of the main axis of the house (see fig. 2), by the 1720s this had ceased to be the case. Gardens such as those at Houghton, although still highly geometric in their individual components, no longer made any serious attempt at achieving overall symmetry (see fig. 3).

The disappearance of enclosing walls, complex parterres, and rigid symmetry and the appearance of serpentine walks within groves are all interpreted in the teleological model as evidence of incipient informality (Hadfield 1960:179–197), a stage in the development from enclosed, geometric gardens to Brown's informal parkland. There may be much truth in this conventional interpretation, but it is nevertheless an oversimplification. Gardens such as these had far more in common with the layouts that preceded them than with the informal parks by which they were replaced. In spite of the twisting woodland walks, they were still dominated by geometric features, and this would have been particularly apparent when gardens were experienced on the ground, rather than in plan. The gardens at Narford and Houghton were drawn in plan by Colen Campbell and at ground level by Edmund Prideaux at roughly the same time, in the mid-1720s. The ground-level sketches show that Houghton had a garden that was strictly geometric in appearance and dominated by clipped topiary, in spite of the serpentine walks that Campbell's plan shows winding through the groves (fig. 4). Indeed, in all Norfolk gardens at this time the designers followed the advice of the influential writer Batty Langley in restricting irregular lines to "pleasant solitary walks in wood, groves, etc. . . ." (1729:38). Elsewhere, in the main body of the gardens, straight lines and geometric shapes still predominated.

Fig. 4. Houghton Hall gardens, as illustrated by Humphrey Prideau, c. 1727. National Monuments Record, London.

Groves and grass parterres had been the principal feature of many English gardens in the previous century. Thus, in reality gardens such as that at Houghton Hall represent a simplified version of late seventeenth-century garden design. This simplification is related most probably to an increase in the size of aristocratic gardens during the early eighteenth century. In the early 1700s the formal garden at Melton Constable extended over less than three hectares, and this was probably one of the largest layouts in the county at this time. At Houghton Hall in 1727, in contrast, the new gardens extended over an area of around nine hectares, and the gardens at Raynham and Narford were probably even larger. In this period of competitive display between aristocratic families, design principles inevitably underwent modification as gardens grew in size. Layouts were simplified, partly perhaps because of maintenance costs but primarily because the larger gardens required rather different principles of organization to create a striking visual effect. Areas of two or three hectares or less could be arranged so that all the different components contributed to an overall, symmetrical plan. Where the area was of six hectares or more, however, the construction of an entirely symmetrical layout was both more difficult and less important, since a garden of this size would not be viewed as a whole.

The disappearance of walled enclosures also seems at least in part to be related to the growth in the area of gardens. Their increased size invited designs based on block planting and broad vistas. Yet it would have been pointless to place such designs within a single, huge walled enclosure, for walls were primarily intended to provide shelter and protection for plants and people, and as the size of an enclosure increased their efficiency in accomplishing this declined. Walls, moreover, interrupted the views out of the garden into the park, which were now being given increasing importance. Indeed, the park was ceasing to be a separate component of the elite landscape and was becoming part of the experience of the garden itself. Not only were there open views from park to garden; the main walks in the garden were now being extended as vistas or avenues far into the park.

These late geometric gardens of the elite in the early eighteenth century had other important characteristics. Many included classical buildings and statues, which proclaimed their owners' knowledge of classical and Renaissance culture and therefore their elite status and fitness to rule. Some of these features and structures alluded to their owners' philosophical views and political affiliations (Clarke 1973; Colton 1974; Rorschach 1983). Indeed, they could form highly complex iconographic schemes. Such gardens were, in addition, often highly compartmentalized—a series of experiences, a collection of routes to be explored. In these respects they differed considerably from the later landscape parks. The latter were much simpler in their design, offering a basically homogenous landscape of tree and sward that ran uninterrupted to the house. The kind of garden laid out around Houghton Hall was thus not so much a herald of the new as an evolutionary dead end. The opening up of views into the parkland was the precursor to the destruction of such gardens and the triumph of the parkland landscape.

THE DEVELOPMENT OF THE LANDSCAPE PARK

This development seems to have occurred on elite sites in the 1750s and 1760s. Straight paths and avenues were removed; geometric groves and plantations were felled or their outlines softened. And at the same time the setting of the far more numerous gentry houses in the county was changing. These too lost their geometric gardens and came to be set in an open parkland landscape, although one devoid of deer. The proliferation of such landscape parks was rapid. By the mid-1790s there were around 120 parks covering an area of fifteen hectares or more; by 1850 this number had risen to nearly 200, and all people with serious pretensions to gentility had their houses set within a park. At this more lowly social level there is little evidence for the supposedly transitional late-geometric phase of garden design exemplified by Houghton Hall. Old-fashioned enclosed gardens were simply swept away and immediately replaced by parks. These new, irregular pleasure grounds differed from the enclosed gardens they replaced not only in style but also in scale: Parks were invariably much larger than the walled enclosures.

Landowners could spend large amounts of money on the creation of new parks or the embellishment, in suitably "naturalistic" fashion, of old ones. Many writers quote the large amounts of money paid to carry out some of Brown's designs—for example, the £4550 paid by the third Earl Waldegrave for the changes at Navestock in Essex or the £5000 paid by Baron Petre at nearby Thornton. But consulting the "genius of the place," to use Pope's famous term—that is, working with rather than against the local landscape and topography—meant that landscapes of this kind were usually constructed rather cheaply. Screening belts were usually planted around the perimeter, but much of the parkland timber originated as existing hedgerow trees, many already ancient. The hedges were grubbed out, with varying degrees of thoroughness, while the more prominent timber was retained. At Raveningham, for example, the park itself was created around 1784, but much of the parkland timber is between one and two hundred years older. Careful inspection reveals that these older trees stand on slight banks—the remains of the former hedges. Such a procedure provided instant parkland timber and added an air of antique authenticity to the creation, making it look as much as possible like the deer parks of the greater landowners.

If a park had a stream or river flowing through it (many did not), damming it was a relatively cheap and easy way to create a lake. Given the topography of minor valleys, the result was inevitably of serpentine form. Often, little was needed in the way of additional revetment or puddling (lining with clay).

We should not push this argument too far. All parks involved some capital outlay. The existing gardens had to be demolished and levelled, and many new plantations were established, particularly on the periphery of the park. Roads often had to be closed, replacements provided, fences erected. Unfortunately, using estate archives (even where these survive) to ascertain the sums involved is often difficult, for the money spent on the various activities is usually subsumed under general accounts for estate labor and purchases. In a few cases, fortunately, the owner maintained a separate, itemized account. One is the "Various Expenses in the Improvements at Hillington" between 1768 and and 1775, drawn up by Edmund Rolfe. This shows that no less than £913.5.1 was spent on the park (denominations are pounds, shillings, and pence). This would certainly have seemed like a lot to Rolfe's gardener, who received only £14 per year at the time. But it is not really that much. The work was spread over eight years, during which time Rolfe's annual income seems to have varied between around £1,200 and £2,300. In other words, in any one year the money expended on the park was between 5 and 10 percent of his annual income. The sum also needs to be compared with that spent on the kitchen garden, which Rolfe began to construct in 1769. This, we are told in a survey of 1773, covered no more than 1¼ acres, but it cost nearly as much as the entire park to construct and equip—£878.7.0, nearly half of which went to the 481,000 bricks used in the walls and greenhouse. In addition, both sums need to be compared with the £4,128.1.4 spent on the new house at Heacham, the construction of which began as work on the park and garden were winding down.

Not only were parks cheap to create. They were also cheap to maintain, for they required only regular grazing by sheep and cattle. Indeed, income could be derived from this and also—as estate accounts make clear—from the systematic commercial exploitation of the woods and plantations that lay within and encircled the parkland.

With the exception of Prince and Williams, few researchers have paid much attention to the economics of parks and gardens (Prince 1967; Williams 1987). This is a serious problem, for the relative costs of different kinds of designed landscape are of crucial importance in their evolution and diffusion. Arguably, the most important feature of the landscape park was that it supplied a cheap way of creating an extensive, ornamental landscape that was ostensibly divorced from agricultural production but that anyone with pretensions to gentility could afford. It demonstrated land ownership and elite status in a highly visible way and carried with it the resonances of the ancient, aristocratic deer park.

But the landscape park, as its style developed during the 1760s and

1770s, offered something more: a measure of privacy, of exclusivity, of divorce from the surrounding countryside. The pre-1750 deer parks had usually allowed views out into and in from the surrounding landscape, as at Holkham Park (fig. 5). But after 1750, as parks proliferated, they were increasingly circumscribed by belts of trees. The creation of parks usually involved the removal of public roads and footpaths, excluding the local population from sight of the house—a process well documented from the 1770s by Road Closure Orders. Sometimes houses and even entire settlements were destroyed to make way for the vast expanses of grass. The result was an extensive, private, insulating space that served to isolate the homes of the landed elite from local communities and their economic activities.

THE SOCIAL CONTEXT OF PARKLAND

The increasing spatial segregation of social classes had been a dominant theme in the development of material culture in England since the late Middle Ages, as Mercer and Girouard have shown with regard to both vernacular and polite architecture (Mercer 1975; Girouard 1978). But the impetus to such segregation seems to have intensified during the later eighteenth century and for good reasons. This was a period of important and rapid social change. The second half of the century saw the beginning of the Industrial Revolution. In the north and west, towns like Birmingham and Manchester grew in size, and canals spread through the landscape. But change was also occuring in predominantly rural areas such as Norfolk. Population increase was rapid, and this, coupled with the impact of the Napoleonic Wars, meant that agricultural prices and therefore farm rents also rose quickly. Together with a gradual shift in the burden of taxation away from land and to consumables, this meant that the second half of the eighteenth century saw an increase in the wealth and importance of the local gentry. Their estates grew in size and became more consolidated as new agricultural techniques and market forces forced many small freeholders into liquidation, a process encouraged to some extent by the large-scale enclosure of open fields and commons. It is arguable that in Norfolk this period saw the final demise of a peasant economy and its replacement with a three-tier system of large estates, tenant farms, and impoverished landless laborers.

Estate consolidation, together with enclosure, worked in a direct and

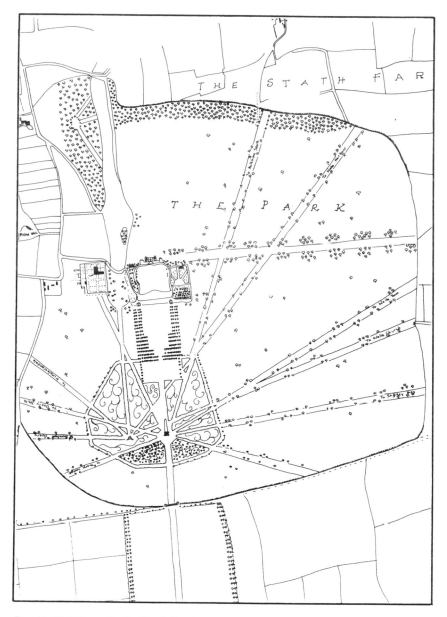

Fig. 5. Holkham Park, Norfolk, from an estate map of 1744. Norfolk Record Office.

practical way to encourage emparking, creating continuous blocks of land that could be used and planted as the owner saw fit. Emparking often came as the finale to a long period of estate consolidation in a parish and was, in some cases at least, a principal motive for it. Once all or a substantial majority of the land in a parish fell into the hands of a single owner, the farms could be reorganized to liberate land for a new pleasure ground. In Docking, for example, William Becher, estate manager for the Ffolkes family, wrote in 1804 that the lord of the manor, Christian Hare, "has a plan for taking land from Barker and his other tennants, to make his own occupation more Parkish if I may be allowed the term, about his house to west, south and east."

With more land at their disposal and with burgeoning economic fortunes, the local gentry were increasingly in a position to emulate in some form the parkland setting of the houses of the very rich. But the need for such a landscape was particularly pressing at this social level at this time. Numerous references in literature, correspondence, and diaries make it clear that the local poor were increasingly regarded as a problem, even a threat, as population growth outstripped employment possibilities in rural areas. This, again, was a problem made worse by the enclosure of common land, which often removed from the rural poor a vital safety net against indigence. Such anxieties on the part of landowners were intensified in the 1790s by events on the other side of the English Channel. It is hardly surprising, then, to find them distancing themselves from social groups with whom they now had little in common, retreating from the realities of rural life, creating an environment that insulated their homes from the economic realities on which much of their wealth was based—a safer pastoral world secluded behind parkland belts.

But landscape parks were not only about the relationships between local gentry and their inferiors. They served to express relations laterally and upward, as well as downward. The great geometric gardens of the early eighteenth-century elite had been appropriate to a rural and hierarchical society in which the power of great landowners was displayed with pride and arrogance, a society that had differed only in degree from the absolutist monarchies of continental Europe. But increasingly, as the century progressed, the ruling elite chose to emphasize a different way of life, often referred to as "polite society." Differences of rank between the great landowners and the broad mass of the local gentry and the wealthier professionals were consciously played down. Instead, emphasis was placed on contact without constraint between members of these groups, regardless of occupation or background. The arrogance of the nobility, the ignorance of the backwoods squire, the ideological motivation of the Jacobite or the Puritan were all anathemas to this wider, easy-going, consumer-orientated ruling group, as they rubbed shoulders amicably at Bath or in the assembly rooms of the provincial towns. Gardens of naked grandeur were increasingly unnecessary and inappropriate in this new, more complex society.

But the smaller geometric gardens around the homes of the lesser gentry were also unsuited to this different world. As their owners flourished and grew closer culturally to the great landowners, they also drew away from their neighbors in the local community. They had less and less in common with their tenant farmers and the local freeholders. Direct hands-on involvement in the kinds of activities that had once seemed fitting to the rural squire—the details of estate and domestic management, including supervision of the gardens—now seemed to smack of the lifestyle of their less exalted neighbors. Gardens were increasingly seen as an inappropriate setting for a polite residence.

By the end of the century, therefore, the earlier division between the landed aristocracy's large semigeometric gardens and deer parks and the local gentry's old-fashioned, enclosed gardens had been largely replaced by a single shared style. The landscape park represented a stylistic game that everyone, local gentry and great landowners alike, could play—one that all could afford and all could understand. It represented the cultural convergence of the landed classes. The new landscape style expressed the common, normative culture that helped define membership of the new, wider elite.

The second half of the eighteenth century was a time of acute social stress, as deprivation and resentment increased among the rural population. But it was also a period in which questions of social definition became particularly pressing, as manufacturers and professionals thrust upward into the ranks of gentry society and members of the local gentry increasingly sought to be identified with their superiors. Parks proliferated because they had a vital function in this changing social system. Landscapes, most visible of all artifacts, became crucial in the definition of social roles.

Of course, this is not the full story. Like other complex artifacts, landscape parks were multipurpose creations, with a range of social functions and meanings. Their form was conditioned by the interplay of many factors, but in a short paper such as this I have intentionally concentrated on those aspects of landscape design absent from or understated in contemporary written explanations. I have tried to let the artifacts speak for themselves.

REFERENCES

Clarke, George. 1973. "Grecian Taste and Gothic Virtue: Lord Cobham's Gardening Programme and Its Iconography." *Apollo* 97:561–571.

Colton, Judith. 1974. "Kent's Hermitage for Queen Caroline at Richmond." *Architectura* 2:181–191.

Girouard, Mark. 1978. *Life in the English Country House: A Social and Architectural History.* New Haven, Conn.: Yale University Press.

Hadfield, Miles. 1960. *A History of British Gardening.* London: Hutchinson.

Hunt, John Dixon, and Peter Willis. 1975. *The Genius of the Place.* London: Elek.

Jacques, David. 1983. *Georgian Gardens: The Reign of Nature.* London: Batsford.

Langley, Batty. 1729. *Practical Geometry Applied to the Useful Arts of Building, Surveying, and Gardening.* London.

Leatherbarrow, David. 1984. "Character, Geometry, and Perspective: The Third Earl of Shaftesbury's Principles of Garden Design." *Journal of Garden History* 4, no. 4: 332–358.

Mercer, Eric. 1975. *English Vernacular Houses: A Study of Traditional Farmhouses and Cottages.* London: Royal Commission on Historical Monuments.

Prince, Hugh. 1967. *Parks in England.* Newport, Isle of Wight: Findhorn.

Rackham, Oliver. 1976. *Trees and Woodland in the British Landscape.* London: Dent.

———. 1986. *The History of the Countryside.* London: Dent.

Rorschach, Kimerly. 1983. *The Early Georgian Landscape Garden.* New Haven, Conn.: Yale Center for British Art.

The Third Earl of Shaftesbury. 1709. "The Moralists." In *Characteristics of Men, Manners, Opinions, Times.* London.

Stuart, David C. 1979. *Georgian Gardens.* London: Viking.

Thompson, E.P. 1975. *Whigs and Hunters: The Origin of the Black Acts.* London: Allen Lane.

Turner, Tom. 1986. *English Garden Design: History and Styles Since 1650.* Woodbridge, Suffolk: Antique Collectors Club.

Walpole, Horace. 1771. "The History of the Modern Taste in Gardening." In

Anecdotes of Painting in England. Reprint. New York: Garland Publishing, 1982.

Williams, Robert. 1987. "Rural Economy and the Antique in the English Landscape Garden." *Journal of Garden History* 7, no. 1:73–96.

Williamson, Tom, and Liz Bellamy. 1987. *Property and Landscape.* London: George Philip.

Willis, Peter. 1977. *Charles Bridgeman and the English Landscape Garden.* London: Zwemmer.

Common Landscapes as Historic Documents

Peirce Lewis

angible objects form a challenging and stubborn kind of historic record. They challenge us because they are there—and because we know, as an article of faith, that those
objects have meaning, if we are only clever
enough to decipher it. They are stubborn because they simply refuse to go away, by their
very presence demanding to be interpreted. To
human geographers no form of material artifact
is more stubborn, more tantalizing, or potentially more illuminating than the vast disorderly collection of human artifacts that constitute the cultural landscape.

The idea is simple to define but daunting in
the enormity of its scope. By *cultural landscape*
geographers mean the total assemblage of visible
things that human beings have done to alter the
face of the earth—their shapings of the earth

with mines and quarries and dams and jetties; the ubiquitous purposeful manipulation of the earth's vegetative cover in farms, forests, lawns, parks, and gardens; the things humans build on the earth, cities and towns, houses and barns, factories and office buildings; the spaces we create for worship and for play. Cultural landscape includes the roads and machines we build to transport objects and ideas, the fences and walls we erect to subdivide land into manageable units and separate portions of the earth from one another, the monuments we build to celebrate our-selves, our institutions, our heroes, and our ancestors. Cultural land-scape, in short, is everything that humans do to the natural earth for whatever purpose but most commonly for material profit, aesthetic plea-sure, spiritual fulfillment, personal comfort, or communal safety.[1]

Human landscapes differ in appearance from place to place for the self-evident reason that all cultures have certain collective ambitions about the way the world should operate and because they possess peculiar means of achieving those goals of profit, pleasure, and safety. Simply because cultures are peculiar, their landscapes are peculiar too. And, of course, because cultures change through time, their landscapes also change. Those landscapes become in effect a kind of document, a kind of cultural autobiography that humans have carved and continue to carve into the surface of the earth.

It follows, necessarily, that if landscape is a document, we ought to be able to read it in a manner analogous to the way we read written docu-ments. We are driven to try to read the language of landscape partly because it is the primary evidence created by people who often left behind no written records of their day-to-day activities and partly because there is so much of it that the validity of its messages can be tested by that most powerful of tests—internal consistency. It does not follow, however, that cultural landscape is an easy document to read, nor does it follow that it is complete. It was, after all, not meant to be read, nor are people accus-tomed to reading it. Large parts of the document are missing (especially the older parts), and our contemporaries are constantly messing with what remains—altering it, erasing it, redesigning it. Cultural landscape has many of the qualities of a gigantic palimpsest, a huge ragged informal document written by a host of people with various levels of literacy, repeat-edly erased and amended by people with different motives and different tools at their disposal. Rarely, however, did the creators of landscape think of themselves as writing a document, nor did they suspect that anyone would try to read it. This quality of artlessness is, to a large degree, what makes cultural landscape such a rich document but also such a valuable one.

But how can one learn to read cultural landscape? What can one expect to learn from the exercise? And how can one test the validity of ideas based on evidence from that landscape?

LEARNING BY DOING: READING THE LANDSCAPE OF A SMALL TOWN

I have been wrestling with these problems for more than twenty years. Every year at Pennsylvania State University I teach an introductory course on the American cultural landscape to a hundred or so undergraduate students, none of them tutored in these matters.[2] The students come from all over campus—from architecture and landscape architecture, mathematics and history, electrical engineering and dairy husbandry; they are, in effect, a random grab from the population of a very large public university. It has not occurred to many of those students that landscape is something other than a disorderly assemblage of miscellaneous objects. To most of them landscape is merely something to cast their eyes across—sometimes in approval, sometimes in disgust—but most often to take for granted, except when particular items in the landscape impinge on ordinary day-to-day life—the location of dormitories and classrooms and dining halls, the pattern of streets and paths that lead most efficiently to a favorite bookstore or disco or pizza joint or romantic liaison. Except under unusual circumstances most students view ordinary landscape simply as a time-consuming obstacle that lies between where they are and where they want to be, to be crossed as quickly as possible but otherwise ignored. It almost never occurs to those students—as it almost never occurs to most Americans—to look at that landscape questioningly, to inquire how it came to be, to ask what it has to tell us about the folk who made it: ourselves and our cultural ancestors.

My job with those students is simple to state but not so easy to execute: to persuade them that landscape can be read and that the enterprise is worth undertaking. Most students are skeptical of both propositions. They do not believe that landscape can be read, partly because it has never occurred to them but, more important, because they have never seen anybody do it. It has never occurred to them that the human landscape can be viewed as a form of cultural autobiography—a source of ideas and information about themselves and their society that is often hard to obtain in other ways.

Over a good many years of teaching the course I have discovered only one effective means of persuading them, and that is to take them physically into that landscape and show them during the course of a one-day field trip what a finite bit of that world has to teach them. Before we sally forth, I ask them to arm themselves with a bit of vocabulary, having mainly to do with the history of American architecture and building technology, and then follow me around for a day while we jointly ask questions about what we see, trying to get some reasonable answers and trying, insofar as we can, to test those answers to see if they are valid.

The place we go to try out these ideas is a small town about a dozen miles from my university campus, a place called Bellefonte, Pennsylvania. Its population is not quite ten thousand, so it is small enough that the mind can get around it and the eye can grasp it as a whole. But it is complex enough to be challenging and old enough (it was founded about two hundred years ago) to contain a good deal of historical diversity. Like many small towns, it does a fair variety of things. It is the county seat of Centre County, and it has been an economic and social hub for a good-sized and fairly prosperous farming district. From time to time it has had its share of manufacturing, chiefly a lively iron industry that flourished for much of the nineteenth century. In sum, it is fairly typical of many semianonymous small American towns.[3]

This essay is a vicarious trip to Bellefonte and is aimed to demonstrate a few things that a common American landscape can reveal. There is some risk in trying to do this. To condense into a short printed essay what takes about eight hours of constant looking and talking and thinking to show the students obviously runs some risk of caricature. And a few black-and-white illustrations cannot really do justice to the multicolored three-dimensional variety and complexity of the real landscape. (Indeed, photographs taken from a single perspective and framed by linear borders cannot help but pull things out of context, something that one constantly seeks to avoid in an enterprise where context is crucial to the understanding of the subject.) But, at the risk of caricaturing the town or, even worse, caricaturing the act of landscape reading, what follows is a small sample of the things one can see on a one-day excursion into the ordinary cultural landscape of an American small town.

PUTTING THINGS IN CONTEXT: THREE LEVELS
OF MAGNIFICATION

If there is a single rule about the interpretation of landscape (or any other artifact for that matter), it is, I submit, to view it in its context of place and time—of geography and history, if you please. Context, of course, is what pathologists look for when they examine cells under a microscope at a low level of magnification but with a large field of vision. Before looking at the details of a cell, pathologists want to see where the cell is, what kind of tissue is around it. Only when they understand that are they ready to increase the level of magnification and look in detail at the cell's internal anatomy.

We approach Bellefonte in the same way by getting two composite bird's-eye views of the town from nearby hilltops—one at a considerable distance, another closer in. Only then do we descend into the streets of the town for a final close-up look.

Fortunately for this exercise, Bellefonte is a fairly hilly place, and a good view of the town can be had from several hilltops nearby. That is not always the case, of course, and that is why students of landscape typically start an exercise of this kind by seeking out a vantage point—a high building or firetower perhaps—to obtain a composite view of the place to be studied. Maps and aerial photographs, of course, serve much the same purpose (fig. 1). At various scales they are wonderfully useful devices to help us simplify and generalize our ideas about large complicated places and, above all, to see them in their larger geographic context.

Two Views from a Distance

From the top of a hill in the prosperous farmland outside Bellefonte one can get a sweeping view of the town and its surroundings (fig. 2). Even at this low level of magnification one can make some educated guesses about the place. The town commands the entrance of a gap in a mountain ridge where a little stream has cut a notch through that ridge. It requires little imagination to guess that the town's prosperity, such as it is, has derived from command of transportation routes through that gap. Prima facie the town seems to be a market center and, one is inclined to guess, a social center too, like so many other American towns that grew up at the junction of roads. What else it may be this distant view does not reveal, but it

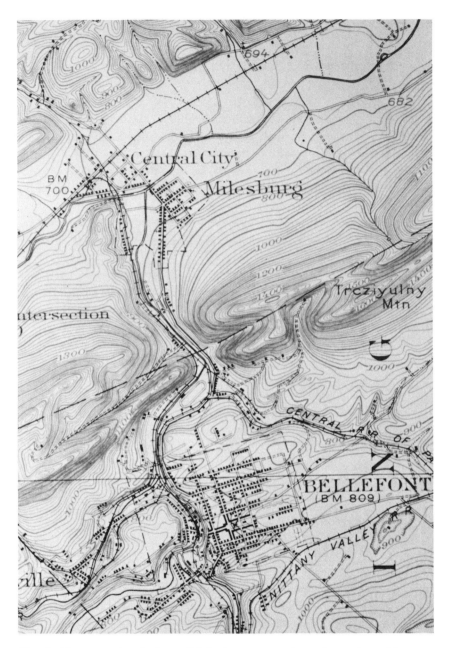

Fig. 1. Maps are singularly useful devices not merely to show where things are located but also to place them in their geographic contexts. This figure is excerpted from the U.S. Geological Survey's 1908 "Bellefonte, Pennsylvania, Quadrangle" (1:62, 500) and shows the town's location with respect to Bald Eagle Mountain, which bisects the map WSW-ENE. Notice the funneling of roads, railroads, and waterways through the watergap carved by Spring Creek between Milesburg and Bellefonte. All photographs in this chapter by Peirce Lewis.

Fig. 2. Panoramic view of Bellefonte from a hilltop about a mile south of town. Rising beyond the town is Bald Eagle Mountain, broken by the water gap carved by Spring Creek (left middleground). The command of routes through the gap gave Bellefonte its economic and social reason for being; like most American cities and towns, it prospered because it commanded a route junction.

invites questions that can be answered only by stepping up the level of magnification and getting a closer view of the town.

From a second hilltop, Half Moon Hill, a knoll that overlooks the railroad station and commercial district, one can make out the general outlines of the town's main industrial, commercial, and residential districts. In the foreground, along Spring Creek and the railroad tracks, is a string of large nineteenth-century industrial buildings, many apparently in an advanced state of decay. (We wonder about what kind of industry flourished there and why it is no more, and we remind ourselves to take a closer look at the banks of the creek when we descend into the town.) On the edge of that industrial district, also near the creek, is the railroad station. The town's main street, High Street, leads uphill from the railroad to the courthouse, a commanding white building with a self-consciously classical porch. Much of the commercial district is strung out along High Street between the railroad station and courthouse. Even at this distance one suspects that those two buildings served as functional anchors— politics at one end of the street, commerce at the other. Indeed, from the hilltop one can make out two bulky hotels: one (the Bush House) across the street from the railroad station, the other (the Brockerhoff) across the street from the courthouse. One is inclined to guess that the railroad hotel might have served commercial travelers—drummers and the like. Equally, it seems plausible that the courthouse hotel was the seat of a good deal of unofficial political activity.

On the hills beyond the commercial district rises the town's main residential area. Even from this distant hilltop there is evidence of residential segregation. To the left (the north side of town) the residential area is a bosky kind of place, and one can spot the characteristic profile of Norway spruces, a tree much beloved by high-style romantic landscape designers of the late nineteenth-century in America. This man-made forest is punctured by several church steeples and mansard roofs, green with verdigris—signs of Victorian money and Victorian good taste. To the right (the south side of town), however, the residential area of Bellefonte is substantially different, even though it lies about the same distance from the center of town and one presumes that it was built about the same time. Landscaping is scantier, and the fashionable late Victorian architecture is totally absent. From the hilltop it is hard to make out much detail, but most of the houses on the south side of town are blocky, unadorned, rectangular two-story houses—the I-houses and watered-down Georgians that had been fashionable in colonial and early national Pennsylvania but had gone out of style among the affluent elite by the time of the Civil War (fig. 3).[4] In short, the north side of Bellefonte was keeping up nicely with late nineteenth-century national styles, as one would expect in the establishment part of town (fig. 4). But Victorian fashion evidently did not reach the south side, and one is led to guess at a substantial schism between the establishment north side and the working-class south side. To be sure, both are parts of the same town, but one suspects that they occupied two very different worlds—different incomes, different ethnic backgrounds, different religions, and different social structures.

Later on, when we descend into the town, those guesses will be corroborated. The fashionable churches of north-side Bellefonte are all establishment Protestant denominations, while the churches of south-side Belle-

Fig. 3. Simple two-story Georgian houses were the fashionable norm in early nineteenth-century Pennsylvania, but they continued to be built and inhabited by unfashionable people almost until 1900, when the elite were emulating the latest Gothic, Italianate, and Queen Anne styles that issued regularly from Philadelphia, New York, Boston, and London. This is blue-collar south-side Bellefonte.

fonte are Roman Catholic and fundamentalist Protestant. We will also learn, later on, when we read the gravestones in the Catholic cemetery in the middle of south-side Bellefonte, that most of those Catholics are late nineteenth-century arrivals: mainly Irish, Germans, and most recently Italian. Most of those Italians, we can learn from conversations on the street, came from the *Mezzogiorno* (Calabria, mainly) and Sicily. That was desperately poor country in the late nineteenth century, of course, and one guesses that those southern Italians who came to Bellefonte were poor folk, hardly people who were plugged into the town's middle-class Protestant society. By contrast, we can get some flavor of the non-Catholic side of town (again later on) by reading the names on Bellefonte's imposing Civil War monument in front of the courthouse. The monument carries hundreds and hundreds of names (supposedly every man who served even

Fig. 4. A sample of fashionable Victorian architecture from affluent north-side Bellefonte, built about the same time as the unfashionable Georgian houses in figure 3.

temporarily in the Union Army is listed), but there are no Italian names on the rolls and few Irish names. One must conclude that early nineteenth-century Bellefonte was inhabited largely by Anglo-Saxon Protestants, and it is natural to suppose that during the nineteenth century at least and perhaps later the town's affluent elite derived from that group.

Maximum Magnification: The View from High Street

We can learn more about the history of Bellefonte by descending from our lofty perch into the streets of the town. By so doing we raise the level of magnification one last notch to discover what can be learned along the three-block stretch of High Street between the railroad station and the courthouse—in effect, the old center of the town.

The railroad station itself, a modest but respectable Stick Style building with Queen Anne touches, plainly dates to somewhere around the beginning of the twentieth century. Across the street is the Bush

House Hotel, a substantial four-story Italianate building that bears a blue plastic sign proclaiming it was built in 1868. Historic signs made of plastic are not always the most reliable sources of information, but this one seems plausible. The architectural style is right for the Civil War decade. Furthermore, for a hotel obviously associated with the railroad station the date is consistent with what we know about American railroad history. The Pennsylvania Railroad's Main Line was finished between Philadelphia and Pittsburgh in the mid-1850s, and it makes sense that branch lines were built to outlying places like Bellefonte within a few years. The size and modest grandeur of the Bush House, in short, is a measure of the railroad's impact on the town's economy, and its dignified facade allows us to conclude that the railroad brought not just money but ideas of Victorian style as well. The railroad, in short, was not merely an economic shot in the arm but also Bellefonte's window on a larger world of ideas and style.

The present railroad station, however, clearly was built twenty or thirty years later than the hotel, and one has to suppose that it was an updating of an earlier station. From the look of the new station Bellefonte as late as the 1890s was trying to keep up with national and international styles of the times and doing so with some success.

A century ago this zone between the hotel and the railroad station was surely a hive of economic and social activity. Today is another story. The railroad station is closed and has been taken over by the Chamber of Commerce, which is using it for offices. The hotel is closed too, except for its bar and dining room, and its current owners have painted the exterior and added the plastic signs, as well as some Williamsburg embellishments obviously meant to signify its historicity. Unlike the original designers of these buildings, who knew very well what they were doing, the current custodians have a fuzzier idea of style and history. Since 1868, one suspects, at least some of the connections with the world of ideas have come unplugged.

Today, the immediate environs of the hotel and railroad station are fairly bleak. The ground floor of the hotel contains a row of shop windows, but only about half of the shops are occupied and those by low-rent occupants: a county relief agency and a cut-rate optometrist. Across the street, in sharp contrast with the Italianate elegance of the hotel, are an ill-tended and optimistically large parking lot and a city park. The park has been planted with grass and a few trees and furnished with a newly built gazebo and a civic fountain. Both park and parking lot are fairly recent, judging from the patina of the asphalt, the size of grease spots on the pavement of the parking stalls, and the modest stature of the Colorado blue spruces on the edge of the park. Even on a nice day, however, the park is not heavily used, and the parking lot is never full, despite the attractive rate of three-hour parking for 25 cents.

Alongside the hotel, however, there is other evidence of those earlier, more prosperous days. In the grass of the city park one can pick out a pattern of old railroad ties that makes it clear that these were railroad yards. Alongside the yards and immediately behind the hotel is a small canal that parallels Spring Creek and is fed by waters impounded behind a dam just upstream. One suspects that this might have been a navigation canal in prerailroad days, but that suspicion is quickly discarded. Standing in the middle of the canal, built Malay-style on pylons in the water, are several buildings that stand as mute testimony to two things: the value of adjacent real estate, which must have been the incentive for this amphibious building, and the unnavigability of the canal (fig. 5). One is left with the necessary conclusion that this was a millrace, generating power for industrial buildings alongside Spring Creek. That, of course, was a typical arrangement during the early days of the Industrial Revolution, and it worked in much the same way as the mills on the Merrimac River at Lowell and Lawrence and Manchester. Today, only one of Bellefonte's mills survives, a large brick vaguely Gothic affair now occupied (as mills tend to be these days) by an up-scale restaurant and a neighborhood bar that offers a variety of imported and designer beers. A set of concrete piers crosses the millrace at an extremely acute angle, requiring one to conclude that a railroad bridge originally connected the mills between the creek and the millrace with the main railroad yards. Here, as in so many other parts of America, history is a ghostly presence, but with the help of artifacts and imagination we can reconstruct the scene in our minds—the constant comings and goings, trains backing and filling amid sulphurous clouds of bituminous smoke, laborers coming and going to work at the now-ruined mills, baggagemen and commercial travelers hauling luggage between the railroad station and the newly built hotel. That century-old image differs wrenchingly from today's scene of desolation and abandonment, but it helps explain the elegance of the hotel and railroad station and a fair number of other buildings in Bellefonte's downtown that were built about the same time.

For Bellefonte was indeed an elegant place, at least in the last third

Fig. 5. Amphibious buildings over the millrace, mute testimony to the high value of adjacent real estate as well as the unnavigability of the canal.

of the nineteenth century. Along High Street between the railroad station and the courthouse are several other commercial buildings executed with care and competence and designed in the latest styles of the times. The Bush Arcade, for example, slightly uptown from the hotel, is a three-story commercial block done in the picturesque-eclectic style of the day and bearing a date stone of 1888 (fig. 6). The arcade is finished with bas-relief tile, finely laid brick, and the same kind of Gothic towers, Romanesque windows, and brownstone piers that were being used in the mansions of Fifth Avenue in New York at about the same time. Like many of Bellefonte's downtown buildings, it exudes pride, optimism, money, and a tone of substantial urbanity. The Bellefonte of 1888, one has to suppose, was a place that was elegantly up to date, knew it, and took pride in the fact.

That prosperous town of the 1880s, however, was a quite different sort of place than it had been earlier in the nineteenth century. One does not need to look far for evidence of that earlier town. In various places

Fig. 6. The Bush Arcade (1888) is one of several imposing eclectic buildings along High Street between the railroad and the courthouse, each built according to the best stylistic canons of the day. The shop windows have recently been "historicized" with snap-in Williamsburg mullions but to little avail. Two of the shops stand empty; the new "historic" tenants include a card and trophy shop, the Bellefonte Area Youth Center, and a karate parlor.

along High Street are four-square Georgian buildings, made of rough-cut local limestone, that obviously predate the episode of Victorian prosperity generated by the railroad. In the middle of town a few of those buildings are more or less intact, although several have been equipped with showcase windows with the help of steel I-beams to keep their upper floors from collapsing. Others of the same vintage were obviously updated in the period of the great prosperity, mostly between 1870 and 1900. That updating took a variety of forms: Many of High Street's most exuberant Italianate buildings, for example, turn out really to be Georgian when viewed from the side (fig. 7). In other instances those older Georgian buildings simply had their roofs raised and were furnished with Queen Anne dormers, fish scales, and a proper Queen Anne roof pitch. But the shape and proportions of those Georgian buildings are unmistakable, even though they are hard to date with any exactitude. We can be sure, however, that they come from pre–Civil War days, since they are of the same style that Pennsylvanians had been building with conservative persistence ever since William Penn set foot on the shore of the Delaware River in 1682 and had continued to build well into the nineteenth century, long after Georgian architectural styles had ceased to be fashionable in Boston and Philadelphia and New York. Here in Bellefonte the best we can say is that they are pre–Civil War, but that is saying a good deal. When we map those Georgian buildings, we can describe a small, conservative, and not very fashionable town, about three by three square blocks (see fig. 1). It is the town that obviously predated the arrival of the railroad, a small agricultural market town of no great wealth and no great pretensions. The arrival of the railroad, then, was not just another incident in the town's ongoing history. It arrived like a barrage of revolutionary cannon fire.

One way to see the effects of that revolution is to stand on the steps of the courthouse and look around. Across the street is the town's largest hotel and most imposing building, the Brockerhoff House, closed in 1958 but recently revamped as a county residence for elderly folk (fig. 8). In architectural style the lower three floors of the Brockerhoff are simple Italianate, just like the Bush House down the street, and it was presumably built about the same time. The upper floor and roof, however, have been redesigned in the manner of the 1890s, and the style can best be called eclectic (to put it mildly): a combination of neo-Gothic and neo-Romanesque with additional Gothic touches that seem to derive from Felipe II by way of the Schwartzwald. If a designer of cuckoo clocks had

Fig. 7. A fashionable Italianate house of the 1870s turns out to be pre–Civil War Georgian when viewed from the side. Georgian architecture had been the urban fashion in Pennsylvania for 150 years but was suddenly eclipsed by the parade of national architectural styles that came crowding in all over America from the mid-nineteenth century onward.

tried his hand at designing hotels, this is presumably what he would have done in 1890—and in Bellefonte did.

The Brockerhoff is a metaphor for the period of Bellefonte's greatest prosperity, for it was finished with modest grandeur after the Civil War and then flamboyantly renewed about the turn of the century. The Brockerhoff, as well as the buildings across the street, is a second redefinition of the small agricultural market town of the early nineteenth century

Fig. 8. The Brockerhoff House, c. 1867. The lower three floors are conventional Italianate, not unlike the Bush House, built about the same time three blocks down High Street. The upper story and roof were remodeled according to picturesque eclectic canons of the 1890s.

whose Georgian fringes are clearly visible from the Civil War monument in front of the courthouse.

There is ample evidence that from the Civil War to the turn of the century Bellefonte was growing bigger but also perhaps more cosmopolitan. Indeed, if Bellefonte's landscape tells us anything, it is that small towns were not necessarily unsophisticated towns. A sign erected in front of the courthouse by the Pennsylvania Historical and Museum Commission notes that Bellefonte was the residence of five Pennsylvania governors during the nineteenth century; one of them, whose statue stands proudly in front of the Civil War monument, was James Curtin, a man who helped keep Pennsylvania loyal to the Union during the grim days between the shelling of Fort Sumter and the Battle of Gettysburg. Curtin was no parochial figure; he was a respected figure in national politics and was appointed U.S. minister to Russia after the war, shortly after the purchase of Alaska. It was no accident that this gifted powerful man called Bellefonte his home. The Bellefonte of 1867 was no backwater.

But it was no paradise either. The county historical society, of course, makes much of Bellefonte's architectural treasures and for good reason. Many are substantial and sophisticated. Along High Street, however, there are elements of the landscape that lead one to suspect that wealth and sophistication were not unmixed blessings. Three institutions, all located within a block of the courthouse, are familiar features in the American small-town landscape: the BPOE, the YMCA, and the WCTU. It is easy to dismiss them all as quaint or insignificant; none seems to possess much social relevance in these closing days of the twentieth century. But it is worth recalling what each of those three institutions did and the social pathologies that each reflected. In nineteenth-century America each performed different functions from those they do today, and taken together their presence on High Street tells a somber story about this picturesque little town.

Consider the BPOE, for example. The Benevolent and Protective Order of Elks was founded for the same reason that the Independent Order of Odd Fellows, the Red Men, and the Woodmen of the World were founded—to care for the widows and orphans of members who had been killed in accidents or died of typhoid and to provide dignified Christian burials that a fatherless family without life insurance could not readily afford.[5] Those fraternal lodges were, in effect, the precursors of life insurance companies and social security agencies. They were invented to help rural folk, who were flocking from farms into the new cities of industrializing America, cope with the unfamiliar physical and social hazards of new cities and new factories—in effect, cope with a whole new society that was being born before their eyes. It was a society that offered unforeseen opportunities but unforeseen perils as well, a cruel, dangerous society in which heretofore rural people needed protection and needed it badly. The BPOE was just one form of such protection.

Across the street the YMCA performed a similar function. Undergraduate students at my university grew up in a twentieth-century world where the YMCA is commonly viewed as a place of recreation for adolescents and where children are taken by their parents on Saturday mornings to learn how to swim. But in the nineteenth century the YMCA was a crucially important institution. It provided safe haven for innocent young men, fresh from the farm, who had come to find new jobs but found as well a quite pathological urban environment. This environment offered opportunities that the overcrowded farmland did not, which is, of course, why the young men came. (Young women came too, and they formed the YWCA.) But the burgeoning cities and towns of nineteenth-century America were easy places for those fresh-faced farm boys and girls to lose their money, their virtue, their health, and even their lives. The YMCA and the YWCA sought to avert such disasters by providing the young single newcomer a clean safe place to sleep, cheap nourishing meals, and some protection against the evils of the street. It is worth remembering that syphilis and gonorrhea were not joking matters before the invention of sulfa drugs and penicillin. The YMCA's safe Christian environment was not a luxury for young people in nineteenth-century American towns: It was an indispensable form of protection against an environment that those innocent rural youngsters had never seen before.

Across the street the WCTU building gives evidence of yet another pathology (fig. 9). The history of prohibition in the United States is a complicated business. One would hardly know that, however, by listening to contemporary pop historians, who have persuaded many Americans (including most of my students) that Prohibition was a silly experiment, imposed on the nation by ignorant extremists. According to that same story, the Women's Christian Temperance Union was largely a collection of hatchet-wielding fanatics.

The WCTU headquarters on High Street in Bellefonte casts considerable doubt on the premises of that pop history. The building, which bears a 1903 date stone, is a large, formal brick and brownstone pile, which bespeaks money, taste, and serious purpose. In Bellefonte, as in many other parts of America, the WCTU was a serious institution, for the simple reason that alcoholism was a serious matter in nineteenth-century America. It is easy enough in the late twentieth century to snicker at those Grant Wood women with their thin lips and grim dedication to the suppression of fun. But institutions such as the WCTU in Bellefonte do not arise without good reason. Indeed, one must conclude that the abuse of alcohol in places like Bellefonte perhaps was not quite as amusing as W. C. Fields later tried to make it seem.

Considered in isolation, none of these three institutions allows profound conclusions about the nature of nineteenth-century Bellefonte. But seen as a group and in the context of a burgeoning urban place, the BPOE, the YMCA, and the WCTU reflect a time and an environment that resembles not at all the roseate image of Norman Rockwell's small-town America. Nor is that the only evidence. All along High Street the shutters

Fig. 9. Petriken Hall, the WCTU Building, bears a date stone of 1903. It be-speaks money, taste, and serious purpose.

of early and mid-nineteenth-century houses are workable things, and they mean business (fig. 10). They are picturesque enough today, and on the town's well-policed streets they are seldom closed. But they do close, and they do work, and one can surmise that in a nineteenth-century town that required the BPOE and the YMCA and the WCTU all in the space of one block to deal with just a few of its social pathologies those shutters were put there for a reason.

Fig. 10. Shutters for street-level windows. The house, which fronts on High Street only a block from the courthouse and the majesty of the law, dates to the early nineteenth century, a time when urban shutters needed to be shuttable. Urban lawlessness did not originate in the twentieth century.

LESSONS FROM THE LANDSCAPE

High Street in Bellefonte is not unique among the main streets of small-town America, and Bellefonte is not unique either. But that is precisely the point. Its ordinary human landscape has things to tell us, not only about one small town in the mountains of central Pennsylvania but also about the larger world of nineteenth-century America. There is evidence all up and down the street that the urbanization of nineteenth-century America was more than just a change in scale of economic enterprise, more than just a shift in population. The Bellefontes of the nineteenth century were often rich, exhilarating places, but they were also wrenching, dangerous places for a nation that, to borrow Richard Hofstadter's words, was born in the country and moved to the city.[6] It was more than just a move from one place to another; Americans, after all, have always been on the move. This was a move from one world to another. And the Bellefontes of America formed crucial stepping stones on America's century-long conversion from a rural world to an urban one.

But that move is over now, and the landscape of Bellefonte's main street makes it obvious that the currents of history have swirled by the town and left it on the shore, beached, like so much other historical detritus in America's throw-away society. Many of its downtown store windows are empty; its downtown parking lots stand waiting for cars that seldom come; buildings such as its old opera house command rents so low that a cut-rate furniture store has taken up residence there and a wholesale beer distributor has its warehouse at the rear (fig. 11). Both these enterprises are (to use the jargon of social science) space-consumptive, which is simply another way of saying that in a prosperous place rents would long since have forced them to the outskirts, where land is cheap. If the WCTU and BPOE are indicators of nineteenth-century social pathology, the location of a wholesale beer distributor and a large cut-rate furniture store on what ought to be prime commercial land is an equally clear sign of twentieth-century economic pathology.

An essay such as this can only hint at the wealth of information that the landscape of a place such as Bellefonte contains. But it suggests, perhaps, some of the benefits and some of the problems of trying to read history from the evidence of ordinary human landscapes.

The benefits, I think, are clear enough. Information derived from

Fig. 11. View at the rear of the opera house-become-furniture store. This was prime space in the nineteenth century. (The light-colored building at the extreme right is the rear of the Brockerhoff Hotel, across from the courthouse.) The large brick rectangular structure is the fly space behind the stage of the opera house. Beer distributors and parking lots are like furniture stores, voracious consumers of space. Their location in the core of downtown, where rents should be high, is prima facie evidence of economic trouble.

direct observation of landscape is, in the old-fashioned sense of the term, primary data; in fact, it is hard to imagine any data that are more primary. Just as important, the data are abundant—indeed, sometimes superfluously abundant beyond any scholar's reasonable needs. But that abundance allows us to assemble huge bodies of data that by their very volume are convincing. Finally, and of surpassing value, the data are in their geographical context. By and large, things are where things were with respect to one another, albeit with some notable exceptions. As geographers have been insisting for a long time, location matters.

And what are the limitations, the defects, in this material geographical record? In my own work and that of fellow landscape readers the most serious defects are likely to reside in ourselves—the occasional failure to remember that landscape, like any artifact, is an incomplete record, that we cannot hope to write a complete history of any place on the basis of artifacts outdoors, any more than archaeologists can hope to write a complete history of Troy, no matter how deeply they may dig, no matter how thoroughly they may sift the diggings. A huge volume of material is simply gone. There is, as well, a common temptation to be glib: to assert relationships between artifact and idea that the evidence itself simply does not support. Rarely in the real world of material objects does "this" mean "that."

Then, too, no scholar can expect to ask questions of the landscape or to get reasonable answers without prior knowledge and without preparation. J. Hoover Mackin, late professor of geomorphology at the University of Washington and perhaps the most brilliant fieldworker I have ever had the privilege of knowing, used to tell his students, "What you get out of fieldwork is in exact proportion to the knowledge you take into the field." Landscape will not provide answers to questions that are not asked, and it cannot be expected to provide good answers unless questions are carefully and intelligently framed. The wise student of landscape reads deeply, thinks long, and plans carefully before sallying forth into the complicated world of geographic reality.

Finally, as with any other method of historical inquiry, reading evidence from landscape demands a constant willingness to be skeptical. Like most artifacts, common landscapes pose more questions than they are likely to answer. But such questions, in turn, can be among the most powerful tools a scholar can possess. Sometimes they force us to look again, to seek other evidence that can corroborate or contradict our hypotheses; sometimes they send us back to the archives to see what others have said about the things we can only suspect on the street; inevitably they send us out to seek first-hand information through careful interviews with knowledgeable old-timers and look again at things we had previously only glanced at.

But in the last analysis, I think, the attempt to derive meaning from common human landscapes possesses one overwhelming virtue. It keeps us constantly alert to the world around us, demanding that we pay attention not just to some of the things around us but to all of them—the whole visible world in all of its rich, glorious, messy, confusing, ugly, and beautiful complexity.

And that, to my way of thinking, may be its greatest virtue.

NOTES

1. There is a considerable literature bearing on this subject. Two avenues into the subject are a collection of essays edited by D. W. Meinig, *The Interpretation of Ordinary Landscape* (New York: Oxford University Press, 1979), and my bibliographic essay, "Learning Through Looking: Geographic and Other Writings about the American Cultural Landscape," *American Quarterly* 35, no. 3 (1983):242–261, reprinted in Thomas J. Schlereth, ed., *Material Culture: A Research Guide* (Lawrence: University Press of Kansas, 1985), 35–56.

2. My course is not unique. Although I know of no university department formally called landscape studies, a small informal band of scholars teaches a variety of similar courses elsewhere in various university departments; examples are those taught by Paul Groth in the landscape architecture department at the University of California at Berkeley, John Stilgoe in the American studies department at Harvard University, John Jakle in the geography department at the University of Illinois, and John Fraser Hart in the geography department at the University of Minnesota. There are many others, but most owe their contemporary form to the pioneer work of John Brinckerhoff Jackson, founder of the magazine *Landscape* and its editor from 1951 to 1968 and himself the teacher of celebrated courses at Berkeley and Harvard. The single best appreciation of Jackson and his work is Donald Meinig's "Reading the Landscape: An Appreciation of W. G. Hoskins and J. B. Jackson," in D. W. Meinig, ed., *The Interpretation of Ordinary Landscape* (New York: Oxford University Press, 1979), 195–244. Meinig's essay contains a fairly complete bibliography of Jackson's seminal work up to 1978.

3. For a historical-geographical profile of Bellefonte, see Peirce Lewis, "Small Town in Pennsylvania," *Annals of the Association of American Geographers* 62, no. 2 (1972):323–351, reprinted in J. F. Hart, ed., *Regions of the United States* (New York: Harper and Row, 1974), 323–351.

4. Fred Kniffen, "Folk Housing, Key to Diffusion," *Annals of the Association of American Geographers* 55 (1965):173–193. See also Peirce Lewis, "Common Houses, Cultural Spoor," *Landscape* 19, no. 2 (1975):1–22.

5. For an excellent account of how these organizations worked, see Richard H. Schein, "A Geographical and Historical Account of the American Benevolent Fraternal Order" (master's thesis, The Pennsylvania State University, 1983).

6. Richard Hofstadter, *The Age of Reform*, especially chapter 1, "The Agrarian Myth and Commercial Realities" (New York: Knopf, Vintage Books, 1955), p. 23.

The New England Cemetery as a Cultural Landscape

Ian W. Brown

"What is the object?" When I attended the History from Things conference I had a button attached to my coat lapel that asked this question. Although acquired at another conference, it seemed an appropriate adornment for this particular meeting, considering the topic. People smiled when they observed it, and when I asked why they were amused the usual response was that it was a good pun. The phrase was certainly ambiguous and could be interpreted differently depending on one's perspective. Was I inquiring about a particular item, or was I making a snide commentary about the session?

Recently I read Antoine de Saint-Exupéry's *The Little Prince* to my nine-year-old daughter. When I turned to the first page and showed her the blob-shaped object, I asked her if she was afraid. She looked at me strangely and said, "Why should I be afraid of a hat?" I turned the page and offered the well-known explanation that this hat of hers was actually a boa constrictor that had swallowed an elephant and suggested that she should therefore be terrified. She laughed and said, "But I didn't see it that way. That's not what the picture said to me."

When found in isolation, divorced from a larger picture, words, images, and objects can indeed be very ambiguous. Give a child a telescope and regard the amazement on her face when she flips it end to end. The same tool is used to view the same object, but one end provides close-up precision and clarity, the other a distant but wider perspective. Different perspectives yield different visions. The more one studies something, the more familiar it becomes. As one's view widens, patterns emerge where before there had been only chaos. Confidence increases as threads of meaning tie together what were once disparate shreds of information. And from these mental deliberations explanatory models derive. But then new information appears that does not fit the pattern. Sometimes the varying messages create only minor ripples and do not disturb the general interpretations, but the wise student does not ignore these messages. Research proceeds by probing inward, asking specific questions to help explain variation, rather than stepping back and continuing to regard overall patterns. In cases where these variations accumulate and remain unexplained, one recognizes that it is time to revise the models.

Objects can tell us much about past and present societies, but their power is seldom realized. Part of the problem is that the objects that so often come under study are in museums, divorced from the social and cultural environment responsible for their existence. Cultural landscapes provide a much better arena for appreciating the value of material culture studies because much of the environment is still in place. Admittedly, much has changed over time to accommodate new ideas and influences, but a careful eye can detect the old behind the new. Lewis in his essay "Common Landscapes as Historic Documents" (in this volume) demonstrates the value of cultural landscape studies in his examination of the town of Bellefonte, Pennsylvania. In this essay I expand on his approach by looking at a cemetery as a different kind of landscape but certainly a related one—a town of the dead. Focusing on a cemetery in Watertown, Massachusetts, I trace the burial arrangement of one family, the Coolidges, through six generations. By changing the angle and focus of a lens, in much the same way that Lewis does in Bellefonte, we detect in the gravestones at Watertown patterns of social relationships not evident in the written record.

When I first examined the Coolidge graves in this cemetery, I recorded a pattern. All but a few of the graves were clustered in one part of the cemetery, which suggested the existence of solid family unity. One of the isolated stones marked the grave of Elizabeth Coolidge, who died of smallpox in 1776. I felt that the spatial separation of Elizabeth provided an interesting social commentary. My interpretation was that this disease was so terrifying to colonial society that even the closely-knit Coolidges were fearful of its effects beyond the grave. This was my perspective from looking in one end of the telescope, but when I flipped it over and focused more closely on the objects in context, I saw that Elizabeth's eternal isolation had nothing to do with the nature of her death. I will return to Elizabeth's case later.

THE POWER OF OBJECTS

In the invitation sent to the participants of the "History from Things" conference, Lubar and Kingery wrote that people who study material culture "aim to read objects in some of the same ways that traditional historians read books." In this way "they hope to add new evidence to that gained from the written record." In his article in this volume Lewis demonstrates that material culture, in this case as seen collectively in a cultural landscape, can indeed be read but not necessarily in the same way that a historian may tackle the documentary record. I believe that three-dimensional objects are very different from written documents, and I am acutely aware of this discrepancy every time I attempt to write an exhibit label for a museum object. No matter how I arrange and rearrange the words, I never seem to capture the essence of the object. Materials have a strength and a power all their own; consequently, as students of material culture we must constantly remind ourselves that our methods are not and will never be the same as those used by historians, and this is not bad. Kouwenhoven correctly notes that "we have been too ready to accept verbal evidence as if it were the equivalent of the evidence of our senses" (1982:81).

Clearly, objects have not been the focal point of much of our understanding of history. Although a number of nineteenth-century cultural anthropologists were heavily involved in material culture analysis, today most are not. A perusal of the principal contemporary anthropological journals reveals that such studies have not played a significant role in our appreciation of the general operation of societies. Hesseltine went so far as to say that objects were of little value to understanding historical processes and showed his disdain for object studies in his article "The Challenge of the Artifact" (Hesseltine 1982). Many sociocultural anthropologists feel the same way toward materials. The real challenge, of course, is to show the utility of such studies. Washburn states, "Too often the university-trained scholar assumes the manuscript in the library can tell him what happened, whereas the object in the museum can merely illustrate the fact" (Washburn 1982:103). Historians often do use objects in their teaching but largely as support materials—as visual examples of facts they have already learned from written documents. Unfortunately objects have contributed very little to developing the main themes of history as perceived by historians (Carlson 1978:42). This is not true for prehistorians, of course, because objects are and probably always will be their basic documents for understanding the past (Washburn 1982:103).

Despite the fact that artifacts have contributed little to the development of main themes in history, they have been used with some success to pull the rug out from under some cherished notions of past happenings: "Objects may make a difference as to how the story is told. . . . Eli Whitney supposedly began making interchangeable parts for guns at his factory in Connecticut. Edwin Battison of the Smithsonian brought together four of these guns and the parts were not interchangeable. So much for that" (Schlebecker 1982:110). This is a fine example of the role of objects as warnings, as corrections to history, but obviously objects can do so much more. People who study objects, or rather material culture, all have a basic assumption: The manufacture or modification of objects reflects something about the beliefs of the individuals who made or used them. It is hoped that such belief patterns, when examined in aggregate form, are a reflection of the belief patterns of the larger society. Material culture, therefore, refers both to the subject of the study, materials, as well as to the purpose of the study, understanding culture (Prown 1982:2; Schlereth 1982:3). Although Beckow does not use the term *material culture*, he does describe the value of such studies: "Men create two products with culture: cultural behavior and artifacts. Culture is neither act nor artifact, but we can discover information about culture by working back from the acts and artifacts which are available for our scrutiny" (Beckow 1982:116).

Of course, if we are to appreciate fully the meaning behind patterns in material culture, we must know the history of object usage—the context. Whom are we investigating when we examine an object? Who is responsible for an object's form—the person who made the object or the person who commissioned it to be made? What about the person who eventually bought it or the person who actually ended up using it? The more we go through the sequence of individuals involved in the life of an object, the more we should see modification in the object itself. Lewis shows us that the Bellefonte BPOE, which was originally founded to care for those who had fallen on bad times, is now a social setting for elderly men on a Sunday afternoon. Similarly, the single surviving mill in this town now provides food and drink for the local young professionals. The buildings are still there, to be sure, but they have been modified, and these modifications reflect the behavior of the individuals who now use them. Changes in society certainly do leave an imprint on the objects in use, but to understand what the imprints signify we must be able to control time and space. Context is indeed the key to understanding what material culture can tell us about historical processes.

Lewis, of course, focuses on the cultural landscape in his essay. I was particularly drawn to his description of students' view of landscape as "a time-consuming obstacle that lies between where they are and where they want to be, to be crossed as quickly as possible but otherwise ignored." His statement reminded me of an off-the-cuff comment that Woody Allen once made: "Half of life is just getting there." And it is true. We all spend a good portion of our lives in transit—either commuting to work, running errands, or taking children to their various social activities. All of us have spent much of our time traveling through space, a space that we rarely focus on. And when we fail to focus, we inevitably fail to see—this is Lewis's important message. As he takes us through Bellefonte, he teaches us (as he teaches his students) how to focus on a town, how to see the changing landscape as a reflection of the people who lived it.

CEMETERIES AS CULTURAL LANDSCAPES

Although cemeteries are just one small part of the total cultural landscape in Lewis's essay, his approach of examining objects in context and looking at landscape on different levels and from different perspectives is certainly applicable to cemetery research in general. Like Bellefonte, a cemetery is a town of sorts—a town of the dead. Also it is not unusual in an area such as New England to find cemeteries, like towns, that have been in use for well over two centuries. The gravestones in these cemeteries changed dramatically over time, and as a result patterns that tell about the changing lives of the local population can be observed. Like most aspects of the cultural landscape, cemeteries were not meant to be read. The inscriptions and epitaphs were supposed to be read, of course, with their various admonitions to the living, but the actual placement of the stones within the cemetery, their shapes, sizes, and distribution in relation to one another were not intended to be read in any real sense. And yet patterns do exist, patterns that can tell us as much about life as death.

Most students of New England cemeteries have tended to focus on the most visible objects—the gravestones themselves—and have generally dealt with them as independent entities. Comparisons among stones are undertaken, of course—for example, to learn to recognize various carving styles (Forbes 1955). Similarly, the messages contained in the symbols that adorn the pilaster and tympanum tell us much about Puritan beliefs (Ludwig 1966), and the inscriptions and epitaphs provide a wealth of geneaological information as well as document the worth of specific individuals in their society. However, with the exception of Deetz and Dethlefsen's (1965, 1967, 1971) studies of style change in New England cemeteries, few people have looked at cemeteries from the perspective of a cultural landscape in which each stone is a part of a larger universe. Individual stones are important, but their significance is enhanced when they are examined in context, compared and contrasted with the markers that surround them.

As Lewis has emphasized, context is critical to an understanding of a cultural landscape, and this is true, too, for cemetery studies. Time, space, and form are three standard dimensions that are with certain limitations controlled quite well in the cemetery landscape. We know the dates of the stones (time), where they are positioned in the cemetery (space), and often who carved them (form). One must be careful to avoid uncritical acceptance of stone date, placement, and carver attribution, but generally the cemetery landscape has many more contextual controls than do most other cultural landscapes. By having these controls one can proceed with the study of a New England cemetery in much the same way that Lewis has done with Bellefonte. Viewing perspective can be altered according to how one adjusts one's lens. Whether one decides to stand back and examine the cemetery from a distance or turn the knob in the opposite direction to magnify certain contexts, it is possible to explore many different aspects of a cemetery.

As an example of the utility of such an approach, it is reasonable to presume that the location of graves in a cemetery reflects to some degree the social relationships of the deceased. Biological relationships are relatively easy to reconstruct from the historical record, but the more subtle emotional relationships (love, hate, friendship, respect, and so forth) are for the most part lacking in the history of a general population. Information of this nature might seem trite in the greater scheme of historical happenings, yet such knowledge might help explain why certain events happened that did indeed influence the course of history. By studying the arrangement of graves it should be possible to say something about social relationships even within the same family. After all, whom one is to lie next to forever could very well be a pressing concern for those approaching their final days on earth. All of this assumes, of course, that the individual who was eventually to occupy a grave (especially an adult) was the main determinant of where he or she would be interred and that there were no substantial barriers as to the choice of plot (designated areas such as tombs, for example, would distort the record because they reduce the possibility of free choice).

Let us look at the Old Burying Ground in Watertown, Massachusetts, as a case study of what can be learned about social relationships from considering the arrangement of graves within a cemetery landscape (Brown 1992; Norris 1925a, 1925b). The Old Burying Ground was established by at least 1642 and was used throughout the early nineteenth century. The cemetery is wedged in a depression at the intersection of Mount Auburn and Arlington streets (fig. 1). The roadbeds have risen gradually over time, leaving the cemetery an obscure and forgotten landscape to all but those few who seek it out. In the mid-nineteenth century William Harris, a Watertown resident whose ancestors are well represented in this cemetery, recorded all the inscriptions and epitaphs on the vertical and horizontal markers (Harris 1869). If one looks from one end of the cemetery to the other, the stones all line up nicely, with the headstones facing west and the footstones east, but from other angles it is clear that there are clusters in this landscape, clusters of stones that reflect certain social features of the population. As might be expected, the clusters are generally reflective of family groupings.

The family I would like to focus on here is the Coolidge family. Not only are the Coolidges well represented in the cemetery; but because this

Fig. 1. A general view of the Old Burying Ground at Watertown, Massachusetts. All photographs in this chapter by Ian W. Brown.

family extends over six generations, it serves as a useful case study for examining how it used the space contained within the boundaries of the cemetery landscape for almost a century and a half. It should be mentioned, too, that the Coolidges buried here are in direct line with President Calvin Coolidge, so even small obscure cemeteries can be keyed into general United States history. Thirty-seven people who once held the Coolidge name are buried in the Watertown Cemetery. All of them were related to the founding parents Iohn (John) and Mary Coolidge (table 1 and fig. 2), both of whom died in 1691. Most of the Coolidges have graves marked by slate stones that stand vertically and face west. Ten people, however, are buried in the Moses Coolidge family tomb. Watertown's revolutionary war hero Joseph Coolidge, who died in 1775, is probably buried in this cemetery, but this is not certain because there is only a modern monument to indicate such. This impressive obelisk could possibly stand above his grave, but the fact that it is situated in the middle of the cemetery far from the other Coolidges suggests that it serves more as a memorial than a marker.

TABLE 1

Coolidge Family Members in the Watertown Cemetery Whose Graves Are Marked by Free-Standing Stones

Name	Date of Death	Number on Stearns's Map	Letter Designation on Figures 2,4,5, and 6
Benoni Coollidge	1754	231	A
David Coolidge	1772	159	B
David Coolidge	1788	163	C*
Dorothy Coolidge	1815	162	C
Ebenezer Coollidge	1750	205	D
Elizabeth Coollidge	1736	71	E
Elizabth Coollidge	1749	205	D
Elizabeth Coollidge	1776	240	F
Hannah Coollidg	1680	59	G
Iohn Coolidg	1691	144	H
John Coollidge	1755	166	I
Joseph Coolidge	1749	72	J
Joseph Coolidge	1754	69	K
Kezia Coolidge	1804	241	L
Lucy Coollidge	1785	161	M
Mary Coolidg	1691	146	N
Mary Coolidg	1700	148	O
Mary Coollidge	1786	158	P
Mercy [Coollidge] Stratton	1749	73	Q
Peter Coollidg	1784	157	R
Priscilla Cooldige	1717	56	S
Richard Coollidge	1732	156	T
Ruth Coollidge	1753	69	K
Samuel Coollidge	1753	69	K
Sarah Tapley Coolidge	1823	164	U
Thomas Coollidge	1737	165	V
Close Relations			
Richard Clarke 1760 (father of Ruth Coollidge [d. 1753])		225	a
Elizabeth Learned 1774 (mother of Elizabeth Coollidge [d. 1776])		90	b
Joshua Stratton 1753 (husband of Mercy Stratton [d. 1749])		74	c

*Stearns's map (1900) shows David Coolidge (d. 1788) and Dorothy Coolidge (d. 1815) under two separate stones, when in actuality they are recorded on the same marker.

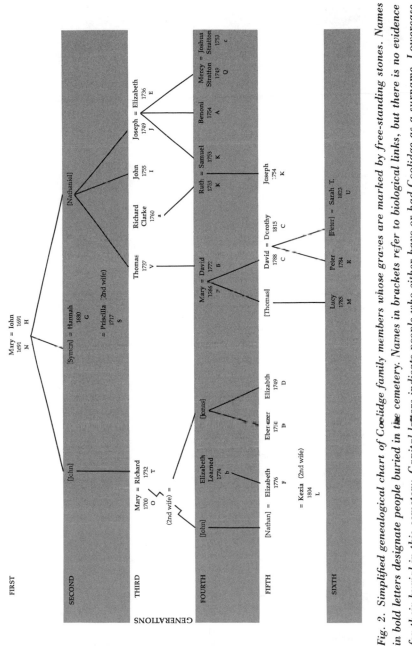

Fig. 2. Simplified genealogical chart of Coolidge family members whose graves are marked by free-standing stones. Names in bold letters designate people buried in the cemetery. Names in brackets refer to biological links, but there is no evidence for their burial in this cemetery. Capital letters indicate people who either have or had Coolidge as a surname. Lowercase letters indicate people who were close to the Coolidge family but who did not have the Coolidge name.

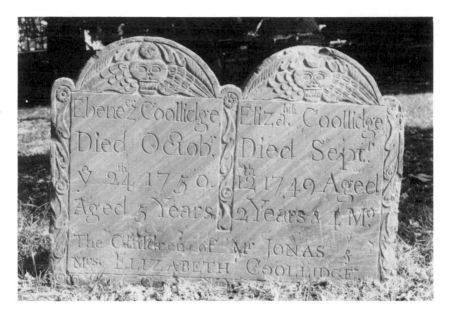

Fig. 3. Combined marker for Ebenezer Coollidge (d. 1750) and Elizabth Coollidge (d. 1749).

Twenty-five Coolidges are buried beneath a total of twenty-one standing stones; the mortal remains of three individuals are grouped under one marker, while four others rest together in sets of two (fig. 3). Mercy Stratton (d. 1749), whose maiden name was Coolidge, is buried here, and she, too, is included in this examination of the Coolidge family. The people in the family tomb are excluded from this case study for the simple reason that once a decision was made to establish a tomb, its presence served as a behavioral straitjacket for subsequent deaths in that branch of the Coolidge family. For economic reasons alone it made more sense to be buried in the tomb, so one would be hard pressed to detect social relations through the material culture in such a situation. Thus, this study involves twenty-six people of six generations of the Coolidge family whose final resting places are marked by twenty-two stones that date between 1680 and 1823. Three additional people who did not bear the Coolidge name appear in table 1 and figure 2, but they were either mates or parents of individuals who did.

Also recorded in table 1 is a number designation from "Stearns's

Map." This refers to a plan of the cemetery formulated by E. B. Stearns in 1900. Because a number of gravestones have been destroyed, eroded, or moved in the twentieth century, Stearns's map has been a major aid in studying spatial relationships. The numbers on his map, however, apply to all the individuals buried in the cemetery. To simplify matters I have arranged the Coolidges alphabetically and given them letter designations. The actual genealogical relationships for the Coolidges considered in this study are depicted in figure 2. Only the first names, dates of death, and letter designations are recorded on this figure. Names in brackets are biological connectors who are not buried in this cemetery (at least there are no surviving markers to indicate their presence).

In general, there are two major branches in the genealogy. On the left in figure 2 is John's line, and on the right is Nathaniel's. The members of these two branches are recorded in table 2, arranged in chronological fashion according to the date of death. The purpose of this particular arrangement is to examine how one death may have affected the next. In other words, once the first grave position was established, what kind of effect might it have had on the location of subsequent graves? The spatial positioning of the Coolidges by generation is presented in figure 4. The first generation consisted of only two individuals—John (N) and Mary (H). They were buried northwest of the main Coolidge family cluster. The second generation, which consisted of the two wives (G and S) of son Symon, were buried far to the south of the main cluster. From the third generation on, all the members descended either from John (Line I) or Nathaniel (Line II), and it is at this point that we can detect a major change in the positioning of the graves. Whereas John's descendants continued the scatter approach of burying their dead in various places throughout the northern half of the cemetery, Nathaniel's descendants decided to enter the afterlife in relatively close proximity. It is quite clear that over the course of four generations (the third through the sixth) they buried their dead in a very tight cluster.

Another way of looking at the relationship between Coolidge family members is to follow grave selection as deaths occurred. Depicted in figure 5 is the progression of death and gravestone positioning for the two main branches of the family. The same basic patterns exist as observed in figure 4, in that the members of John's line do not appear to have been influenced to any degree by where earlier family members had been buried. As for Nathaniel's descendants, burial placement was indeed important; the members were positioned close to their ancestors in what seems to have

TABLE 2

Coolidge Family Members Arranged by
Subfamily Groupings and by Order of Death

I—John's Line				Thomas's Line		
Mary	1700	O		Thomas	1737	V
Richard	1732	T		David	1772	B
Elizabth	1749	D		Peter	1784	R
Ebenezer	1750	D		Lucy	1785	M
Elizabeth	1776	F		Mary	1786	O
Kezia	1804	L		David	1788	C
				Dorothy	1815	C
II—Nathaniel's Line				Sarah	1823	U
Elizabeth	1736	E				
Thomas	1737	V		Joseph's Line		
Joseph	1749	J		Elizabeth	1736	E
Mercy	1749	Q		Joseph	1749	J
Ruth	1753	K		Mercy	1749	Q
Samuel	1753	K		Ruth	1753	K
Benoni	1754	A		Samuel	1753	K
Joseph	1754	K		Benoni	1754	A
John	1755	I		Joseph	1754	K
David	1772	B				
Peter	1784	R				
Lucy	1785	M				
Mary	1786	P				
David	1788	C				
Dorothy	1815	C				
Sarah	1823	U				

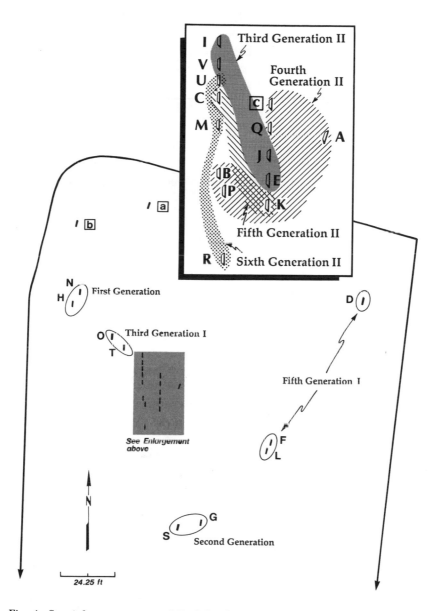

Fig. 4. Spatial arrangement of Coolidge family members through six genera-tions. For the third through sixth generations I signifies John's line whereas II signifies Nathaniel's line.

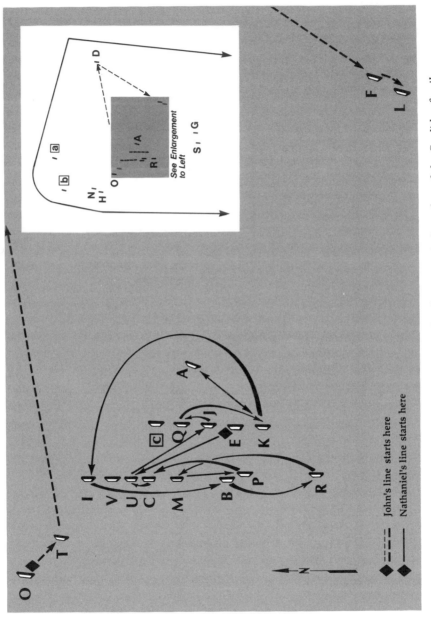

Fig. 5. *Progression of death and burial placement for the two main branches of the Coolidge family.*

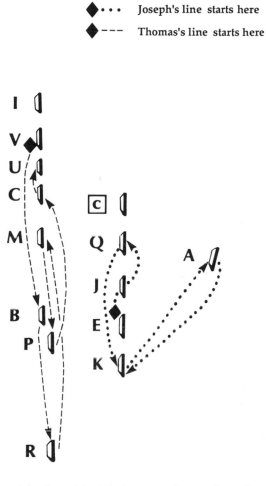

Fig. 6. A more focused view of death and burial placement for members of Nathaniel Coolidge's line. Thomas and Joseph were Nathaniel's sons.

been a spiral burial pattern. The pattern becomes even more defined if we move further down the branch and look at two of Nathaniel's sons. Starting with Thomas (V) and Joseph (J) and tracing their lines (table 2), we come up with the pattern depicted in figure 6. From this view it is now evident that what was thought to be a spiral arrangement for Nathaniel's line (from figure 5) is actually a linear arrangement when the focus is narrowed. Here again, as one turns the lens back and forth in viewing a cultural landscape, different patterns emerge.

By looking at the Coolidge family as a whole within this cemetery landscape, it has been possible to see marked differences between the two main branches of the family. For at least four generations one branch of the family (Nathaniel's) appears to have maintained much closer social relationships than the other (John's). Armed with this knowledge, one can avoid certain interpretations that might seem logical but can be quite erroneous. As I noted at the beginning of this essay, when I first began my study of the Watertown cemetery I quickly learned to appreciate the clustering of the Coolidges and made note at the time of what seemed to me to be an unusual position for one of the graves. When Elizabeth Coollidge (F) died in 1776 (fig. 7), she was buried by herself far to the east of the main Coolidge family cluster. Clearly stated in her inscription was the cause of death—smallpox—which provided a ready explanation for her isolation. Obviously, the other Coolidges were fearful of this dreaded disease and did not wish to be contaminated by poor Elizabeth, either in life or in death. Such an interpretation could have sowed the seed for speculation about eighteenth-century attitudes toward disease and the afterlife. After considering the Coolidge family as a whole in this cultural landscape, however, it is evident that my initial interpretation was wrong. Because the remote placement of Elizabeth was perfectly consistent with the way in which all the members of John's line were treated, there is no longer any reason to believe that she received special treatment because of the nature of her death.

Although the patterns presented here have come from an analysis of the material record—gravestones, which can be arranged in time and space—it should be noted that without the documentary record I would not have been able to establish the genealogical relations with any confidence. And that is because only a segment of the Coolidge family is actually buried in the Watertown cemetery (or at least has standing gravestones). The written documents provided me with categories of related people, and once these culturally meaningful categories were established I was able to examine the distribution of the gravestones across this landscape. The relative positions of the dead provide a view of relationships that one would never be able to appreciate by studying genealogies alone. Here again it is necessary to repeat Lewis's comment that location matters. For any study of objects in a cultural landscape it is absolutely

Fig. 7. When Elizabeth Coollidge died of smallpox in 1776, her grave was dug far from the Coolidge family cluster. Her eternal isolation, however, was unrelated to the nature of her death.

fundamental that "things *are* where things *were* with respect to one another." It is the context, including the control of time, space, and form, which provides the power generated in material culture research. Without context our contributions to history are indeed minimal, but with it we can view the people of the past in ways that could have never been anticipated by students of the written record.

At the next History from Things conference my button will read "What is the object and context?" It will not receive as many smiles, but its meaning will be far clearer.

REFERENCES

Beckow, Steven M. 1982. "Culture, History, and Artifact." In *Material Culture Studies in America*, edited by Thomas J. Schlereth, 114–123. Nashville, Tenn.: The American Association for State and Local History.

Brown, Ian W. 1992. "The Lamson-Carved Gravestones of Watertown, Massachusetts." In *The Art and Mystery of Historical Archaeology: Essays in Honor of James Deetz*, edited by Anne E. Yentsch and Mary C. Beaudry, 165–191. Boca Raton, Fla.: CRC Press.

Carlson, Cary. 1978. "Doing History with Material Culture." In *Material Culture and the Study of American Life*, edited by Ian M. G. Quimby, 41–64. New York: W. W. Norton & Company.

Deetz, James J. F., and Edwin N. Dethlefsen. 1965. "The Doppler Effect and Archaeology: A Consideration of the Spatial Aspects of Seriation." *Southwestern Journal of Anthropology* 21, no. 3:196–206.

———. 1967. "Death's Head, Cherub, Urn and Willow." *Natural History* 76 no. 3:29–37.

———. 1971. "Some Social Aspects of New England Colonial Mortuary Art." In *Approaches to the Social Dimensions of Mortuary Practices*, edited by James A. Brown, 30–38. Memoirs of the Society for American Archaeology, no. 25.

Forbes, Harriette M. 1927. *Gravestones of Early New England and the Men Who Made Them 1653–1800*. Reprint. 1955. Princeton, N.J.: The Pyne Press.

Harris, William T. 1869. *Epitaphs from the Old Burying Ground in Watertown*. Boston: Privately printed.

Hesseltine, William B. 1982. "The Challenge of the Artifact." In *Material Culture Studies in America*, edited by Thomas J. Schlereth, 93–100. Nashville, Tenn.: The American Association for State and Local History.

Kouwenhoven, John A. 1982. "American Studies: Words or Things?" In *Mate-

rial Culture Studies in America, edited by Thomas J. Schlereth, 79–92. Nashville, Tenn.: The American Association for State and Local History.

Ludwig, Allan I. 1966. *Graven Images: New England Stonecarving and Its Symbols, 1650–1815*. Middletown, Conn.: Wesleyan University Press.

Norris, Wilfred A. 1925a. "The Gravestones in the Old Burying Ground at Watertown, Massachusetts: Their Decorative Carving, Lettering and Symbolism." *Old-Time New England* 16, no. 2:65–74.

———. 1925b. "The Old Burying Ground at Watertown, Mass." *Old-Time New England* 16, no. 1:3–9.

Prown, Jules D. 1982. "Material Culture and the Use of Artifacts as Cultural Evidence." *Winterthur Portfolio* 17:1–3.

Schlebecker, John T. 1982. "The Use of Objects in Historical Research." In *Material Culture Studies in America*, edited by Thomas J. Schlereth, 106–113. Nashville, Tenn.: The American Association for State and Local History.

Schlereth, Thomas J. 1982. "Material Culture Studies in America, 1876–1976." In *Material Culture Studies in America*, edited by Thomas J. Schlereth, 1–75. Nashville, Tenn.: The American Association for State and Local History.

Stearns, E. B. 1900. "Plan and Register of Burials in the Arlington Street Burying Ground, Watertown." Appendix to *Watertown Records: Comprising the Third Book of Town Proceedings and the Second Book of Births, Marriages and Deaths to End of 1737*. Watertown, Mass.: Press of Fred G. Barker.

Washburn, Wilcomb E. 1982. "Manuscripts and Manufacts." In *Material Culture Studies in America*, edited by Thomas J. Schlereth, 101–105. Nashville, Tenn.: The American Association for State and Local History.

Artifacts as Expressions of Society and Culture: Subversive Genealogy and the Value of History

Mark P. Leone and
Barbara J. Little

This essay has three purposes. One is to show that using artifacts enables us to ask questions and produce tentative answers that would not typically arise through the use of documentary materials; thus, we hope to establish the primary importance of objects, not as opposed to documents but as parallel to written material. Our second aim is to work with two important products of the Federal era (c. 1780–1825): (1) the Maryland State House and its surroundings as redesigned after the American Revolution and (2) paintings by Charles Willson Peale, including those of his natural history museum in Philadelphia in the 1820s. We argue that the similarity of these artifacts is based on a dual assumption: first, that the citizens of the new state were to teach themselves a way of thinking, or a discipline, that was to make each one a self-watching individual under his or her own surveillance; and, second, that acceptance of this way of thinking was so complete as to be thought natural and beyond challenge. Our third aim is to consider how surveillance mechanisms, to apply Foucault's (1979) term, have come down to us today, particularly in the descendants of Peale's natural history museum, which not only imprison us through their presentations of history but also enable others to challenge successfully our own integrity.

When addressing the matter of the primacy of objects, we serve two constituencies. One is a group of scholars, some of whom are associated with museums, who attempt to teach and learn through objects as a source of primary knowledge. These scholars all know that meaning is established in a scholarly or scientific dialogue in which people and objects are treated as independent data with separate epistemologies. They also know that artifacts by themselves do not produce questions, discourse, or answers. But since museums of all kinds feature things, how do we use these things to produce new knowledge? This question is more serious than asking how a library produces knowledge, since we have accepted answers to the second question, but we do not have a set of well-defined answers, discipline by discipline, for the first question. The dilemma facing scholars who use artifacts as their primary source of information no longer confronts prehistoric archaeologists with much force since effective methods leading to widely respected results exist in that field.

This observation leads us to historical archaeology, also a field within anthropology, and our second constituency. Historical archaeology struggles with how it creates knowledge. What is the epistemological role of historic artifacts within this field? How does the field create knowledge? Our response, like that of others (for example, Deetz 1988), is that our contribution is to provoke questions and provide data not anticipated by other scholars and unavailable through other disciplines. This ability provides the reason for studying both the Maryland State House and Peale's paintings as artifacts.

We argue that our data—the State House in Annapolis and its landscape, as both were redesigned in the 1780s, and Peale's paintings—have as their conscious aim to provide universal views of life. The objects we have chosen may seem unrelated, but they are closely connected in time and philosophy. We hold that the State House dome, built after the Revolution and in response to the triumph of the theory of individualism embodied in the Bill of Rights, is a panopticon, an all-seeing eye of the state watching and being watched by fellow citizens who are liberty-loving and liberty-endowed individuals. Peale's museum, on the other hand, offers a view unrestricted to a particular place: a universal view, over both space and time in the present and the past. In our argument, then, these artifacts represent the totalizing institutions of the new state, those institutions that intend to affect all of social life. They were intended as surveillance mechanisms to see everyone and everything in every place and through all time.

Our third argument is that the theory behind these artifacts is alive today. Since most of us still believe these theories and their representations, we do not use the past to see through the arbitrary claims they sustain or the surveillance they establish. Nor are we able to respond successfully to claims made against our values by others who *do* see through the arbitrariness of our two-centuries-old official history.

This third issue is, we acknowledge, the most difficult and probably the most controversial. It has several parts but begins with the assumption that the purpose of knowing about things historically is to be able to know consciously or criticize the society we live in now. This purpose is not the only reason to know things historically, but in our opinion without this kind of knowledge the rest of the reasons do not stand easily on their own. Therefore, the purpose of historical knowledge, including that of things, is to allow for critical knowledge of our own society.

Because we Americans are still embedded in Peale's philosophy about how to think and behave as citizens by learning from an "accurately" and "naturally" presented past, which has led inevitably to our present condition, we as "naturally free" and "independent" individuals are trapped in a social presentation of history that forecloses an ability to use history to see our own society in a different way. Furthermore, and this is our most practical point, our imprisonment within an old and conventional presentation of history has enabled others—for example, Native Americans seeking the return of museum collections and the closing or redesigning of exhibits—to indict our uses of these collections by indicting our own origins as portrayed within the collections. Because our natural history presentations rank Native Americans as natural rather than as heroic or aesthetic, Native Americans have been classed with and presented alongside whales and geodes, not with George Washington, for example, or Peale's art. This intellectual artifact of our own history, this function of our own self-created and self-imposed genealogy, when turned against us indicts us by saying that we think Native Americans have more in common with natural species than with the rest of American citizens. At least this was the case before the passage of P.L. 101-601, the Native American Graves Protection and Repatriation Act, in November 1990.

Let us turn to Annapolis as we have come to know it as archaeologists since 1981. The plan for the city of Annapolis was created by Maryland's second royal governor, Sir Francis Nicholson, after he moved the colony's capital from St. Mary's City in heavily Catholic southern Maryland to Protestant Annapolis in 1694. This move was accomplished after William and Mary became sovereign and Protestants consequently assumed power in England. Lord Baltimore, a Catholic, temporarily lost his proprietary right to the colony founded by the Calvert family in 1634.

Annapolis had existed as a small town under other names as early as the 1650s (Baker 1986:192), but it had no special status. In 1683, as part of an effort to encourage the growth of towns, the legislature declared the settlement a port of entry (Papenfuse 1975:8; Baker 1986:192). Richard Beard surveyed the existing streets in 1684. His survey does not represent a planned town, but it does describe some of the layout with which Nicholson had to work. Beard was commissioned to do another survey and lay out Nicholson's plan in 1694. Although the survey was burned along with other public records in the State House fire of 1704, enough references to it remain to confirm that the major features of the Nicholson plan were surveyed in the 1690s (Baker 1986:193).

Reps (1972:121) notes that the Nicholson plan for placing streets and buildings follows the concept of baroque design, with certain classic features: formal symmetry, imposing open spaces, vistas leading to important structures, and major buildings placed on commanding sites. Reps (1972:123) also comments that the baroque principles were imperfectly applied in Annapolis. Although he attributes the geometric imbalance to Nicholson's incomplete understanding of the principles (1972:125), it is perhaps more likely that Nicholson was accommodating his understanding of baroque design to preexisting streets (Ramirez 1975:38ff).

The best existing representation of the early town plan is a copy of the Stoddart survey done in 1718 (fig. 1). The most obvious feature of the town plan is the placement of two circles on two hilltops with the larger circle enclosing the State House and the smaller enclosing the Anglican, or state, church. From these circles radiate streets, creating vistas that lead to the centers of royal and religious authority.

We know a good deal about this plan through archaeology. As a result of digging at almost two dozen locations on the larger circle surrounding the State House, we know that over the centuries the circle has been

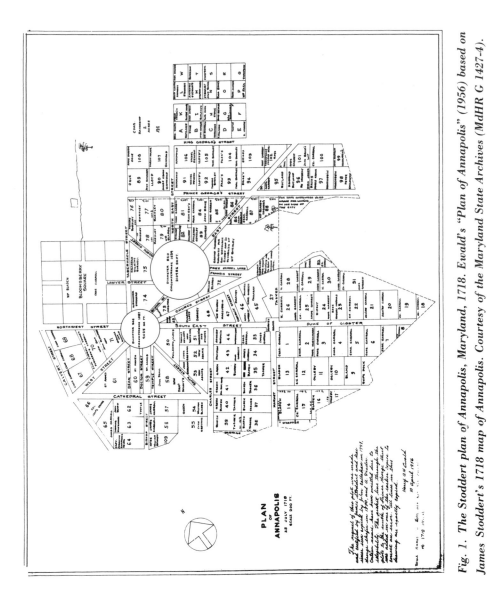

Fig. 1. The Stoddert plan of Annapolis, Maryland, 1718. Ewald's "Plan of Annapolis" (1956) based on James Stoddert's 1718 map of Annapolis. Courtesy of the Maryland State Archives (MdHR G 1427-4).

shifted to the north and east and at least since the 1830s has been a nearly perfect geometrical egg. To be more precise, it has been made up of four connected arcs drawn from four centers, three of which make a triangle and one of which is in the middle of the triangle's base. The smaller circle that encloses the Anglican church has been constricted into an ellipse whose true geometry we do not yet know. The State Circle hill had its top leveled in the eighteenth century and its sides steeply terraced in the nineteenth century to provide the appearance of height. The land around the church has been lowered and the street level of Church Circle raised, effectively lowering the church's locale, especially in relation to the State House grounds (Leone and Stabler 1991; Read 1990; Shackel 1988; Leone and Shackel 1986).

Neither the circles nor the major streets radiating from them have been interrupted to block the vistas. In one case a street off Church Circle was blocked when William Reynolds built on top of it in 1747, but the view from other streets was not compromised. Other streets occasionally have been added. We know from archaeological evidence gathered from monitoring hundreds of yards of utility trenches in the streets in the city's core that the streets have been raised, extended, and crowned but not bent, curved, or otherwise changed so as to alter the vistas. Therefore, except for the land encompassed by the U.S. Naval Academy after 1845, the basic plan of the whole town has stayed virtually intact for three centuries.

The Nicholson plan, with its foci on the structures of church and state, is an artifact of baroque urban planning. It concerns institutions that were hierarchical, with the parts being subordinated to the whole (that is, to the authority of state and church). The plan taught and reminded inhabitants and visitors of the centrality and ultimate authority of the state and church. It presented an order for political and social life that appeared inevitable.

Nicholson's plan served as a vehicle for placing Maryland's State House at the highest point in the town, visible to the waterfront, as a focal point of the built environment. There have been three state houses on this rise of land since the 1690s. The current building is the third, built originally in the early 1770s. The building is not in the center of the surrounding circle; rather the circle, which is an egg that appears circular to the traveler on the ground, is looped unevenly around the building. Eight streets and alleys radiate from the circle and control the view, especially as one approaches the State House on foot.

In the 1780s the current eight-sided, multistoried domed tower was placed on the building, replacing a lower, open lantern. The tower still offers commanding views of the town and can be seen everywhere from within the city. We focus here on the combination of the 1780s tower with the continued use of the 1690s baroque street plan to argue that until the Revolution the idea of the state expressed in Annapolis was to focus the views of people upward to authority. But with the acceptance of a theory about the state based on assuming individual rights of citizenship, the opposite view—the view down from centers of authority—became equally and possibly more important.

Our suggestion is that the multisided, panoptic State House was intended to express and simultaneously create the view that a citizen's obligation was both to watch the state and to act as the watchful state, since the citizen was embodied in the very nature of the state's foundation. The discipline of self-watching, or self-discipline, was essential in the citizen's role; an individual took it upon himself or herself to learn how to think and behave in a disciplined way. Not coincidentally, during this time in Annapolis lessons were advertised and taken in arithmetic, penmanship, horticulture, music, dancing, physics, medicine, and almost anything else that could be learned, including etiquette and rules for being a lady, a gentleman, a noble citizen. The people doing all this were self-watching individuals, who as the foundation for the new government needed to be ever watchful of both self and other citizens.

The second major artifact is a trio of pictures by Charles Willson Peale. Peale was born in Maryland, was raised on its Eastern Shore, and did his early painting in Annapolis. He finished his life's work in Philadelphia, having founded the nation's first natural history museum. That museum is the subject of the first painting of the trio, *The Artist in His Museum*, done in 1822 (fig. 2). The preliminary sketch that accompanies this painting is *The Long Room* (fig. 3), also done in 1822; it shows the main museum room, which appears as one of the subjects of the Peale masterpiece. The third picture is Peale's *The Exhumation of the Mastodon*, 1806–8 (fig. 4). We argue that in this trio of pictures Peale showed his contemporaries how to apply the rules of equality, graduation, and predictability to the living animal world, the past of the natural world (that is, fossils), and human personality and moral standing, using as examples revolutionary war heroes.

Peale created his museum for the public to use for its education. Without much difficulty, it is possible for us to look at his two pictures of

Fig. 2. The Artist in His Museum, *by Charles Willson Peale (American, 1741–1827), oil on canvas, 1822. Courtesy of the Pennsylvania Academy of the Fine Arts, Philadelphia. Gift of Mrs. Sarah Harrison (The Joseph Harrison, Jr., Collection)*

Fig. 3. The Long Room, Interior of Front Room in Peale's Museum, *by Charles Willson Peale, watercolor, 14 by 20¾", 1822. Courtesy of the Detroit Institute of Arts; Founders Society Purchase, Director's Discretionary Fund.*

this museum's central hall and see that what he intended is a version of what we still think of as a natural history museum. It seems old-fashioned now, but it is clearly recognizable. Both the museum cases and the arrangement of them to order the world in a graduated way are familiar and important elements. Actual measurements of Peale's cabinets are not necessary to see that the cabinets are in rows, are all the same size in any one row, and tend to get smaller as they ascend. There is a basic measure and orderliness that encompasses all the units in the overall plan. At the top of Peale's Long Room are two rows of revolutionary war heroes. These are his own paintings, which make the room a major intellectual and artistic *tour de force*. We believe that a key to understanding the room is that all the paintings are in identical frames, so they too are a function of the same basic desire to measure, which orders the museum cases. The geodes, rocks, and sea shells, as well as Native American artifacts, are in cases that have compartments all the same size for each kind of item, so that all

Fig. 4. The Exhumation of the Mastodon, *by Charles Willson Peale, 1806–8. Courtesy of the Peale Museum/Baltimore City Life Museums.*

such items are in equal rows, are fronted by equal panes, and are equidistant from one another. They are either equal or in spaces that are multiples of each other. The paintings of heroes are also equal in scale and size.

"With this museum, Peale set out 'to bring into one view a world in miniature' " (Richardson et al. 1982:83). Since everything except the paintings was the size it was in nature, except stuffed or preserved, "miniature" meant that the whole order of nature was so comprehensive that it was possible to use a sample of natural forms to encompass and teach the rules of similarity, graduation, and natural precision in one space. His effort was to array many parts of nature so that the Great Chain of Being was visible with rocks, insects, shellfish, birds, Native Americans, and heroes having precise relationships to one another. The museum was a model of the world. Peale was putting nature on display so that people could learn the natural principles, obey them, and use them to shape nature. One could either let nature speak through one and accept one's role humbly or encounter nature as an adversary and shape it aggressively using its own rules (Penn, pers. com. 1988). In any case it is clear that Peale intended his museum to be a place for citizens of the new republic to learn the rules of nature so that they could play an active and enlightened role in shaping the republic, which could also be seen as a natural form.

Peale attempted to order all of living nature in his museum, but he did more. He ordered both the paleontological past and the human character, and he used and taught the principles by which all could be unified. *The Exhumation of the Mastodon* and the place of the assembled mastodon in *The Artist in His Museum* are enough to show us his attempt to introduce systematics into North America's past. Peale was the first person in North America to excavate a major fossil in a scientific way. He reassembled it with the missing pieces restored so that the whole could be appreciated.

Richardson, Hindle, and Miller comment on Peale's intent and originality:

> When the French scientist Cuvier published the mastodon as a representative of an extinct species, it was a dramatic demonstration of the fact that over geologic time species could become extinct, an issue that was still being debated at that time. Peale, through his own perseverance, had found scientific information that had not been known before. (Richardson et al. 1982:85)

We argue that Peale was attempting to create a paleontological past for North America. His drawings, notes, mounting of the skeleton, and parading of a reconstructed mastodon through Europe demonstrate this point. Peale's paleontology can be linked to the archaeology of Thomas Jefferson, his friend and correspondent, who is credited with the first systematic excavation of a Native American mound. Jefferson's excavation and investigation of the hypothesis that modern and ancient indigenous peoples formed a cultural continuum are well known (Jefferson 1787). Crucial here is the link between fossils and Native Americans in Peale's museum and Jefferson's archaeology. As new categories were being created for past time in the New World, both the fossils and the Native Americans were thought to be part of "native" natural history. Obviously the histories were not native from the viewpoint of the subjects, nor were they tied to the present through any device offering to explain continuity or disruption. Peale and Jefferson were rationalizing past time for the natural order, which included Native Americans. They created an orderly precision in their plan for building a history of nature. At the same time, however, what they perceived as natural for themselves were their rights, especially their liberty, rather than their history or historical tie to the North American continent.

A final categorization made by Peale is one of his most innovative. His paintings of revolutionary war heroes were to be sketches of character, meant to teach the personal attributes needed by citizens in the new republic. Peale's portraits are still considered sharp, incisive studies of personalities, and most of them will still convince a viewer that the subject has a set of traits that *are* interesting. The point is that Peale intended his heroes to teach character traits such as leadership and scientific thoughtfulness to the visiting public. Peale's objective was to enumerate human characteristics and then put them on display with the assumption that they could be copied and mastered by individuals. With this effort Peale was attempting to segment and rationalize the human personality. Thus, we can see that Peale's museum displays were not only shapes; they also implied rules for equivalencies, gradations, and precise divisions whose rules probably aimed to exclude nothing from their domain. Here was expressed an explicit hierarchy of physical beings, past and present, progress, and individuals' moral standing.

Peale's representation of the order of natural and human life and the State House of Annapolis as redesigned after independence are similar in several ways. Both create and present a way of categorizing based on the individual as well as a vision of order. Both used volume: one to control space, the other to use objects to present a realistic view of time and all nature juxtaposed to its own parts. Nicholson's plan of 1694, as it remained in use with the renovation of the State House in the 1780s, intended to use vistas to direct sight and in doing so appeared to alter space so as to make objects appear bigger or smaller, taller or shorter, than they were. Peale's painter's quadrant, a *camera obscura*, allowed the representation of three dimensions in two with the appearance of accuracy. Thus, one technique involved in both artifacts was the use of Renaissance rules of perspective to control vision. To include Peale's museum in this argument we must assume that vision includes seeing *into* nature, the past, other cultures, and the human character.

We believe it is fair and necessary to ask, If the State House and

Peale's museum were organized as we suggest, were they recognized as such, were they successful, and did they create protests against their totalizing intent? Given diverse social classes—including enslaved and free African Americans, paupers, women as well as men, country people and city dwellers—who did and who did not accept and reject these surveillance mechanisms? We are not now able to establish for whom this surveillance worked. We do not attempt answers to these important questions here; the questions are themselves new to us. Our originality stems from the question itself, which comes from our discovering that the State House and its surrounding landscape not only were planned and executed as a unit but also were planned and reexecuted several times, probably using different ideas of what their purpose was. Our novel contribution, which raises these other questions about impact and influence, is what the postrevolutionary State House and Peale's museum have in common, not yet whether or not they worked in their time in the way we suggest. We argue that these questions reveal the fruitfulness of historical archaeology.

On the other hand we are firmly convinced that they have worked in our own day and for many generations preceding ours just as we have hypothesized they were supposed to have in the Federal era. We believe that both artifacts have served in particular ways to represent the genealogy of two key elements of American ideology. Both have been made into historical statements not only about the way things were but also about how they came to be that way. This point represents the third part of our argument. It contains a dual proposition: first, that the State House and the descendants of Peale's museum philosophy are effective today; and, second, that because they are used to ground our rights as citizen-individuals (as the State House does in self-watching) and our dominant position on the continent in nature (as natural history museums do), these are imprisoning ideological devices.

Our argument is based in part on a provocative article by Shklar (1971), who explores creation myths as subversive genealogies that in themselves hold the possibility of subverting the society they were intended to uphold. She examines the caricatures of creation myths written by Hesiod, Rousseau, Nietzsche, and to some extent Freud, all of whom expressed bitter disgust with the pervasive suffering of humankind and tried to account for it with their explanations of the origins of that sad condition. Questioning the origins of social relations and authority is subversive and dangerous because it calls into question the status quo. Shklar writes:

> Since Hesiod's day the myth of origins has been a typical form of questioning and condemning the established order, divine and human, ethical and political. The myth of creation that Hesiod devised out of the depth of resentment has been a model for writers of similar inspiration. . . . In the modern age both Rousseau and Nietzsche, to name the most notable, used creation myths to express their unlimited contempt for their world. (Shklar 1971:130)

In his genealogy of the gods of Olympus, Hesiod found the origins of human suffering in the character of Zeus and in the fourth age, that of the Men of Iron, who were doomed to suffer. Much later Rousseau traced humanity's lot to the inequalities that came about in the fifth age, that of grain and iron, with the development of a division of labor and the gap between wealth and poverty. For Rousseau society was the evil ancestor that determined humankind's fate. Nietzsche attributed nihilism to the age of the "men of iron . . . the age of the slave spirit triumphant" (Shklar 1971:142).

In Nietzsche's philosophy, memory, an awareness of the past and of history, is an illness and a torment (cf. Lowenthal 1985:65; Nietzsche 1873–76). Yet it is part of a persistent desire for control. Memory is argued to be necessary to understand and dominate society and control the future (Shklar 1971:144). Knowledge of history provides the power to create genealogy, and such power is the key to control. Genealogy here is to be seen as the version of history that suggests the inevitability of the present social order. Thus genealogy becomes a political necessity because it legitimizes the tie between the present and the past. Shklar's argument recognizes that within genealogy the past and the present are identical. Connections between past and present are inevitable, determined, or epigenetic, implying that the present could not be other than it is. These are ties that appear to be central because they are based on assumptions such as biological kinship, natural right, or evolutionary development.

Peale's museum and the Maryland State House fit into this model of genealogy. Peale was not an evolutionist; he represented the hierarchical and static Great Chain of Being and humanity's place in it. Nonetheless, all succeeding such museums from the 1870s and 1880s not only used his organization but also added the dynamic of evolutionary development to explain how all those items in all those cases merged into one another over eons of time, culminating in European humanity. The inevitability of the arrangement is the genealogical aspect; the arrangement still dominates museum presentations of evolutionary development. Peale is important here because he initiated the process of explaining to the public, with reference to the surrounding world in space and time, why they as people were here now. While the Great Chain of Being has been rejected as an idea, most of Peale's ideas are so completely intact that it is virtually impossible today to imagine any alternative museum presentation of the things, creatures, and cultures within them, their interrelationships, or reasons for being. In this implied inevitability lies a problem.

The Maryland State House in the 1780s was a political rather than a historic statement. However, since early in this century, when the building was subject to the colonial revival style and some of its original eighteenth-century appearance was restored, it has become historical. We do not know whether the original panoptic intention of its prominent tower was ever known or realized. Instead, the tower is now thought of as a remnant from another era, and this essence, plus its prominence, constitutes its chief meanings. But because it is a product of the revolutionary period, it has been made into a direct ancestor for modern government. As such it cannot invite a question about origins, because the origin is given. Thus it is a historical citation that can neither illuminate its own origins nor explain any of the problematical relationships that may come from current circumstances.

Such genealogical history is uncritical, which is why both Rousseau and Nietzsche had contempt for history as a self-justifying form of knowledge (Shklar 1971:142) and why they wrote their own creation myths as a subversive way of questioning the origins of human suffering. They expressed their outrage at life's circumstances by writing genealogical histories that communicated the inevitability of the evils of the world. However, "both saw the inescapability of the inheritance whose origins they had so mercilessly exposed" (Shklar 1971:146). When genealogical creation myths insist that the past could have led to one and only one possible present, they allow for no human choices in history. Thus, we suggest that history and genealogy do not necessarily serve the same purpose. Shklar notes that the creation myth has to appear to be "prehistorical"—that is, not part of history—otherwise the contingencies and accidents of history would be apparent and humans would have freedom and choice and thus power.

Genealogy, as Shklar explains it, expresses the past as an integral part of the present: "Genealogy deals with the ever-present, indestructible actualities" (1971:146). Through effective genealogy the present is inevitable and was contained in the origin. When stated this way, this view implies that there is no effective challenge to the present through precedent. There are instead the pessimistic creation myths that recognize necessary evils: "It [the myth] permits defiance and rejection, without arousing the slightest hope or impulse to action" (1971:141). History, however, may illuminate current conditions whereas genealogy merely justifies them.

As Barbara Clark Smith (pers. com. 1989) suggests, Jacoby's (1975) idea of social amnesia may be useful for characterizing the uncritical nature of creation myths. Afflicted with social amnesia, people forget that their own society has a historical past and must conclude that whatever is is natural and inevitable. It must be understood, however, that personal shortcomings do not create social amnesia. People do not actually forget; they never know.

Marxian critical theory holds the possibility of human action and people's control of their own history as they come to understand the self-justifying genealogies that have been taught to them. Feenberg writes:

> The ultimate dialectical "mediation" of reified social reality consists in the real practical subversion of the social order through the breakdown of the boundaries of its partial subsystems. Making connections between the artificially isolated subsystems is the most threatening oppositional strategy for this reified social order. . . . It is through such subversive mediation that the human community, conscious of itself, assumes control of its own history. (Feenberg 1981:70)

Making connections both among artifacts and between our genealogies and artifacts, therefore, is one way of exposing origins and laying claim to history.

Shklar suggests that genealogical myths may be an enduring form of polemical discourse, which in turn must be expressed metaphorically to be shared and understood. She argues that creation myths make evident what is abstract, that these myths act as "psychological evocation." They are mnemonic devices that must rely on familiar experience and are effective because of a shared cultural literacy. In our argument those devices are the museums and the State House, which are widely shared although by different audiences, by experience, and by being the centers of continuous "historical" discourse. Myths express, evoke, and translate cultural pretensions into realities through common experiences. This insight allows us to connect objects with presumed genealogies where both are created to be believed and obeyed and where both are effective social and political statements. With such connections we can return to the artifacts described earlier, indeed to material culture in general, and ask how political discourse, social rules, and cultural literacy were expressed.

How were the rules that created a social order expressed in material culture? How were they lived out and realized? And who rejected them? They were internalized through designing, constructing, and inhabiting buildings; eating according to certain rules; and looking, seeking, talking, and keeping time in equal, graduated units that covered and included potentially all things. They composed a way of life, a "version of everything," to use Peale's own term.

Most modern Americans do not see natural history museums as pessimistic or imprisoning, but Native Americans, Aleuts, and native Hawaiians do, because in them they inevitably rank below modern Western human beings. The ranking is inevitable because through genealogy it has been made to appear so, as if it were the natural consequence of evolutionary progress. What Native Americans have successfully done to natural history museums and disciplines such as anthropology used within them is to attack the museums by attacking the origins of the evolutionary and genealogical tie within them. Their argument has been that they are not like stones, insects, fish, or birds. They are not below other Americans; instead, as fellow citizens, they have equal rights. Thus, as fellow citizens not only are they to be treated equally, but also the very material used to prove their naturalistic status was stolen property, another violation of their natural rights. Their indictment has been powerful because they could use their status as liberty-loving and liberty-endowed individual citizens to say that if this was how we classified them—that is, as equals— then they could not also be inferiors, as our American genealogical myth told us they were. Thus, our genealogy was not just incorrect; it was corrupt. They took the institutions in which we housed, celebrated, taught, and demonstrated our natural history, our reasons for being here now, and indicted the conditions society placed them in. The indictment stuck, is recited in P. L. 101-601, and is addressed throughout the provisions of the law. This is, of course, our reading of the situation and the complex new law whose regulations have not yet been finalized.

Although we cannot be sure how Peale's museum, the 1780s Maryland State House, modern natural history museums, and the modern Maryland State House actually communicate their ideas, we assume they are significant in the process as artifacts and institutions, particularly since millions of people annually are told about them and their meanings by guides, teachers, films, guidebooks and maps, docents, and other means. What, then, do people know about them? The central fact is that in neither a natural history museum nor the Maryland State House is its own history presented. Those histories are rarely open for examination.

There are two points to be drawn from an archaeological view of the artifacts we have chosen. The first point is methodological. Using historical archaeology within the discipline of anthropology, the aim of this analysis has been to take material culture and analyze it along with parallel written material. The archaeology shows material representations and reifications. The documents provide ethnographic intention and some meanings. Working with several sources we created hypotheses about the rules that certain parts of society used to create order and sense and about how these rules were experienced and internalized. Work yet to be done involves showing how the rules operated and on whom.

The second point is that the work we have begun challenges existing genealogies. Material culture might support the subversion or criticism of self-justifying genealogies by making criticism concrete, understandable, and testable. Such endeavors might make the structure of our artificial surroundings understandable at different levels. The Maryland State House is currently lightly interpreted, its long history totally ignored. But there are questions to be asked of that history. Why should the building sit within a surrounding circle that has twice been redesigned as an egg shape? Why do seven of the eight streets and alleys leading to it narrow or converge to highlight the view when no other streets in town do? Why is it the centerpiece of an optical illusion? And why, after 1780, did an all-seeing eye get mounted on top of the structure? We believe that the purpose of this latter occurrence in particular was to encourage surveillance—that is, to convince the new citizens that they were the power behind the state, rather than the power base under those who ran the state. Thus, it is possible that the newly redesigned State House deepened the illusionary basis for authority and then, when in the first decade of the twentieth century it all became washed with historicity, the illusion was buried in the wisdom of the founding generation and enhanced by the still-present ideology of individualism and citizens' rights. In this way the State House became a genealogical artifact.

Just as Hesiod's genealogy of the Olympian gods can be understood as either innocent mythology or a subversive challenge to the gods and the order of things, material culture can be understood in a straightforward, functionalist manner or in a way that integrates symbolism and the appropriate cultural associations that place things in their cultural context. The audience for criticism need not be universal, although every individual may claim some understanding and reaction.

The redesigners of the State House in the 1780s used antiquity and Palladian proportion to justify their plans, and Peale cited nature to show a unified system. Both were based on a particular vision of rationalized order and a categorization that enclosed, segmented, and judged both natural and artificial phenomena. Both started to universalize order by imposing it on time and space.

These artifacts are early illustrations of a process that by the late nineteenth century was taken as inevitable: the seamlessness of the continuity between past and present and the acceptance of Darwinism as characterizing the social world, including the idea of cultural evolution. The implication was that the past was somehow present now, so that genealogy referred to both past and present simultaneously. The artifacts we have analyzed are quite different in form, yet they are both concrete expressions of the value of the individual citizen and the individual's place in nature. The artifacts themselves do not call such values into question, but they can provide evidence of their origins and thus provoke a critique of these values.

It is possible for those frustrated with such current presentations to subvert the genealogies presented and use them as an indictment of parts or all of social life today:

> To destroy the prestige of convention, nothing will do so well as to
> show that it really is not what it appears and pretends to be. If begin-
> nings were sordid, surely its essence cannot be worthy. To unmask is
> to display an ambiguous parentage at best. Since we accept the ori-
> gins, that is the motives, of actions as their moral definition it makes

sense to show up these less than admirable beginnings. (Shklar 1971:148)

To summarize and conclude: Native American claims to museum collections have drawn their force from attempting to show the scientific worthlessness of the use of the remains. In addition, Native Americans have claimed that both scientific practices and the holding of collections violate the First Amendment guarantees for freedom of religion. They also have indicted the morality of archaeologists and physical anthropologists. These accusations depend for their force on their ability to indict the foundations of the disciplinary claims that justify the collections, including the associated sciences. A challenge has been made to an Anglo-American way of categorizing and ordering the world in such a way that Native Americans are linked with birds and sea shells and not treated as equal citizens. These claims constitute a subversive genealogy that invokes history to critique the present. Since the now successfully subverted genealogies depend for their own origins on such creations as the Maryland State House of the 1780s and the organization offered in Peale's paintings, the claim can be analyzed, questioned, and transformed.

Our final point concerns the place of history within our society, particularly its political function. To begin, we make two assumptions. The first is that history can be used to illuminate current conditions, to explain current circumstances, to ground our understanding of modern life, and, in short, to educate. This education includes offering critiques of our own society. History has the capacity to tell us why we are here now. Second, to achieve this aim we argue that history has to be able to criticize itself, since it is frequently turned into the sort of self-justifying genealogical myths we have associated in this essay with Peale and the uses of the Maryland State House. We already know that it can be made subversive, since Native Americans have recently done this.

One problem is that many historians associated with museums or operating in local historical contexts focus so completely on accuracy and completeness that they are unwilling to see their work as so embedded in the status quo that it is obfuscating rather than illuminating and, indeed, basically a prop of the status quo. We claim to be able to situate artifacts, or things, within their genealogical contexts so that their self-justifying qualities are seen more clearly and their potentially subverting qualities can be called on and developed. Thus, our position is not antihistorical, nor is it unpatriotic; it is both optimistic and quite traditional.

NOTE

Barbara Clark Smith contributed significantly to this essay through criticism of the original version, presented by Mark Leone at the conference "History from Things," April 11, 1989.

REFERENCES

Baker, Nancy T. 1986. "Annapolis, Maryland, 1695–1730." *Maryland Historical Magazine* 81, no. 3:191–209.

Deetz, James. 1988. "American Historical Archaeology: Methods and Results." *Science* 239:362–367.

Feenberg, Andrew. 1981. *Lukacs, Marx, and the Sources of Critical Theory.* Totowa, N.J.: Rowman and Littlefield.

Foucault, Michel. 1979. *Discipline and Punish.* New York: Vintage Books.

Jacoby, Russell. 1975. *Social Amnesia: A Critique of Conformist Psychology from Adler to Laing.* Boston: Beacon Press.

Jefferson, Thomas. 1787. *Notes on the State of Virginia.* London: John Stockdale. Reprint. Chapel Hill: University of North Carolina Press, 1954.

Leone, Mark P., and Paul A. Shackel. 1986. *Archaeology of Town Planning in Annapolis, Maryland.* Final report to the National Geographic Society. NGS grant no. 3116-85.

Leone, Mark, and Jennifer Stabler. 1991. "The City Center of Annapolis and the Kind of Economy It Reflects." Presented at the annual meeting of the Society for Historical Archaeology, Richmond, Virginia.

Lowenthal, David. 1985. *The Past Is a Foreign Country.* Cambridge: Cambridge University Press.

Nietzsche, Friedreich. 1873–76. *The Use and Abuse of History.* Reprint. Indianapolis: Bobbs-Merrill, 1957.

Papenfuse, Edward C. 1975. *In Pursuit of Profit: The Annapolis Merchant in the Era of the American Revolution, 1763–1805.* Baltimore: Johns Hopkins University Press.

Ramirez, Constance Werner. 1975. "Urban History for Preservation Planning: The Annapolis Experience." Ph.D. diss. Ann Arbor, Michigan: University Microfilms.

Read, Esther Doyle. 1990. *Archaeological Excavation of State Circle, Annapolis, Maryland.* With contributions by Jean Russo, George Logan, and Brett Burk. Principal investigators: Mark P. Leone and Barbara J. Little. Report for the City of Annapolis submitted by Archaeology in Annapolis, a cooperative project between the Historic Annapolis Foundation and the University of Maryland, College Park. On file at the Maryland Historic Trust.

Reps, John W. 1972. *Tidewater Towns: City Planning in Colonial Virginia and Maryland*. Williamsburg, Va.: The Colonial Williamsburg Foundation.

Richardson, Edgar, Brooke Hindle, and Lillian Miller. 1982. *Charles Willson Peale and His World*. New York: Abrams.

Shackel, Paul A. 1988. *Excavations at the State House Inn, 18AP42, State Circle, Annapolis, Md*. A final report with Joseph W. Hopkins and Eileen Williams. On file with the Historic Annapolis Foundation, Annapolis, Md.

Shklar, Judith N. 1971. "Subversive Genealogies." In *Myth, Symbol, and Culture*, edited by Clifford Geertz, 129–154. New York: W. W. Norton.

Why Take a Behavioral Approach to Folk Objects?

Michael Owen Jones

I t is axiomatic nowadays that things do not exist in a vacuum. Made and used by people, artifacts relate to human values, needs, and concerns past and present. They may reflect the spirit of an age, the beliefs of a society or a subgroup, or the experiences of an individual. They can embody notions of how to survive in the physical world, serve as indexes of social relations, or be forms of emotional coping and adjustment. Their use may be instrumental and utilitarian, sensory and aesthetic, expressive and symbolic, or a combination of these. In sum, both the manufacture and use of artifacts are rooted in historical, sociocultural, and psychological conditions and processes.

Early research on objects was largely descriptive. Then artifacts were used as supplementary data and corroborative evidence for ideas derived from analysis of verbal sources. Eventually things were viewed as links to socioeconomic structures and cultural values (Jones 1976, 1987:1–9; Schlereth 1985). Increasingly, however, researchers seem to be headed toward a behavioral approach in studying what people make and how they use these things. A recent example is Bronner's *Chain Carvers: Old Men Crafting Meaning* (1985), which he labels behavioristic because of its preoccupation with motivations, symbols, and meanings.

In this essay I focus on the field with which I am associated, that of folklore studies. Using some of my own research data as illustration, I suggest how a behavioral approach seems appropriate, even inevitable. First, however, let me give some terms and trends.

"Folklore" was coined in England in 1846 to replace "popular antiquities" and "oral traditions," terms used in previous centuries. Other designations include the French *traditions populaires;* the German *Volkskunde* (literally, goods of the folk), coined in 1803; and the Swedish *folkliv* (folklife), in use since at least 1847. In 1909 the latter term was combined with the Swedish word for research to yield the name of a field of study— *folklivsforsning.* Both "folklife research" and "folkloristics," popular in America since the mid-1960s, refer to the study of folklore rather than to the subject matter itself (Bronner 1986; Dorson 1972; Oring 1986; Toelken 1979).

Among the "genres" of folklore are jargon, argot, proverbs, traditional sayings, and nicknaming; myths, legends, and anecdotes; jokes and kidding; rumors and gossip; costume, the making of things by hand, and the personal decoration of space; recreation, games, and play; celebrations, festive events, parties, and cooperative work effort; ceremonies, rituals, and rites of passage; singing, dancing, and music making; and customs and social routines.

The forms, processes, and examples of behavior labeled folklore tend toward the expressive or symbolic. They are learned and manifested largely in people's firsthand interaction. And they exhibit continuities and consistencies through time and space. Because of the latter quality, they are said to be "traditional" or simply "traditions" (Georges 1983; Jones 1990).

"The folklore of material culture is one of the most neglected fields of American folklore study," contended Wayland D. Hand in his presidential address to the American Folklore Society in 1958. "This work has fallen largely to museum people, who follow it as a collateral interest . . ." (Hand 1960:4). Earlier Fife had speculated about the reasons "the folk-

lore of material culture has been neglected": "It derives from the fact that
the pursuit of folkloric research has largely been an appendage to literary
and linguistic study. This means that the folk tale, the folk song and
ballad, the proverb, and many other forms of literary folklore have made
first demands on our interest." Moreover, "engineers, architects, farmers,
domestic economists, artists, etc. have remained peculiarly uninterested
in the historic or folk aspect of their respective domains" (Fife 1957:110).

The past thirty years have witnessed an astonishing growth in folklore research on objects and their makers and users. Typical perspectives
include the historical, sociocultural, and psychological (Jones and Greenfield 1984). But also emerging is a behavioral orientation emphasizing
basic cognitive, communicative, and interactional processes and concentrating on the circumstances in which certain behaviors are conceptualized and brought into existence (for examples, see Bronner 1983, 1985;
Jones 1975, 1989; Greenfield 1986).

To illustrate these orientations I will refer to some of my research on
chair making in southeastern Kentucky in the late 1960s. Other researchers have pursued certain kinds of questions on the subject. There is a
body of literature on the technology of chair making—the tools, materials, and construction techniques that typically are used (Anon. 1969;
Milnes 1986). Some works categorize chair designs into types or styles,
going so far as to try to establish patterns of historic and geographic
development and distribution (Cummings 1957; Glassie 1968; Lyon 1931).
Yet others are more sociological or cultural in approach, concerned with
the institutions of apprenticeship or of production and exchange or with
general values and norms (Mayes 1960; Trent 1977; Vincent 1962).

I discovered early in my fieldwork that every chair had a story. The
craftsman commented on each piece of furniture, remarking on the circumstances in which it was made or purchased, identifying the woods
used, describing construction techniques or problems, giving reasons for
specific features, and occasionally passing judgment on the work. Customers referred to the approximate date or other matters attending the purchase (including perhaps the price paid or relationship with the craftsman), mentioned uses of the chair, and sometimes expressed opinions
about the object or its maker through word or deed.

I began to lose sight of these stories and their implications, however,
when attempting to organize or interpret data according to one or another
analytical approach current at the time. For instance, I tried to establish
periods as units of development—an accepted technique in art history

(Thompson 1969:158)—and account for traits in objects with respect to evolution in style. I asked the chair maker Chester Cornett, whose works over a forty-year career I had struggled to organize into periods, what had caused him to change from making chairs with vertical slats in their backs to making chairs with horizontal slats. "In the chairmakin' business you make all kinds of different chairs an' different types of backs," he said. "I've made different types of chair seats. Chair seat like that chair you're settin' in there is a different chair." He went on to explain various principles of construction and design, some of which he did not always follow. So committed was I to the concept of style periods and the theory of evolution in art that I thought the chair maker had not answered my question. In reality, I failed to understand his response. I had been looking for answers in a realm outside the particulars of traditional utilitarian art.

To illustrate further I will discuss the works of a chair maker named Aaron. Some of his chairs have vertical backs while others have horizontal slats. Two "settin' chairs" are remarkably similar yet slightly different. The rocking chairs exhibit considerable range of variation; most notable are the differences in the design of the back and the arm rests. How can one account for these features?

Born in 1926, Aaron saw service in the military in World War II. He studied for two years at a local community college. He taught elementary school in the area for three years but intensely disliked teaching; he let his certificate lapse to force him to find some other kind of employment. Then for several years he wandered from one northern city to another, working at various semiskilled jobs such as operating a drill press and making television cabinets and stands. Disillusioned and unhappy, he headed back to the hills of Kentucky to live with his brother's family, initially to drink but eventually to make chairs.

In 1962, out of desperation for something constructive to do, Aaron attempted to infer how a neighbor, no longer living, had managed to build a chair using a few simple tools and techniques. Aaron measured Harry's work exactly and duplicated as closely as he could the chair's features and dimensions; on the basis of information from his father and other men, he built his own "settin' chair" of maple and ash (fig. 1).

The two chairs are not quite the same. Harry put a large peg in each end of the top slat, whereas Aaron used small pins of wood that blended with the chair. The posts of Harry's chair flare backward in a fashion that would never appeal to Aaron, who was soft-spoken and tended to be personally undemonstrative. The distance between the top of the back

Fig. 1. Chair made of maple and ash by Aaron, about 1962. Photograph by Michael Owen Jones.

posts and the bottom of the legs is more nearly equal in Aaron's chair, again suggesting greater containment in expressive quality.

One day in mid-1962, while recovering from a weeklong bout with the bottle, Aaron heard that the local community would soon reactivate a chair shop established in the 1930s; it would need chair makers. Several men had already signed up to work under the supervision of Verge, a part-time farmer and one of the original chair makers in the shop when it was active earlier. A teacher who had befriended Aaron encouraged him to accept the job. Verge and his son Hascal were amazed at Aaron's skill and knowledge when he joined them, and they remarked to me about his diligence and his talent as a craftsman—when he worked. Often he drank.

By 1964 he was again without a job. He began to make chairs at home once more, at first to support his drinking habit but later to help overcome it. By the time I met him he was firmly on the wagon, with a tight rein on his problems, and the empty half-pints lining the walk to his house were like ruts in a road, covered with more than a year's accumulation of dust.

The form of a black walnut rocker made about 1962 and owned by Aaron (fig. 2) is typical in many ways of works produced at the inception of his career. It is a panel-back or vertical-back chair with indistinctly defined turnings. The back posts have stiles, or flat surfaces, because the post on the right had a structural fault, which Aaron removed with a drawing knife, and because he happened to like stiles at that time.

Another black walnut rocking chair, made in 1963 or 1964, has more distinctly developed turnings and a more sharply defined form, suggesting greater self-certainty in its maker. The rockers are still rounded on the top edge, a design element that Verge's son Hascal claimed to have developed. The academy dean "wanted something a bit different" and suggested the idea, said Hascal, who claimed that he then developed the technique although he did not like the design himself.

Both these chairs resemble those I found in the chair shop made by Hascal or his father Verge, but they differ somewhat in having less taper to the posts. Made from black walnut, they are of a more fragile, expensive, and "pretty" wood than Verge would ever permit in the shop. They reveal a definite interest in ornamentation. And they exhibit the unusual trait of a hole in the top slat, which Aaron admitted was his trademark.

Some customers would like all the slats in a chair to have a notch in the center, said Aaron, but the notch weakens the slat or panel and should not be there at all, he told me. Why make the notch then? He said he made

Fig. 2. Black walnut panel-back rocking chair by Aaron, 1962. Photograph by Michael Owen Jones.

some chairs with it and others without; potential customers always chose the chairs with the notch. Therefore, he began making all chairs with a notch in the center of the top edge of the slat. But he was also seeking to develop his own distinctive kind of chair.

"I like that chair," remarked Verge about Aaron's earlier work reminiscent of chairs produced in the shop under Verge's supervision. "But for myself I wouldn't have them rings and nubs. But you gotta make it how the customers want," he said, not realizing that Aaron was making the chair as *he* wanted. "I like the round arms," concluded Verge. The rounded arm was the only major element of Verge's and Hascal's chairs that Aaron maintained in his later works, though he hoped to depart from it.

Chester Cornett remarked that the chair in figure 2 "needs patchin'—you need to patch the gaps in 'twixt the bark." The gaps in the seat were formed when the splints drew away from each other as they dried. Only Chester used winter bark ("skinned" or stripped from the tree with a drawing knife in early fall). Aaron and other men in his area used summer bark, which has more sap and consequently shrivels up more when it seasons. In addition, Aaron and others stripped off and discarded the top half of the inner bark (fig. 3); thus the splints were only half as thick as Chester's, and the edges turned down as they dried, leaving gaps between the splints.

Chester was more impressed with Aaron's recent works, as was Aaron himself. "That's a new design on me," Chester said about a chair made in 1967 (fig. 4). "I've never seen that decoratin' before on a chair. Whoever made this chair's interested in makin' somethin' differ'nt." Chester had never met Aaron or seen his chairs; rather, he selected these works for special comment from a stack of photographs of chairs I had given him.

"The wood in them backs has been sawed," he continued. "It's not been riven out 'cause the grain in each slat's differ'nt. Can't tell 'bout the postees. . . . Hit's a well-built chair like the other'n; there's nothin' outta line. That's the reason I'm sure he's an old-time chair maker."

That remark would have pleased Aaron, who was generally content with his recent works, which he thought were "kinda pretty" in form and design. Aaron's brother said that the dining and rocking chairs were pretty because "they got all them knobs on 'em." Referring to a black walnut rocker he made in late July 1967, however, Aaron muttered to himself, "It ain't the prettiest one I ever made." He said that it showed

Fig. 3. Aaron separating the bottom half of hickory bark from the top, which he discards. Photograph by Michael Owen Jones.

knots and white wood and that the grain was not straight on all the pieces. To Aaron—the perfectionist—the component elements should have matched in all respects.

For the most part, however, Aaron felt that his chairs were attractive in their harmony of design and form. The spools were of the proper shape and number and in the proper location on the chair. The wood was inherently pretty. The chairs were of good proportions and the design elements unified. By the time I met Aaron, in 1967, he was making rocking chairs on which the turnings had become quite clearly delineated, the rockers and slats were sharply defined, the form—slat-back rather than panel-back—no longer resembled factory-made chairs (which looked "cheap" according to him), and the back posts had been made smaller in diameter, increasing the elegance of the chair. In other words Aaron was executing works that were distinctly his own with only a nod of recognition to his predecessors—chairs in which, from his point of view, all the elements were perfectly integrated.

Then why did he make a dining chair in August 1967 with flat arms

Fig. 4. Black walnut slat-back rocking chair by Aaron, June 1967. Photograph by Michael Owen Jones.

that obviously were not in harmony with the rest of the chair? The barrel arms still disturbed Aaron because they were like Verge's; he had wanted to use some other design but had no idea what. In mid-July I had shown Aaron photographs of some of Chester's works, a few of which he examined closely, but he remarked only on the arms of two of the chairs. "Both of 'em's pretty," he said. "That armrest's pretty and it'd be easy to make."

I did not realize at the time why he had singled out the armrests for comment or suspect what he had in mind. In late August a niece of Aaron's asked him to make some end tables and eight dining chairs, one of which was to have some arms although Aaron usually made such chairs without arms. His niece thought that the surface area of the arms should be larger than that of the barrel arms. Aaron agreed, so he tried to make them like the armrests on Chester's chairs. The results disappointed and embarrassed Aaron, who became apologetic. Although his niece seemed satisfied, Aaron said the arms were too thin, the small ends of the arms that fitted into the posts were not small enough, and the inside of the curve was too deep. In essence, the chair could "be improved on."

Aaron felt the design had potential, but it was a problem he would have to address later. That he had the patience for such a task was obvious. He measured each chair post with a handmade micrometer to get every two exactly alike. "Get 'em all alike and you don't have to worry about whether they'll set right or not," he said. Aaron sanded each piece while it spun on his homemade turning lathe, using fine sandpaper and emory cloth, despite his contention, "I dislike this job worse'n any job of chair making—too dusty." He carefully measured the angle of every hole he drilled in the posts, tested the smoothness of each slat he sawed to shape and sanded, and turned the rounds twice a day as they seasoned above the wood-burning stove in the kitchen. "If you don't turn 'em like an ole hen turns her eggs," he warned, "they get a crook in 'em."

"He's experienced as a chair maker," said Chester as he examined photos of Aaron's chairs. "He must be a slow worker an' a sure worker." Aaron, in fact, seemed to be second only to Chester in his willingness to "fool" with chair making—that is, to take it seriously (for more information about both men, see Jones 1975, 1989).

I could have limited my research to typologizing these chairs and others in the South and East. As researchers were then doing with traditional houses, outbuildings, and hay derricks (respectively, Glassie 1968; Fife and Fife 1948). I could have postulated the origins and distribution of chair types over time and space—treating the objects as diffusible entities that changed according to certain "laws" (for example, Kniffen and Glassie 1966). Had I done this, I would have been following the precedent of earlier historic-geographic research on folk tales and ballads (compare the essays in Dundes 1965). I had data on the values and ways of doing things of some people in the hills of southeastern Kentucky. Following the lead of other researchers who had studied Hispanic wood carvers, African American graveyards, and Kachina sashes (Briggs 1980; Vlach 1977; Wade and Evans 1973), I might have been able to use chair making as an index to Appalachian culture, contending it was interrelated with general norms, religious values, subsistence livelihood, and other aspects of the culture. Like art historians who had written about styles of epochs and great masters, I could have continued attempting to identify periods of development and postulating origins in earlier trends and conditions.

Instead, I asked myself why the chairs had particular features and how their design related to the men's experiences, personalities, and relationships with others. In seeking answers I considered the implications and ramifications of the stories that craftsmen and customers told about the objects. This forced me to consider the immediate circumstances in which the chairs were conceptualized, built, sold, responded to, and used. Historical and sociocultural processes constituted the backdrop against which were displayed various psychological, communicative, and interactional processes. Whether I wanted to or not, I had to consider craftsmen's relationships with others, including not only customers but also family members and neighbors. I had to probe for self-concepts, personal aspirations, and individual motivations. I was forced to examine the making of each chair as a unique occurrence.

By concentrating on the actual circumstances in which objects were conceptualized and brought into existence, I came to postulate at least four matters that need to be considered when trying to explain the traits of handmade objects (Jones 1989). They are as follows:

1. Technology. The tools, techniques of construction, and materials as well as the ends to which the object is to be put and the means for achieving these objectives.

2. Producer. The craftsperson's self-concept, motivations, and aspirations; knowledge of and skill at this endeavor; values; and intentions and criteria of formal excellence in addition to preferences and predilections on the basis of which a characteristic mode of execution, construction, and presentation develops.

3. Consumer. Customer stipulation of form, materials, and design elements as well as selection and treatment of and comments about the object or objects from which the craftsperson is likely to infer values, attitudes, preferences, and associations that inform expectations, satisfaction, and uses or functions.

4. Product-Producer Interface. Models and precedents for a work, the requirements of useful design (for example, appearance, access, strength, and durability), the process of conceptualization as it affects and is affected by implementation and the craft identity, activity, or product as a vehicle of expression or locus of symbols.

None of this excludes the impact of historical conditions or the operation of sociocultural processes. But a behavioral approach—focusing on specific circumstances and incorporating principles of psychological, communicative, and interactional processes—seemed essential to my research. Moreover, it appears to me that folklore studies have been moving increasingly in the direction of the behavioral and experiential (see Bauman 1969; Bronner 1980, 1988; Jones 1982; Laba 1979; Quigley 1987).

While we can view the production of objects as a reflection of historical processes, as an element of culture, or as an index of social conditions and processes, we can also investigate some things in their immediate situation of manufacture as aspects or manifestations of human behavior. This approach has the potential of revealing a great deal about why certain objects were made, what they mean, and why they have the features they do. For those interested in such questions, a behavioral perspective should seem promising.

REFERENCES

Anonymous. 1969. "An Old Chair Maker Shows How." *Foxfire* 3:11–16, 53–55.
Bauman, Richard. 1969. "Towards a Behavioral Theory of Folklore: A Reply to Roger Welsch." *Journal of American Folklore* 82:167–170.
Briggs, Charles. 1980. *The Wood Carvers of Cordova, New Mexico: Social Dimensions of an Artistic Revival.* Knoxville: University of Tennessee Press.
Bronner, Simon J. 1980. "An Experiential Portrait of a Wood Carver." *Indiana Folklore* 13:30–45.
———. 1983. "Links to Behavior: An Analysis of Chain Carving." *Kentucky Folklore Record* 29:72–82.

————. 1985. *Chain Carvers: Old Men Crafting Meaning*. Lexington: University Press of Kentucky.

————. 1986. *American Folklore Studies: An Intellectual History*. Lawrence: University Press of Kansas.

————. 1988. "Art, Performance, and Praxis: The Rhetoric of Contemporary Folklore Studies." *Western Folklore* 47:75–101.

Cummings, John. 1957. "Slat-Back Chairs." *Antiques* 72 (July):60–63.

Dorson, Richard M. 1972. *Folklore and Folklife: An Introduction*. Chicago: University of Chicago Press.

Dundes, Alan. 1965. *The Study of Folklore: An Introduction*. Englewood-Cliffs, N.J.: Prentice Hall.

Fife, Austin E. 1957. "Folklore of Material Culture on the Rocky Mountain Frontier." *Arizona Quarterly* 13:101–110.

Fife, Austin E., and James Fife. 1948. "Hay Derricks of the Great Basin and Upper Snake River Valley." *Western Folklore* 7:225–239.

Georges, Robert A. 1983. "Folklore." In *Sound Archives: A Guide to Their Establishment and Development*, edited by David Lance, 134–144. Milton Keynes, England: International Association of Sound Archives.

Glassie, Henry. 1968. *Patterns in the Material Folk Culture of the Eastern United States*. Philadelphia: University of Pennsylvania Press.

Greenfield, Verni. 1986. *Making Do or Making Art: A Study of American Recycling*. Ann Arbor, Mich.: UMI Research Press.

Hand, Wayland D. 1960. "American Folklore after Seventy Years: Survey and Prospect." *Journal of American Folklore* 73:1–9.

Jones, Michael Owen. 1975. *The Hand-Made Object and Its Maker*. Berkeley and Los Angeles: University of California Press.

————. 1976. "The Study of Folk Art Study: Reflections on Images." In *Folklore Today*, edited by Linda Dégh, Henry Glassie, and Felix J. Oinas, 291–304. Bloomington, Ind.: Center for Language and Semiotic Studies.

————. 1982. "Another America: Toward a Behavioral History Based on Folkloristics." *Western Folklore* 41:43–51.

————. 1987. *Exploring Folk Art: Twenty Years of Thought on Craft, Work, and Aesthetics*. Ann Arbor, Mich.: UMI Research Press.

————. 1989. *Craftsman of the Cumberlands: Tradition and Creativity*. Lexington: The University Press of Kentucky.

————. 1990. "A Folklore Approach to Emotions in Work." *American Behavioral Scientist* 33:278–286.

Jones, Michael Owen, and Verni Greenfield. 1984. "Art Criticism and Aesthetic Philosophy." In *American Folk Art: A Guide to Sources*, edited by Simon J. Bronner, 31–50. New York: Garland.

Kniffen, Fred, and Henry Glassie. 1966. "Building in Wood in the Eastern

United States: A Time-Place Perspective." *The Geographical Review* 56: 40–66.

Laba, Martin. 1979. "Urban Folklore: A Behavioral Approach." *Western Folklore* 38:158–169.

Lyon, Irvin Phillips. 1931. "Square-Post Slat-Back Chairs: A Seventeenth-Century Type Found in New England." *Antiques* 20:210–216.

Mayes, L. J. 1960. *The History of Chairmaking in High Wycombe*. London: Routledge and Kegan Paul.

Milnes, Gerald. 1986. "West Virginia Split Bottom: The Seat of Choice." *Goldenseal* 12 (Fall):9–15.

Oring, Elliot, ed. 1986. *Folk Groups and Folklore Genres: An Introduction*. Logan: Utah State University.

Quigley, Colin. 1987. "Creative Processes in Musical Composition: French Newfoundland Fiddler Emile Benoit." Ph.D. diss. University of California at Los Angeles.

Schlereth, Thomas J., ed. 1985. *Material Culture: A Research Guide*. Lawrence: University Press of Kansas.

Toelken, Barre. 1979. *The Dynamics of Folklore*. Boston: Houghton Mifflin.

Thompson, Robert. 1969. "Abatan: A Master Potter of the Egbado Yoruba." In *Tradition and Creativity in Tribal Art*, edited by Daniel P. Biebuyck, 120–182. Berkeley and Los Angeles: University of California Press.

Trent, Robert F. 1977. *Hearts and Crowns: Folk Chairs of the Connecticut Coast 1720–1840 as Viewed in the Light of Henri Focillon's Introduction to Arte Populaire*. New Haven, Conn.: New Haven Colony Historical Society.

Vincent, John Robert. 1962. "A Study of Two Ozark Woodworking Industries." Master's thesis, University of Missouri.

Vlach, John Michael. 1977. "Graveyards and Afro-American Art." *Southern Exposure* 5, no. 2–3:161–165.

Wade, Edwin, and David Evans. 1973. "The Kachina Sash: A Native Model of the Hopi World." *Western Folklore* 33:1–18.

Machine Politics: The Political Construction of Technological Artifacts

Steven Lubar

O bjects are cultural artifacts, shaped by the society that uses them. They form the boundaries between us and the natural world we inhabit. They mediate our experience of our environment. Even as they separate us from the world, they stabilize our place in it, providing us with a touchstone against which to measure the rest of the world. The objects around us, Hannah Arendt suggested in *The Human Condition*, allow us to define ourselves as separate from the world of nature, to fix our place in the world (Hickman 1988:161–163). They do this not as mere passive intermediaries but rather as agents, always creating the world anew. They define nature, the world, and ourselves. Objects change the world, and we constantly rediscover and redefine the world through objects.

Even more than most objects, machines modify the world. Machines continually reconstruct a new world based only partially on the social relations of the old. They define life, constrain it, focus energies, and thus structure possibilities. Because of the place of machines in industrial society, at the intersections of the interactions of groups as well as the interactions of individuals, they are among the most revealing of cultural artifacts.[1] Machines are the material culture of politics in its broadest sense: politics as the interactions between groups of people. I shall call this "machine politics": the ways in which machines modulate, influence, and intermediate the interactions of groups.

Some examples: Production machinery is the battleground where managers and workers struggle. The constant change in production machinery, as it is modified by those groups, helps determine the outcome of the battle between them. The machinery of agriculture and the exploitation of natural resources are perhaps the most important places where people meet the environment around them. This is where the environment is reshaped to meet human needs and human needs are shaped to the needs of the machinery. Household machinery is often where the expectations of the genders clash and plays a role in determining the outcome of that clash. Machines as objects of consumption are the meeting point between buyers and sellers; in most instances the technology reflects not only that relationship but also the relationship of consumers to their friends and colleagues and to the world around them. Transportation systems mediate not only our physical view of the world but also our relationship with what we see. Communications systems are the less-than-completely-transparent contact between their users; they mediate what we hear. Computer systems mediate what we think.

In this essay I will look first at the ways in which culture is revealed in machines, giving a few examples and applying to machinery some of the categories developed by historical archaeologists and cultural geographers to describe cultural change. Then I will look at the ways machines shape culture, the ways they mediate the interactions of people with the world around them. And finally I will suggest a way of looking at technology—a "pattern language" for technology—that might allow us better to understand the relationships among technology, culture, and politics and that might provide us a new way of looking at the technological artifacts that surround us, define our world, and shape our lives.

MACHINES REVEALING CULTURE

Many factors shape machines. Those that first come to mind—the reasons that make machines machines—are the technical ones. These include the science of the thing—the laws of motion and the nature of materials, for example—as well as its "pure engineering"—the stress analyses, the calculations of the flows of electrons, the interactions of molecules in retorts.

Technical in another sense, not quite so clearly defined, is the efficiency of the design. Efficiency is a socially constructed and relative concept that straddles the borderline of technology and economics. Economics clearly plays an enormous role in technical design. An entire school of economic historians has grown up around the economics of machine design, reducing the design process to an exercise in balancing what these econometricians delight in calling "factor endowments." Machine designers and purchasers, they claim, take the costs of labor, energy, and materials into account in designing and choosing machines, picking the mix of factor endowments to make the machine cheapest to make or most profitable to use (Noble 1977:33–35).

Econometricians would like to think that technology and economics provide sufficient explanation of technological choice. But I think we need to go further, to pass through the economic and enter into the domain of the social and cultural and, ultimately, the political. Hidden under the veneer of economics we find social and cultural reasons for technical design. (Costs, after all, are determined by, at the very least, supply and demand, which in turn is dependent on traditions, the relative wages of skilled and unskilled workers, the desire for certain products, and so on—all cultural and social factors.)

Production machines give the clearest examples of the social aspects of technological design. Consider the types of stop-motions used in two different industries. A textile spinning frame from Lowell, Massachusetts, employs stop-motions, devices that bring the spinning frame to a halt when a thread breaks. (If the machine keeps going after a thread breaks, a great deal of work is ruined.) This mechanism meant that a worker could attend more than one machine. These stop-motions were soon found on almost every textile machine, making possible the "stretch-out" that defined the labor politics of the American textile industry (Jeremy 1973). The pin industry of Connecticut, by contrast, never added stop-motions to its machines, although they were subject to exactly the same problems of ruined work if a machine got out of control. Instead of using stop-motions, pin-packing machines left unautomated the start of each motion, demanding, one inventor wrote, "the whole attention of one person to see that the pins are properly delivered." This, he claimed, was "more convenient" than a stop-motion—by which he meant that it better fit the social and cultural traditions of the industry (Lubar 1987).

From social and cultural aspects of machine design it is easy to slip into the political aspects of machine design, to move from the social and cultural construction of machines to their political construction—the "machine politics" of my title. Karl Marx suggested that "it would be possible to write quite a history of inventions, made . . . for the sole purpose of supplying capital with weapons against the revolts of the working-class." Indeed, there are many examples of inventions made for the sake of taking power from workers by incorporating their skills into the mechanisms of the machine. Machine politics is the use of machines to mediate between groups with differing political interests.[2]

Perhaps the best-known exposition of machine politics is Noble's *Forces of Production* (1984), a history of two competing types of computer-controlled machine tools. The winner in the competition was the design that took control of the process out of the hands of machinists and put it into the hands of management, reinforcing ongoing trends in the politics of the factory. Here the question of design is really the question of choice between two designs. This is often the most politically revealing, and it answers the question technologists so often raise about the issue of the politics of technology: How might it have been otherwise?

Machines as weapons in the battle over the control of the workplace, with machine designers usually on the side of managers and owners, suggest the extent of the possible political dimensions of machinery. But even in less extreme cases there is often a politics to machine design, a negotiation between the social groups involved in its creation and use and those affected by it. Each of these groups brings its own wants and its own traditions to the technology, and the clash of these wants and traditions is a political battleground in machine design (Pinch and Bijker 1987:30; Staudenmaier 1988).

The politics and philosophy of a community rather than a factory play the main role in the next few examples. A steam engine (fig. 1) installed in the Charleston, South Carolina, shops of the Southern Railroad in 1851 partook of the Greek Revival architecture of its day, and like that style it had a politics. Charleston was a city opposed to industry in

Fig. 1. Steam engine built by the Harlan and Hollingsworth Company, 1850. Photograph courtesy of National Museum of American History, Smithsonian Institution.

general and steam engines in particular but one that looked kindly on the sort of republicanism represented by the Greek Revival. The steam engine's design was, no doubt, a political attempt to fit the new technology into the accepted forms of everyday life. (A similar argument, about the architecture of Rhode Island textile mills, is made in Kulik [1981].) The Shaker villages of Canterbury, New Hampshire, had a very unusual water-power system. The Shakers built an extensive system of canals and ponds, bringing water where there had been none and sharing it equitably among several villages (Starbuck 1986). It was a cooperative system that reflected elements of the Shaker philosophy—simplicity, functionality, and sharing—also found in other Shaker artifacts. A very different community politics can be found in the bridges on Long Island parkways. Robert Moses, builder of so much of New York City's infrastructure, wanted to keep poor people away from the Long Island beaches. Poor people traveled by bus, and so Moses designed the parkways leading to the beaches with bridges too low for a bus to pass under. The politics of the day are nicely embodied in the artifact (Winner 1986:22–23).

These examples reflect local politics, the details of interactions of groups that were directly involved in the design or the use of the machine. There is another, much broader category of cultural influences on machinery. These are the overarching cultural traditions that depend on national boundaries—more generally, cultural regions—and on changing beliefs about the order of the world.

National styles of technology can be illustrated quickly; a glance at locomotive design makes the point. English locomotives of the turn of the century look like a substantial building—very solid, very establishment; French locomotives are of a rational, extremely efficient design that shows off all their scientific improvements; and American locomotives are practical, easy to repair, only superficially decorated.[3] The styles are sufficiently distinctive that it is easy to identify a locomotive's country of origin after looking at only a few exemplars. The design desiderata of all three locomotives are similar, but the designs are different, reflecting local beliefs and traditions, as well as environmental and economic conditions (William Withuhn, pers. com. 1989; more generally, Hughes 1979). That there are social and cultural influences in design is easily seen in cross-cultural comparisons such as these.

The second of my general categories, the historical ones, require more explanation. I suggest that historians of technology can make use of a set of periodizations of culture that have been suggested by historical archaeologists and cultural geographers, periodizations that these scholars have found reflected in a vast range of material culture. These "orders," as Groth calls the periodizations of culture, are sets of "unconscious rules and oppositions which underlay a culture's spatial organization." And not just its spatial organization; these rules, he suggests, following Henry Glassie, mediated not only the construction of space but also architecture, pottery, and folk tales (Groth 1985).[4] If this is true, then we can begin to see not just the details of workplace negotiations in the machines but also the same general shifts in thinking, the same broad trends in material culture—and, as Leone (1988:237) has pointed out, the politics that goes along with these beliefs—that affect other cultural constructions of the day.

I believe that these orders show themselves in machines as well. Georgian houses are characterized by symmetrical façades with virtually identical, interchangeable rooms. Georgian cities were platted in interchangeable lots. The Georgian countryside was laid out according to a

Fig. 2. Samuel Slater's spinning frame, 1790. Photograph courtesy of National Museum of American History, Smithsonian Institution.

rectangular grid. What would a Georgian machine look like? I suggest that Samuel Slater's spinning frame (fig. 2), with its repetitive elements and its periodic operations is a Georgian machine. Textile machines from Lowell, too, are Georgian. The lathe of figure 3, made in Massachusetts in 1829, is Georgian in the uniformity of its design and, especially, the symmetry of its reversing gear.

There is a subclass of Georgian machines that suggests some of the richness this line of argument can include. The 1830s and 1840s saw a surge of interest in rotary machines, machines making use of circular elements in design and operation. Dozens of rotary steam engines, rotary pumps, and rotary production machines were patented in the 1840s. John Howe's pin machine, with its rotary tables and radial spacing, is one such machine (fig. 4). The machine reflected styles found in other artifacts of its day and its cultural milieu (Lubar 1987:261–265).

Fig. 3. Lathe built by James Wheaton Bliss in Massachusetts, 1829.
Photograph courtesy of National Museum of American History, Smithsonian
Institution.

What of the other orders? What would a eunomic machine look like, or a mononomic one? The history of steam engines suggests the sorts of changes that might be linked to changing cultural orders. A Newcomen engine, with its slow-moving parts and one-at-a-time mechanical actions, is eunomic; a Corliss engine, its rotary valve gear breaking the actions of the engine into tiny, more or less equal pieces, is isonomic or Georgian; and a uniflow engine, with its simplified, unitary design, is mononomic. The periodization fits nicely with factory design, too—an argument Groth (1987) has made in some detail. These three categories might well be applied to, successively, the shop of a skilled craftsperson, the interchangeable-parts manufacture of the government armory, and the steady flow of an assembly line.

Now this is clearly an off-hand appraisal of the possibilities of putting technological artifacts into the categories that describe other cultural artifacts, and other schemes of categorization are certainly possible.[5] But the specifics of the categories are not the point here. Rather, I hope to suggest that technological artifacts partake enough of culture and politics to allow

Fig. 4. John Howe's 1845 pin machine, overhead view. Photograph by Eric Long, courtesy of National Museum of American History, Smithsonian Institution.

them to be lined up and categorized with other cultural and political artifacts.

Staudenmaier (1988:154) has suggested why this is so: "Successful technologies come in clusters, each embodying the same set of values, the entire cluster reflecting the technological style of its culture of origin." This is not surprising: The designers of technologies, or at least the people who pay those designers, are a small group and a group that generally holds "cultural hegemony" in the society; they tend to view the world from the same perspective. Mumford (1934:110) in his own periodization of civilization into three categories—eotechnic, paleotechnic, and neotechnic— started with the machines and argued that "the machine cannot be divorced from its larger social pattern; for it is this pattern that gives it meaning and purpose." At the very least this suggests that there is more to technology than the technical. And it suggests some of the ways in which we can find history in technological things.

These examples suggest to me that there are always cultural and political reasons that help account for machines being as they are. I think that the inverse is also true: If you look closely enough at the machines, you can almost always find something about the politics of the situation in which they were used or designed. War, von Clausewitz wrote, is "politics by other means." It is a different way of settling issues. What I am suggesting is that technology, too, is a way of settling issues; it too is politics by other means. The use or nonuse of stop-motions, the choice of automatic control on machine tools, the height of the Long Island bridges, Georgian machines and the world view and politics they reflect—all are extensions of politics, of culture, into artifacts. The job of the student of material culture is to read the equation backwards, to find the politics in the artifacts.

CULTURE REFLECTING MACHINES

Demonstrating that there are social and cultural influences on technology is only the first step in my argument. The next step is to show the effects of those machines and, thus, those influences on society. I am not going to claim that technology determines the nature of society. Rather, it reinforces those elements of society that played a leading role in designing and developing it—the groups that won the battle of machine politics.

What sort of general inferences might we be able to make from examining the politics of technology as it is captured in the artifact? Are there, as Winner (1986:27) suggests, some artifacts that are "inherently political," human-made systems that "appear to require or to be strongly compatible with particular kinds of political relationships"? Or does politics shape the technology in its use, allowing a given machine to take on the politics of its day?

Winner, in suggesting that some technologies require certain politics, is echoing a classic argument in the history of technology: Mumford's suggestion that there are two basic types of technology, one "authoritarian"—"system-centered, immensely powerful, but inherently unstable"—and one "democratic"—"man-centered, relatively weak, but resourceful and durable" (1964:2). Mumford suggests that the technologies of civilization—from water power to war—are by their nature authoritarian, requiring a centralized political control that rested on "ruthless physical coercion, forced labor and slavery" and that turned people into standardized, re-placeable, interdependent parts. The technologies of the small farmer, on the other hand, are "democratic" technologies, technologies that allow for individual choice. (One wonders what Mumford would think of the Shaker water-power system![6])

There is a strong Marxist tradition, too, which suggests that some technologies demand certain politics. Engels, in *On Authority*, wrote that "the automatic machinery of a big factory is much more despotic than the small capitalists who employ workers ever have been." Marx was less certain about the matter: Sometimes he treats machines as "subject to abuse by capital but not in their design inherently capitalist"; at other times he speaks of some machines as being a "specifically capitalist form of production" (MacKenzie 1984:30).

The Marxist line of argument, like Mumford's, comes close to deter-minism, suggesting that the machines *require* certain social systems. This is an extreme form of machine politics, a form that does not leave much leeway in the structuring of the relationships of technology and society and that does not offer much hope for a sophisticated reading of the material culture of technology. It is an ahistorical argument, too; there is not much room for historical interpretation when there are only two categories of technologies.

I would like to suggest a less deterministic relationship. Technology, I claimed in the first part of this paper, is the physical embodiment of social order, reflecting cultural traditions. It is part of culture, and as such it mediates social relationships. There are at least five types of social relation-ships that machines-as-culture mediate: personal relationships, worker-manager relationships, community relationships, buyer-seller relation-ships, and human-nature relationships. Rather than go into details here, I will try simply to suggest in a general way the nature of the technological artifacts' role.

"Mediation" is a key word here. It is more than suggestion but not determination; it is a weak sort of causation. Machines mediate because they are the physical parts of those political structures, of larger systems. In a factory, for example, there is a system of discipline, of rules, of politics in the traditional sense. The forms of machines help enforce these rules; they suggest the easiest possibilities to those who use them. They mediate between the people who make the rules and the people who have to follow them.

Factory machines thus help enforce discipline. So too, though in a less literal way, do all machines. Alexander (1979:72, 92), speaking about architectural space, puts it rather nicely: He suggests not that "space creates events, or that it causes them" but rather that "people know how to behave in certain spaces." A particular space, like a particular technology, is "the precondition, the requirement, which allows the pattern of events to happen." White (1962:28) used an architectural metaphor: Technology, he said, opens the door but does not require us to enter. But, of course, open doors are tempting.

The result of the mediation of machines, the temptation they provide, is a change in people's actions and beliefs. Shanks and Tilley write: ". . . material culture is structured by agency and once the labour becomes objectified in material reform it acts back to structure practices. . . . Structured patterns of action and consciousness become retained in objects as significations of the practice that produced them" (1987:131). In other words, objects reflect past actions and constrain future actions. They continue: "Material culture . . . may be particularly productive in serving power strategies at a practical or non-discursive level of consciousness. That which is contingent may appear to be natural. . . . Consensus may seem not only to be natural but actually spontaneous" (1989:133). Machines reflect the structures of society, and because they play a mediating role in personal and community relationships, they help structure political situations. By suggesting the resolution of political disagreements, they serve as cultural bulwarks. They establish patterns and make it easy for us to follow those patterns; they tempt us with the possibilities beyond the open door.

AN EXPLANATION FOR TECHNOLOGICAL STYLES

In the first part of this paper I suggested that machines are, in part, determined by culture; in the second I suggested that they in turn influence society, mediating the interactions of individuals and groups and the natural world. In this third and final part I suggest a way of thinking about the internal construction of technology that might allow us to understand its relationship to society and culture.

The notion of technological style allows us to understand the place of culture and politics in the technological artifact. Prown (1980:197–198) defines style as the expression of the widely shared beliefs of a society—its assumptions, attitudes, and values. In technological artifacts, style reflects the cultural values of the people who invent, shape, and use them. In Layton's phrase (1984:195), machines carry "all kinds of implicit assumptions about man, nature, and society."

These assumptions are hard to get at, but recent work in architectural theory suggests a possibility. It might be useful to think of technological style using the notion of a "pattern language," as that term is used by Alexander. In *A Timeless Way of Building* and *A Pattern Language*, Alexander outlines a generative grammar of building, a list of 253 "patterns" that, taken together, help determine good regional and urban planning, good architecture, and good building. These patterns are not specific plans, not "an image like a drawing or a blueprint or a photograph." Rather, they are part of a "system of patterns which functions like a language." Some examples give the flavor of these patterns: "ceiling height variety," "thick walls," "light on two sides of every room" (Alexander 1979:178–179).

A pattern language for one field of technology exists. Teague of the National Institute of Standards and Technology has derived a group of patterns for precision measurement machines. These rules include "design for repeatability," "incorporate symmetry to the maximum extent possible," and "make the path from the test probe to the workpiece as short as possible" (Teague and Evans, n. d.) A second field of technology, lathe design, has been analyzed in a way that reveals underlying patterns. Danko and Prinz (1988) suggest a method of modeling the historical transformations of lathe design that allows the isolation of the major patterns of design. They do not use the same form as Alexander and do not suggest that the "rules" they isolate are indeed the rules used by the designers and inventors, but their work suggests possibilities for historicizing the notion of a pattern language.

The nature of patterns, whether architectural or technological, suggests something of the thought patterns of the practitioner of those fields. They provide a grammar not of the finished products but of cognitive strategies, a series of mental templates to guide the work of design. Cognitive anthropologists Dougherty and Keller (1985) call them "task-oriented constellations of knowledge" and suggest that they change as the contextual frames of the practitioner change, as he or she contemplates the design or construction task at hand. These mental templates, based on past experience and on both general theoretical knowledge and specific practical knowledge, guide the work and shape the artifact.

Alexander suggests that his rules are "timeless," which I doubt. Dougherty and Keller are not interested in change over time, though their system of "taskonomy" certainly allows for change. I believe that any such system must allow for change over time, that the pattern languages of architecture and artifacts, including machines, are a historical as well as cultural matter. Indeed, I would suggest that the changing cultural orders of the historical archaeologist reflect fairly small changes in these patterns. If we historicize these patterns, they become useful for understanding not only the changing styles of technology but also the relationship of technology and culture. It is these underlying rules that help the makers of artifacts determine what seems proper at any given time—that is, what an appropriate style is for a given cultural order, individual, or nation. They are outlines of the political, social, and cultural forces that shape design.

The general form for Alexander's patterns is:

context $\longrightarrow$ conflicting forces $\longrightarrow$ configuration

A pattern works, he claims, when we can express it "as a conflict among forces which . . . cannot normally be resolved within that context" and when the pattern "solves the problem." Patterns arise from conflict; they are successful patterns when they resolve that conflict (Alexander 1979:282–285).

With the mention of contexts and conflicting forces, we have come full circle, back to my initial statement of technology as a way of resolving political, social, and cultural problems among groups of people: politics by other means. The interaction of these groups, the battle they wage over the shaping of technology, shapes their pattern language, which in turn resolves the conflicts by shaping technological artifacts and systems. The patterns derive from past practice and current problems. Patterns are the elements of style, the resolution of cultural interactions, the culmination of the battles of machine politics.

If there is something to this deep structure of technological artifacts, it suggests a new goal for the history of technology: to understand the patterns of technology. Alexander was content to list the patterns of architecture, but historians must go further than that and find the context and conflicting forces that create them. Only then can we really understand the reasons technological artifacts are the way they are and appreciate their role in the world.

NOTES

1. Students of material culture often leave technologies out of their studies. Tools and machines, they imply, are somehow different from other artifacts of material culture. They are willing to analyze the artifacts of everyday life for hints about the culture they contain but draw the line at technological artifacts. Machines, it seems, obey a higher law: the laws of scientific and technological necessity—or, at the very least, the laws of economic necessity. They do not seem to be cultural artifacts in quite the same way that dishes or landscapes or houses are. (See, for example, Prown 1980:197–198.) I suggest that these authors take too narrow a view of culture, leaving out much that is of interest to the historian and anthropologist. They imply that technological and economic effects are not cultural or at least not interesting.

2. Marx had in mind the self-acting mule, invented to break the power of the mule-spinners' union. The quote is cited in Paynter (1988:419). For other examples, see Braverman (1975) and Bennett (1989). On the social construction of technology, see Bijker, Hughes, and Pinch (1987).

3. These generalizations are based on the locomotive drawings in Nock (1969), especially figures 75, 15, and 18.

4. Authors vary in the details and the names of the orders. The details are not important here; what matters is that all find a fairly small number of styles of cultural organization in the history of the European settlement of North America. Groth distinguishes five periods: "Open order" landscapes were the landscapes of the frontier. Eunomic, or "good order," landscapes were found in New England towns and tidewater Southern plantations of the eighteenth century. Isonomic spaces—what James Deetz has called the Georgian order—stretched from about 1750 to 1850. Mononomic (single-ordered) spaces were built from about 1850 to the present. Multinomic (many-ordered) spaces are the new spaces of the age of video and computers.

5. Staudenmaier (1988:154) lumps Ford's assembly line, Taylor's scientific management, Sperry's servomechanisms, and tear gas into a single category, all of them "integrated systems to control potentially chaotic exogenous variables." For a description of the military technology of World War I—poison gas, the zeppelin, and the U-boat—as modernist, see Eksteins (1989).

6. Another categorization of this sort is found in Ley (1987), who follows Martin (1981) in distinguishing between "expressive" and "instrumental" landscapes, which correspond in many ways to Mumford's democratic and authoritarian technologies.

REFERENCES

Alexander, Christopher. 1977. *A Pattern Language*. New York: Oxford University Press.

———. 1979. *A Timeless Way of Building*. New York: Oxford University Press.

Bijker, Wiebe E., Thomas P. Hughes, and Trevor J. Pinch. 1987. *The Social Construction of Technological Systems: New Directions in the Sociology and History of Technology*. Cambridge, Mass.: MIT Press.

Braverman, Harry. 1975. *Labor and Monopoly Capital: The Degradation of Work in the Twentieth Century*. New York: Monthly Review Press.

Bennett, Stuart, Harold Closter, Nanci Edwards, Peter Liebhold, Steven Lubar, Harry Rubenstein, and David Shayt, curators. 1989 "Workers and Managers: The Crises of Control in American Manufacturing." Exhibition at the National Museum of American History, Smithsonian Institution, Washington, D.C.

Danko, George M., and Friedrich B. Prinz. 1988. "An Analysis of Lathe Development Using Artificial Intelligence Techniques." *History and Technology* 5, no. 1:1–29.

Dougherty, Janet W. D., and Charles M. Keller. 1985. "Taskonomy: A Practical Approach to Knowledge Structures." In *Directions in Cognitive Anthropology*, edited by Janet W. D. Dougherty, 161–174. Urbana and Chicago: University of Illinois Press.

Eksteins, Modris. 1989. *Rites of Spring: The Great War and the Birth of the Modern Age*. New York: Peter Davison, Houghton Mifflin.

Groth, Paul. 1985. "Landscape Orders: Frameworks for American Cultural Landscape History." Paper presented at the Association of American Geographers.

———. 1987. "Making the System First: Engineering Cultural Change in Twentieth-Century Factory Complexes." Paper presented at the American Studies Association meeting, New York.

Hickman, Larry. 1988. "The Phenomenology of the Quotidian Artifact." In *Philosophy and Technology. Vol. 4: Technology and Contemporary Life*, edited by Paul T. Durbin, 161–176. Dordrect, Netherlands: D. Reidel.

Hughes, Thomas. 1979. "Regional Technological Styles." In *Technology and Its Impact on Society; Tekniska Museet Symposia* no. 1, 1977:211–232. Stockholm: Tekniska Museet.

Jeremy, David. 1973. "Innovation in American Textile Technology during the Early Nineteenth Century." *Technology and Culture* 14:40–76.

Kulik, Gary. 1981. "A Factory System of Wood: Cultural and Technological Change in the Building of the First Cotton Mills." In *Material Culture of the Wooden Age*, edited by Brooke Hindle, 300–355. Tarrytown, N.Y.: Sleepy Hollow Press.

Layton, Edwin. 1984. "Style and Engineering Design." In *Bridge to the Future: A Centennial Celebration of the Brooklyn Bridge*, edited by Margaret Latimer, Brooke Hindle, and Melvin Kranzberg, 173–181. New York: New York Academy of Sciences.

Leone, Mark. 1988. "Georgian Order and Merchant Capitalism." In *The Recovery of Meaning: Historical Archeology in the Eastern United States*, edited by Mark Leone, 235–262. Washington, D.C.: Smithsonian Institution Press.

Ley, David. 1987. "Styles of the Times: Liberal and Neo-Conservative Landscapes in Inner Vancouver, 1968–1988." *Journal of Historical Geography* 13, no.1:40–56.

Lubar, Steven. 1987. "Culture and Technological Design in the 19th-Century Pin Industry: John Howe and the Howe Manufacturing Company." *Technology and Culture* 28:253–283.

MacKenzie, Donald. 1984. "Marx and the Machine." *Technology and Culture* 25:473–502.

Martin, Bernice. 1981. *A Sociology of Contemporary Cultural Change*. New York: St. Martin.

Mumford, Lewis. 1934. *Technics and Civilization*. New York: Harcourt, Brace and Co.

———. 1964. "Authoritarian and Democratic Technics." *Technology and Culture* 5:1–8.

Noble, David. 1977. *America by Design: Science, Technology, and the Rise of Corporate Capitalism*. New York: Knopf.

———. 1984. *Forces of Production*. New York: Knopf.

Nock, O. S. 1969. *Railways at the Turn of the Century*. London: The Macmillan Company.

Paynter, Robert. 1988. "Steps to an Archeology of Capitalism." In *The Recovery of Meaning: Historical Archeology in the Eastern United States*, edited by Mark Leone, 407–434. Washington, D.C.: Smithsonian Institution Press.

Pinch, Trevor J., and Wiebe E. Bijker. 1987. "The Social Construction of Facts and Artifacts." In *The Social Construction of Technological Systems: New Directions in the Sociology and History of Technology*, edited by Wiebe E. Bijker, Thomas P. Hughes, and Trevor J. Pinch. Cambridge, Mass.: MIT Press.

Prown, Jules David. 1980. "Style as Evidence." *Winterthur Portfolio* 13: 201–210.

Shanks, Michael, and Christopher Tilley. 1987. *Re-Constructing Archaeology: Theory and Practice*. Cambridge, England: Cambridge University Press.

Starbuck, David R. 1986. "The Shaker Mills in Canterbury, New Hampshire." *IA: Journal of the Society for Industrial Archeology* 12, no.1:11–38.

Staudenmaier, John M., S. J. 1988. "The Politics of Successful Technologies." In *In Context: History and the History of Technology, Essays in Honor of*

Melvin Kranzberg, edited by Stephen H. Cutcliffe and Robert C. Post, 150–171. Bethlehem, Pa.: Lehigh University Press.

Teague, E. Clayton, and Chris Evans. n.d. *Patterns for Precision Instrument Design (Mechanical Aspects).* Gaithersburg, Md.: National Institute of Standards and Technology.

White, Lynn. 1962. *Medieval Technology and Social Change.* Oxford, England: Clarendon Press.

Winner, Langdon. 1986. "Do Artifacts Have Politics?" In *The Reactor and the Whale: A Search for Limits in an Age of High Technology,* 19–39. Chicago: University of Chicago Press.

Technological Systems and Some Implications with Regard to Continuity and Change

W. David Kingery

We think of ourselves as living in an increasingly technological world in which technology consists of "codified ways of deliberately manipulating the environment to achieve some material object" (National Academy of Sciences Committee on Science and Public Policy 1969); we have to agree that "since the beginning everything has involved technical knowledge" (Braudel 1977:14). From Paleolithic times to the present, technology has mediated between human behavior and its material environment. Technology covers the spectrum from continuing, rather dull everyday tasks to esoteric revolutionary innovations affecting humankind's circumstances and behavior. It involves the design, creation, distribution, and use of an enormous variety of artifacts. I hope to show that learning

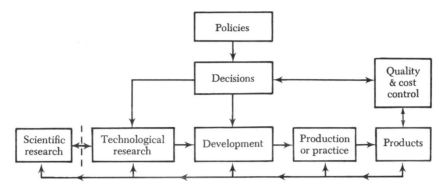

Fig. 1. Flow diagram of technological process (Bunge 1979:265).

from these artifacts is more effective if one thinks of technology as an interrelated system.

A TECHNOLOGICAL SYSTEM

When one uses the word "technology" with a group of archaeologists or art historians, the image that first comes to their minds is almost always the manufacturing process. In contrast, with historians of technology the image is generally the design process, be it a simple object or a complex system. As historians and philosophers of technology cope with the science-technology nexus and focus on technology as a science-based cognitive endeavor, the central role of design is reinforced. An indication of this mindset is seen in the flow diagram for a technological process proposed by Bunge (1979:265), which ends with the creation of a "product" (fig. 1). Here I propose first to define a somewhat more complete technological "system" and then examine a historical development in my field of ceramic technology, which leads to some observations on the nature of technological continuity and change.

I have previously discussed (Kingery 1989) how technology and its history have come to be studied in categories more or less reflecting the department structures of university schools of engineering. Remembering that the encyclopedists of the eighteenth century changed the way people thought about branches of knowledge (Lough 1971), there may be value in considering alternative classification schemes. The usual industry-focused

	Generalized Technology	Textile Technology	Electronic Technology	Civil Engineer Technology
Materials Acquisition Technology	Starting Material	Silk Fiber	Silicon Powder	Iron Bar
Materials Engineering Technology	Shaped Object	Silk Thread	Silicon Crystal	Iron I-beam
Device Production Technology	Intermediate Devices	Silk Cloth	Transister Chip	Iron Truss
Product Manufacture Technology	Product	Wedding Gown	P.C. Computer	Railroad Bridge
System Design Technology	System	Marriage System	Publication System	Transportation System

Fig. 2. The usual industry-focused classifications of technology (vertical columns) and task-focused classifications (horizontal rows).

classifications are shown as vertical columns in figure 2. Peer groups based on academic discipline join professional societies, attend professional meetings, are elected to national academies and otherwise reinforce the scheme. Another equally rational classification is what I call task-focused and is illustrated by the horizontal rows in figure 2. In every industry there is a series of tasks of increasing structural complexity that begin with materials acquisition, preparation, and shaping. Materials are assembled to form products and devices that are the industry's output. Products are used in systems that may be based on one or several different industries. Task-focused departments of materials science and engineering, manufacturing engineering, and systems design are now in place or becoming established as engineering departments at many universities. One advantage of a task-focused classification is that it recognizes commonalities in the design, manufacture, and use of different product lines. Task focusing achieves an industry-free generality and allows industry-craft-archaeology-ethnography continuities and comparisons to be seen more easily.

A different and equally rational classification is to focus on the technological system associated with a specific artifact—a ceramic capacitor, a semiconductor chip, a temple, a television set, an energy system. This product-focused technology is a particularly natural scheme for material culture studies; it implies the existence of a technological system consisting of materials acquisition and distribution, design, manufacturing, product distribution, reception, perception, and use as well as various possible reuse and discard technologies. The product is in the middle, not at one end. A generalized illustration of such a system is shown in figure 3. In contrast with the two previous typologies, this product-focused classification has little to offer in a direct way for the organization of technologist training or for professional societies. It has more to offer in understanding how technology exists as a system within society and the central role of material culture.

Each of the activities forming a part of this system—design, manufacturing, distribution, and use—requires human perceptions, human cognition, social organization, and human interactions as well as artifacts for its performance. This is more than context; it is an integral part of technology itself. In fact, every human activity includes these components of action; through the use of artifacts, technology permeates all human activities and behavior. Activity analysis is central for understanding technological influences on behavioral activities and change (Schiffer 1989) and the influence of culture on technology.

Each of these technological activities manipulates the environment in ways that not only are utilitarian—for example, Binford's technomic (1962)—but also have social and ideological functions (sociotechnic, ideotechnic). In addition, I believe there is an important category of aesthetic function. Bunzel, in her study of Pueblo potters noted that "these potters constantly invent new patterns . . . because it is as easy as painting the old ones and very much more enjoyable" (1929:57). As Smith and others have emphasized (Smith 1970; Huizinga 1970; Ehrmann 1968), people do things, search for and discover things, and use things simply for the pleasure attending these activities. In recent times science fiction fantasies have played an important role in setting the stage and creating a social imperative for technological change. Aesthetics are particularly important in understanding the invention and acceptance of new technologies (Smith 1970; Hatfield 1948).

PAINTERLY CERAMICS OF THE ITALIAN RENAISSANCE

In my special field, ceramic technology, many studies have shown that ceramic traditions of form and manufacture are conspicuously conservative and resistant to change. This perhaps relates to the fact that pottery is not an essential product for effecting warfare, major cultural changes, or much else. Pottery is a follower, not a leader, of social and cultural change

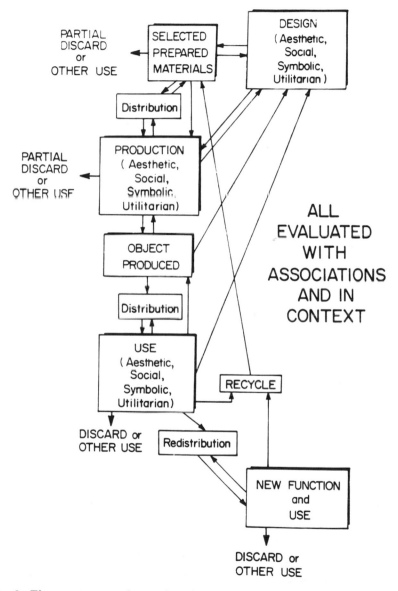

Fig. 3. The components of a product-focused classification of technology as they interrelate and interact to form a technological-social system.

(Kingery 1984). Uses of ceramics as containers and cooking vessels have been as conservative as their method of manufacture (I believe the two are related). Studies by Vandiver (1989) of the "software horizon" (Dyson 1965) in the Near East have shown that a "sequential slab" method of ceramic fabrication extended from circa 7000 to circa 3000 B.C. The method was originally based on sound technical considerations but continued to be used long after the material restraints that led to its adoption had disappeared. Other similar examples are Greek pithoi (Cullen and Keller 1989) and the pottery of the Andes (Tschopik 1950), central Mexico (Charlton 1968), and Nubia (Adams 1979). This has been true for ceramic technology to the present century and is perhaps rational and unsurprising since the consequences of changing raw materials or altering processing techniques have been notably unpredictable; they are not modified without some strong impetus.

In light of this conservatism the development of ceramic maiolica as an art form in central and northern Italy during the last quarter of the fifteenth century was quite remarkable (Liverani 1960; Cox 1974; Wilson 1987; Kingery and Aronson 1989). A type of ware in which the painting of narrative and historical scenes took precedence over shape, form, and texture—*istoriato* ware—came to be widely produced. An outstanding example of the new genre is the Perseus and Andromeda plate, now at the Boston Museum of Fine Arts, which was painted for Isabella d'Este by Nicola da Urbino about 1524 (fig. 4). In the view of Cox (1974), "the pictorial and narrative element which was entirely out of place on pottery became dominant and most destructive to the art. The Italians never seemed to grasp the beauty of an object in itself, but always had a yen to wrap it with stories, sentiments and emotions." In contrast Wilson (1987) holds that "this was the time that ceramics, one of the so called 'minor arts' came perhaps closer to the 'major arts' than at any point in the long history" of ceramics. It seems that there is no accounting for taste. What is clear is that there was a parallel development of a new ceramic technology along with new ceramic painting techniques, which the new art form demanded or perhaps which made it possible (Kingery and Aronson 1989). The new technology also developed into a new industry; many pottery centers developed in central and northern Italy. During the sixteenth century Italian potters emigrated to establish manufactories throughout northern Europe. The product came to be called faience in France, delftware in Holland.

The essence of the new technology was a multilayer glaze system

Fig. 4. Perseus and Andromeda plate. Otis Norcross Fund, Museum of Fine Arts, Boston.

comparable to modern, thick-film electronic devices. A fired bisque pottery shape was dipped to form a white-ground glaze coating opacified with tin oxide (*bianco*). For the underlying ground to be translucent rather than completely opaque, some feldspathic sand was added to the mixture. The painting was executed directly on the unfired white ground. Traditional blue and green pigments dissolve in the glaze and form a diffuse watercolor-like effect. New white, black, red, yellow, and orange pigments were insoluble and behaved more like oil paints, maintaining their position during firing and allowing the development of depth, gradation of

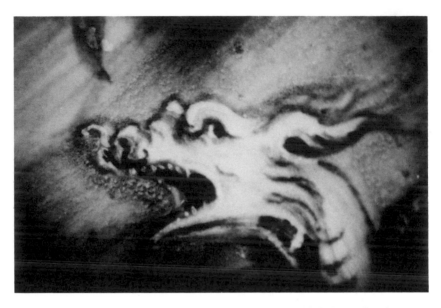

Fig. 5. Magnified view of the dragon Cetus, Perseus and Andromeda plate.
Otis Norcross Fund, Museum of Fine Arts, Boston.

tone, and a precision of painting impossible with the previous ceramic materials and technology. After being painted, the ware was dipped or sprinkled with a lead silicate coating (*coperta*), which wetted out the pigments to form a smooth, highly reflective surface. The entire three-layer structure was fired together. The result was an unprecedented combination of drawing precision, bright color, depth, and brilliance.

To obtain precise control of line and color, it was essential to have pigments that would not flow but would still be wetted by the overlying *coperta*. In his 1557 treatise on pottery making, Piccolpasso devotes almost half his text to pigments and painting, a startling change in the potter's craft. A magnified detail of the dragon Cetus shows how the pigment under the overglaze retains its position and allows a precision of drawing not previously possible (fig. 5).

As is shown both by correspondence and by ware shapes (Mallet 1981), these objects were decorative art meant for both use and display. The Perseus and Andromeda plate was commissioned by Isabella d'Este, marchioness of Mantua. Microscopic examination shows that after four hundred years there are signs of wear only at the lip and the internal bowl edge. This piece was perhaps used as a serving bowl; had it been used for anything more vigorous, its relatively soft lead silicate *coperta* would be scratched and worn.

Of the glaze-system components the underlying white *bianco* ground had been used in Islam since the tenth century and in Italy since the thirteenth. In the fifteenth century the principal luxury ceramic coming to Italy was lustre ware over a white ground imported from Valencia. It had decorative designs rather than pictorial painting. The new pigments began to be used as early as the 1430s. About the same time a *coperta* overlayer seems to have first been used on tile subject to abrasive wear. The precise dates are less than certain, but the basic elements of the new technology were being used half a century before the appearance of *istoriato* ware.

The combination of these elements—painting with the new insoluble pigments on a *bianco* ground covered with a lead silicate *coperta*—appeared in the last fifteen years of the fifteenth century and rapidly developed into a widely accepted innovative art form. The essence of the new technology was a combination of the evolving traditions of pottery technology with the evolving traditions of Italian drawing.

This new maiolica technology should not be seen in isolation. There was a parallel development of colorful, precise pictorial representation in the medium of enameled glass (Gasparetto 1958) as well as in painted enamel on metals (Verdier 1967; Forman 1962). New innovations and new levels of excellence were seen also in sculpture, painting, architecture, woolens, silks, furniture, and metalwork.

The reasons that this efflorescence was possible are rooted in the growth of the Italian economy beginning in the thirteenth century and the development of an urban elite that replaced the feudal aristocracy (Luzatto 1961). Trade, banking, and commerce became the main sources of wealth, allowing a certain degree of social mobility. New standards of urban behavior developed in which splendor became a virtue and the acquisition and appreciation of things, the achievement of both refined private luxury and public display, were respected achievements. In the cities there was excess disposable income, and an incipient consumer society developed (Goldthwaite 1984, 1987, 1989).

The development of decorative art was reinforced by the pricing system. Prices were based on labor and materials. The annual labor cost of the best sculptors, architects, painters, goldsmiths, and furniture makers was about 100 ducats; to this was added the cost of materials. In contrast, the cash profits of banking, commerce, and trade were measured in thousands of ducats; in 1500 there were more than two hundred banking operations in Florence alone. In concert the strong demand for fine things and their reasonable cost led to outstanding work in all the decorative arts (and transformed the craft of painting into the realm of artistic creation).

But the course of development of the maiolica industry was exceptional compared with that of enameled glass or enamels on metals, which remained luxury items made in relatively limited amounts. This resulted from two factors. One was the change in dining habits that accompanied a more refined way of life and made tableware a product with a much expanded market (Goldthwaite 1989). The second factor was the thick-film multilayer technology, which allowed firing many hundreds of decorative pieces at one time in one furnace loading. Because of standardized painting, painterly maiolica became relatively inexpensive and eminently affordable by the growing middle class as well as the rich. By 1550 the two ducats that Isabella paid for the commissioned Perseus and Andromeda plate would suffice for an entire high-quality service. Much less expensive ware was being made to accommodate the changed eating habits of first Italy and then Europe north of the Alps (Braudel 1973).

CONTINUITY AND CHANGE

Archaeologists are fond of pointing out that the plasticity of clay can give rise to innumerable possibilities and that ceramic forms are a matter of choice, not necessity. Invention of a new technology is essentially an individual achievement (see, for example, Usher 1954) that recurs from time to time but rarely becomes part of the archaeological or historical record. It is only when innovation brings an invention into technological practice that we see its spoor; this sort of innovation has usually been treated by economic theorists (Schumpeter 1934; Schmookler 1966; Fellner 1971) as involving both perceived utility and entrepreneurial action. Once adopted, an accepted empirical successful technology invariably becomes conservative and subsequent modifications are gradual and incremental (Sahal 1981). This slow continuous process has allowed archaeologists and anthropologists to see changes occurring in technology and culture over time as analogous to Darwinian natural selection (Thompson 1977; Dunnell 1980; Leonard and Jones 1987). Basalla (1988) has recently extended and elaborated this analogy, beginning with the point that novelty is part of the artifactual world and that technological evolution is a selection process choosing particular artifacts for replication and addition to a diverse technological inventory. He shows that if one looks one can always find antecedent artifacts; all made things have historic or prehistoric predecessors. Nothing comes out of the blue.

A quite different world view sees technological discontinuities as corresponding to revolutionary change, to a conceptual turnabout. This would correspond to the scientific revolutions that Kuhn (1962) has described. In Kuhn's picture a confrontation between two different world views (such as the Copernican heliocentric conception and the Ptolemaic earth-centered viewpoint) forces choices based on arguments that are less than certain on either side. A model achievement produces a paradigm that is subsequently confirmed by a community of believers. This model has been applied to rapid technological change—for example, the transformation from propeller-piston to turbojet aircraft engines (Constant 1980). However, unlike science, which deals with observations and ideas, technology cannot be seen as right or wrong but merely as appropriate for a particular social and cultural environment. After all, we still have propeller-piston aircraft engines. It is also true that if we look hard enough, we can find lots of antecedents for turbojet engines (Basalla 1988).

The dramatic and unique change in Renaissance ceramics could easily be described as evolutionary; after all, the basic elements—white opaque tin glaze, the pigments, and clear lead silicate glazes—had all been used for a hundred years or more. In the manufacture of tile, plaques, and some pottery the three-layer combination had occasionally been used for half a century before the appearance of *istoriato* ware. The use of pottery as a medium for narrative art could also be seen as a revolutionary paradigm shift in the history of ceramics. In a decade or so pigment and glaze preparation became the potter's most important technology and painting the most important skill for top-of-the-line ceramics. Unquestionably there was a paradigm shift in ceramic technology, but there is no hint of confrontation except for competition with wares imported from Valencia.

With respect to the process of technological transformation, this rapid change is perhaps best seen as a joining together of two previously distinct craft technologies. The lineage of the potter combined with the lineage and traditions of Italian drawing. The painterly technique used

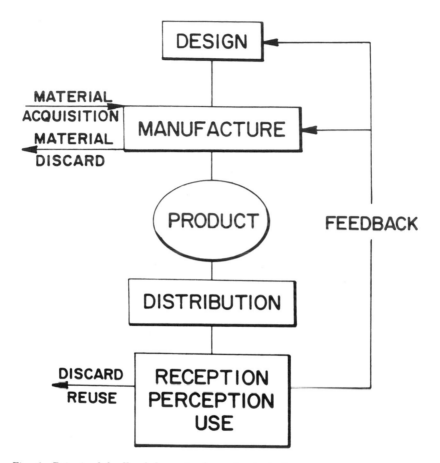

Fig. 6. Principal feedback loops in the technological system.

for *istoriato* maiolica was not invented for the purpose; it was the product of a long evolutionary development in Italian art (Murray and Murray 1963; Wackernagel 1981). Interbreeding between different species is forbidden to Darwinian evolution but seems to be a critical process allowing rapid technological change to occur. Interbreeding provides a way of getting around the barriers of learned motor and cognitive behavior that would otherwise be difficult, perhaps impossible, to overcome.

The rate at which any change occurs depends on the driving force and the system inertia. As we have discussed, the impetus leading to *istoriato* maiolica was a changed perception of the value and role of technical expertise in the urban society of Renaissance Italy. In this case and many others the perceived utility of these objects and a change in use technology led to new design and manufacturing technology, as is rather crudely illustrated in figure 6. Divorcing use from design and manufacturing cannot lead to satisfactory archaeological or historical interpretations and explanations. Indeed, we can propose as a basic tenet of material culture that a radical change in design technology (not style) or manufacturing technology invariably implies a change in use technology and vice versa.

However, I have to accept that this remains much too naive a picture; the acts of reception, perception, and use are conditioned by a wide variety of cultural, economic, and social concerns. Design, manufacture, distribution, and use are all activities involving cultural constraints and social organization. Technology proceeds in increments with the source of individual modifications coming from a variety of directions over a period of time. The effects of technology on culture and the influence of culture on technology are multidimensional. An internalist approach looking toward technology as applied science with a product as the final output is simply wrong.

REFERENCES

Adams, William Y. 1979. "On the Argument from Ceramics to History: A Challenge Based on Evidence from Medieval Nubia." *Current Anthropology* 20:727–744.

Basalla, George. 1988. *The Evolution of Technology.* Cambridge, England: Cambridge University Press.

Binford, Lewis R. 1962. "Archaeology as Anthropology." *American Antiquity* 28:217–225.

Braudel, Fernand. 1973. *Capitalism and Material Life*, Chapter 3. Translated by Miriam Kochan. New York: Harper and Row.

———. 1977. *Afterthoughts on Material Civilization and Capitalism*, translated by Patricia Ranum. Baltimore: Johns Hopkins University Press.

Bunge, Mario. 1979. "Philosophical Inputs and Outputs of Technology." In *The History and Philosophy of Technology*, edited by G. Bugliarello and D. B. Dover, 262–281. Urbana: University of Illinois Press.

Bunzel, Ruth L. 1929. *The Pueblo Potter.* New York: Columbia University Press. Reprint. 1972. New York: Dover.

Charlton, Thomas. 1968. "Post-Conquest Aztec Ceramics." *Florida Anthropologist* 21:96–101.

Constant, Edward W., II. 1980. *The Origins of the Turbojet Revolution.* Baltimore.

Cox, William E. 1974. *The Book of Pottery and Porcelain.* New York: Crown Publishers.

Cullen, Tracey, and Donald E. Keller. 1989. "The Greek Pithos through Time: Multiple Functions and Diverse Imagery." In *Ceramics and Civilization V; The Changing Roles and Functions of Ceramics in Society from ca. 26,000 B.P. to the Present,* edited by W. David Kingery, 183–210. Westerville, Ohio: American Ceramic Society.

Dunnell, Robert C. 1980. "Evolutionary Theory and Archaeology." In *Advances in Archaeological Method and Theory,* vol. 3, edited by M. B. Schiffer, 35–99. New York: Academic Press.

Dyson, Robert J., Jr. 1965. "Problems in the Relative Chronology of Iran, 6000–2000 B.C." In *Chronologies in Old World Archaeology,* edited by R. W. Ehrich, 215–256. Chicago: University of Chicago Press.

Ehrmann, Jacques, ed. 1968. *Game, Play, Literature.* New Haven, Conn.: Yale University Press.

Fellner, William. 1971. *The Economics of Technological Advance.* New York: General Learning Press.

Forman, Werner F. 1962. *Limoges Enamels.* London: Arita.

Gasparetto, Astone. 1958. *Il vitro di Murano.* Venice: Neri Pozza.

Goldthwaite, Richard A. 1984. "The Renaissance Economy: The Preconditions for Luxury Consumption." In *Aspelti Della Vita Economica Medievale,* 659–673. Florence: Pisa-Prato.

———. 1987. "The Empire of Things: Consumer Demand in Renaissance Italy." In *Patronage, Art and Society in Renaissance Italy,* edited by F. W. Kent and Patricia Simons with J. C. Eade, 153–175. Oxford, England: Clarendon Press.

———. 1989. "The Economic and Social World of Italian Renaissance Maiolica." *Renaissance Quarterly* 62, no. 1:32.

Hatfield, Henry S. 1948. *The Inventor and His World.* West Drayton, Middlesex, England: Penguin.

Huizinga, Johan. 1970. *Homo Luderis: A Study of the Play Element in Culture.* New York: Harper and Row.

Kingery, W. David. 1984. "Interactions of Ceramic Technology with Society." In *Pots and Potters,* monograph no. 24, edited by Prudence M. Rice, 171–172. Los Angeles: University of California at Los Angeles, Institute of Archaeology.

————. 1989. "Ceramic Materials Science in Society." *Annual Review of Material Science* 19:1–20.

Kingery, W. David, and Meredith Aronson. 1989. "On the Technology of Renaissance Maiolica Glazes." *Faenza* 5:221–224.

Kuhn, Thomas S. 1962. *The Structure of Scientific Revolutions*. Chicago: University of Chicago Press.

Leonard, Robert D., and George H. Jones. 1987. "Elements of an Inclusive Evolutionary Model for Archaeology." *Journal of Anthropological Archaeology* 6:199–219.

Liverani, Guiseppe. 1960. *Five Centuries of Italian Majolica*. New York: McGraw Hill.

Lough, John. 1971. *The Encyclopedie*. New York: McKay.

Luzatto, Gino. 1961. *An Economic History of Italy*. Translated by Phillip Jones. New York: Barnes and Noble.

Mallet, John V. C. 1981. "Mantua and Urbino: Gonzaga Patronage of Maiolica." *Apollo*, July, 162–169.

Murray, Peter, and Linda Murray. 1963. *The Art of the Renaissance*. New York: Thames and Hudson.

National Academy of Sciences Committee on Science and Public Policy. 1969. *Technology: Processes of Assessment and Choice*. Washington, D.C.: U.S. Government Printing Office.

Piccolpasso, Cipriano. 1557. *The Three Books of the Potter's Art*. Reprint. 1980. Translated by R. Lightbown and A. Caiger-Smith. London: Scolar Press.

Sahal, Devendra. 1981. *Patterns of Technological Innovation*. Reading, Mass.: Addison-Wesley.

Schiffer, Michael B. 1992. "Technology and Society." Chapter 6 in *Technological Perspectives on Behavioral Change*. Tucson: University of Arizona Press.

Schmookler, Jacob. 1966. *Invention and Economic Growth*. Cambridge, Mass.: Harvard University Press.

Schumpeter, Joseph A. 1934. *The Theory of Economic Development*. Translated by Redvers Opie. Cambridge, Mass.: Harvard University Press.

Smith, Cyril S. 1970. "Art, Technology, Science: Notes on Their Historical Interaction." *Technology and Culture* 11:493–549.

Thompson, Michael W. 1977. *General Pitt-Rivers: Evolution and Archaeology in the Nineteenth Century*. Bradford-on-Avon: Moonraker Press.

Tschopik, Harry. 1950. "An Andean Ceramic Tradition in Historical Perspective." *American Antiquity* 15:193–218.

Usher, Abbott P. 1954. *A History of Mechanical Inventions*. Cambridge, Mass.: Harvard University Press.

Vandiver, Pamela B. 1989. "Sequential Slab Construction: A Conservative

Southwest Asiatic Ceramic Tradition, ca. 7000–3000 B.C." *Paleorient* 13, no. 2:9–35.

Verdier, Philippe. 1967. *Catalogue of the Painted Enamels of the Renaissance.* Baltimore: Trustees of the Walters Art Gallery.

Wackernagel, Martin. 1981. *The World of the Florentine Renaissance Artist.* Translated by Alison Luchs. Princeton, N.J.: Princeton University Press.

Wilson, Timothy. 1987. *Ceramic Art of the Italian Renaissance.* London: British Museum Publications.

Replication Techniques in Eastern Zhou Bronze Casting

Robert W. Bagley

For more than a thousand years, from about the fifteenth to the fifth century B.C., bronze vessels played a leading role in Chinese religious ritual and state ceremony. From our vantage point today the bronzes represent the major art form and the most sophisticated technology of their time, and their study leads in many directions. A comprehensive account of their history would necessarily be centered on events that took place inside the workshops, above all on the complex and changing relationship between technology and design.[1] Decisions taken within the workshops must always have been constrained by external parameters such as vessel function and manufacturing cost, however, and in the present paper I should like to focus on a technical innovation of the fifth century B.C. which raises puzzling questions about economic pressures and workshop organization. To a historian studying ancient metal technology it is very satisfying to figure out how a tricky technique worked but somewhat distressing not to know why the technique was used.

The bronze vessel shown in figure 1, a *hu* now in the Freer Gallery in Washington, D.C., was cast early in the fifth century B.C. Since no written records from the Chinese Bronze Age tell us anything about casting technique, to discover how the Freer *hu* was made we must turn to the object itself. But although careful study of the vessel might enable us to decide how *we* would make it, we cannot assume that a method which seems reasonable to us also seemed reasonable to the ancient founder, who had different training and worked in very different circumstances. Our present understanding of the technique used to cast the Freer *hu* depends not only on painstaking study of that vessel and its relatives but also on hard-won and still only partial knowledge of the millennium of Chinese bronze casting that preceded it.

Let me try briefly to explain what we know about the procedure used to cast the Freer *hu*. I will concentrate on mold making, the most interesting part of the procedure, and chiefly on the method employed to decorate the mold.

The starting point for the vessel proper was a model. (Ignore the handles of the vessel; they were made separately from the vessel proper and I will not be concerned with them.) The model was exactly the size and shape of the finished vessel, but it was blank; it had no decoration. The first step in preparing a mold was to pack clay around the model. This envelope of clay was then sliced open vertically, along the axes of the handles, and removed from the model in two large shells. The result was a blank, undecorated two-piece mold, like two halves of a large avocado with the pit removed. The caster proceeded to apply decoration to the interior of this mold but not by carving or otherwise working the mold surface directly. He made the decoration separately: one by one units of decoration were slip-cast in pattern blocks and then set into the mold.

Thirty years ago examples of the pattern blocks used in this procedure came to light during excavations of an ancient foundry site at Houma in Shanxi province.[2] Figure 2 shows one of the Houma pattern blocks. Made of very fine clay, it was carved with a single unit of decoration and then fired hard so that it could be used repeatedly. To decorate a mold the craftsman filled the pattern block with wet clay and then peeled the clay (now bearing a negative imprint of the decoration) off the block and plastered it into the mold. He did this again and again, working his way

Fig. 1. Bronze hu vessel cast early in the fifth century B.C., perhaps at the Houma foundry. Height 44.8 cm. Freer Gallery of Art, Smithsonian Institution, Washington, D.C.

Fig. 2. Clay pattern block from the Houma foundry site. Width 32.8 cm. Late sixth or early fifth century B.C. After catalogue no. 132, The Chinese Exhibition: A Pictorial Record of the Exhibition of Archaeological Finds of the People's Republic of China *(Kansas City, Mo.: The Nelson Gallery-Atkins Museum, 1975).*

around the mold, wallpapering it with clay negatives. The bronze cast in the resulting mold carried horizontal bands of decoration, each band composed of identical replicated units. Such decoration has often been described as stamped, but long pattern units on curved surfaces could not in fact have been produced with stamps. Since moist clay negatives taken from a flat pattern block could be bent and trimmed to fit the contours of any mold section, the pattern-block technique was far more versatile than any stamping technique.

But notice that the technique cannot be inferred from the pattern blocks themselves: They are by no means self-explanatory objects, and indeed the excavators who found them were not able to explain how they were used. The key to their function is supplied by the bronzes they

Fig. 3. Peripheral photograph of a hu, *one of a matched pair in the British Museum, London. The British Museum vessels are similar to the Freer* hu *but have lids which bear an inscription securing a date of ca. 482 B.C. On both of the British Museum* hu *the foot and most of the body below the main register are modern restoration. Courtesy of the Trustees of the British Museum. Copyright British Museum.*

helped to make. The basic elements of the pattern-block technique were worked out fifteen years ago by Barbara Keyser in a meticulous study of a matched pair of bronze vessels; had the Houma blocks not already been discovered, she could have predicted their existence.[3] The feature which allowed her to reconstruct the technique is perhaps most easily explained using peripheral photographs. Peripheral photography is a way of unwrapping a cylindrical object. The object is set on a turntable and photographed with a special camera. Instead of the usual aperture, the camera has a vertical slit, and as the object slowly rotates on the turntable, a piece of film is slowly moved past the slit. Figure 3, a photograph of a *hu* in the British Museum very similar to the Freer *hu*, gives a good idea of what a peripheral photograph of the Freer vessel would look like. Each band of

Fig. 4. The Freer hu, *the same band as shown in figure 5, detail centered on the incomplete interlace unit with which laying of the band ended. Freer Gallery of Art, Smithsonian Institution, Washington, D.C.*

decoration is made up of units taken from a pattern block, and all the units in a given band are identical except for one: Unless the mold maker was lucky, when he had wallpapered his way around the mold and returned to his starting point the last negative would not fit. Unperturbed by this difficulty, Houma mold makers simply cut the last clay negative short to fit the available space. Figure 4 shows the chopped-off unit in one band of the Freer vessel. In figure 5, which shows a detail from elsewhere in the same band, the interlace is continuous. The narrow vertical slice of a dragon visible just to the right of center in figure 4—nothing of him but his snout—is an error of sorts, but the interlace is so complicated that no ordinary patron would be likely to spot the error; even for observers very familiar with these patterns the incomplete units can be difficult to find. Given that fifth-century fashion called for continuous bands of decoration, a certain degree of intricacy must actually have been a precondition for the emergence of the pattern-block technique. Pattern blocks could

Fig. 5. The Freer hu *of figure 1, detail showing the third band of dragon interlace (numbering the bands downward and counting the petals at the top of the vessel as the first band). The strips of braid, like the interlace bands they separate, come from pattern blocks. Freer Gallery of Art, Smithsonian Institution, Washington, D.C.*

not become an acceptable way of generating decoration until designs in which incomplete units would pass unnoticed had come into vogue.

The foregoing description introduces the basic features of the pattern-block technique, but in some respects it is oversimplified. Parts of the decoration of the Freer *hu* were in fact taken off pattern blocks which had themselves been generated from other, smaller pattern blocks. And the negatives for the main register, the register at the widest part of the vessel, came not from a single pattern block but from two blocks used in alternation. The dimensions of those two blocks moreover seem to have determined the circumference of the vessel, for on a vessel of this shape it was essential to the designer that the pattern units in the main register should come out even: The four staring faces had to be complete and oriented toward the front, back, and sides.[4]

From even the briefest description it should be clear that the Houma founder's technique demanded extraordinary ceramic expertise. The handling and laying of the negatives must have been a very delicate operation, and the finished mold for the Freer *hu* consisted of nearly a hundred pieces of clay which somehow bonded together quite perfectly when the mold was fired. The rationale for so complex a technique is not obvious. Before the Eastern Zhou period mold making normally began with a fully decorated model of the vessel to be cast, and if at some point it had occurred to a founder to increase efficiency by means of replication, presumably he could simply have reused the decorated model to make duplicate molds and hence duplicate vessels. Yet this most straightforward replication process seems to have been studiously avoided. Early founders seem always to have made matched bronzes from models decorated independently; even paired inscriptions on the lid and body of a single vessel were made independently. And when in the Eastern Zhou period replication did finally make its appearance, reusable decorated models were employed only for making vessel appendages (perhaps the handles of the Freer *hu*) and a few special items such as animal-shaped bronzes.[5] For most purposes the pattern-block technique was preferred.

How are we to explain these technical choices? Perhaps the mold-making procedures employed before Eastern Zhou involved some crucial step that made reuse of the model impossible; perhaps what looks to us like an obvious shortcut was in fact ruled out by a technical consideration we are unaware of. Since the Houma caster did on occasion reuse decorated models, however, his normal preference for pattern blocks must have depended not on some single technical factor but on a balancing of practical considerations that we know too little about to weigh properly. We do not have his experience with clays, nor do we know what labor and material costs he faced. No doubt he took some techniques for granted simply because he had learned them as an apprentice. Lacking all information about the economics of the Houma foundry, we can only guess at the advantages of pattern blocks.

Two possible advantages suggest themselves. First, pattern blocks allowed the mold maker to achieve perfect uniformity in repetitive decoration. By itself this does not seem an important enough advantage to account for their use, however, since there is ample evidence that Houma founders could execute patterns freehand with a high degree of uniformity (and if they had executed the patterns freehand they could have made all registers come out perfectly, eliminating incomplete units). A second possible motive for replication is to increase output or productivity. This seems more promising, but it requires us to consider the issue of workshop organization, for it is not obvious that so delicate and involved a ceramic technique did save labor.

Because casting involves many distinct stages which can be assigned to different workers, all casting processes lend themselves to efficient division of labor.[6] Until the pattern-block technique was invented, however, the production process included one long and exacting stage, the carving of a decorated model, that could not easily be parceled out to several different workers. The pattern-block technique allowed that stage to be efficiently subdivided. It made the best use of the most highly skilled worker, the one who carved decoration onto pattern blocks, because his work could be mechanically replicated: One carver could decorate thousands of bronzes. The pattern-block procedure was also more versatile than simpler replication techniques. Forming two or more identical molds on a single decorated model could only produce duplicate vessels; the pattern-block technique allowed decoration from a single block to be applied to an unlimited range of vessel shapes. These advantages must somehow have outweighed the difficulties of the technique.

One conclusion that can surely be drawn from the use of pattern blocks is that in the fifth century B.C. bronze casting was not a craft pursued in small workshops by independent artisans. At Houma large numbers of workers must have been organized in a factory system under some kind of central authority. The operations of the Houma foundry can be quite properly described by the term "mass production" as long as we bear in mind that this rather misleading term normally signifies not so much the production of goods in large quantity as efficient production, high efficiency being obtained through division of labor.[7]

Unfortunately we do not know much about the society that supported the Houma foundry. The fifth century B.C. in China is in most respects not very well documented. We do not know how wealthy a patron had to be to buy a bronze like the Freer *hu* (if it was bought at all in our sense of the word), we do not know how many people could afford such luxuries in the fifth century, and so on. But from the Han period a few centuries later some very interesting documents have survived. One is the inscription written on a lacquer wine cup made in the year A.D. 4 in a state-operated lacquer factory (the earliest such inscriptions have dates about a century earlier). We know when and where the cup was made because it has a "quality-control" inscription of sixty-seven characters on the underside. Roughly translated, the inscription says:

> Made in the fourth year of the Yuanshi reign period at the Western
> Factory in Shu Commandery. Imperial pattern. A lacquered, carved,
> and painted wood cup with gilt-bronze handles. Capacity one *sheng*
> sixteen *yue*. Priming by Yi, lacquering by Li, outer coat by Dang,
> gilding of the handles by Gu, painting by Ding, inscription carved by
> Feng, cleaning and polishing by Ping, inspected and passed by Zong.
> Director, Zhang; Manager, Liang; Deputy, Feng; Assistant, Long; Chief
> Clerk, Bao.[8]

This inscription testifies in no uncertain terms to division of labor and highly organized workshops. Outside China it is difficult to think of anything comparable before the Industrial Revolution. But in China this kind of factory organization clearly goes back at least to the fifth century B.C., when the Freer *hu* was made. Although the inscription on the wine cup speaks more vividly than the bronze, the bronze is five hundred years older than the cup. The early history of industrial organization and mass production depends entirely on inferences made from bronze vessels. The pattern-block technique is not explained in ancient sources; it was worked out during the last fifteen years by scholars studying bronze vessels at the Freer Gallery.

NOTES

1. I have described the early evolution of this relationship in "Shang Ritual Bronzes: Casting Technique and Vessel Design," *Archives of Asian Art* 43 (1990), 6–20, and in more detail in the introduction to *Shang Ritual Bronzes in the Arthur M. Sackler Collections* (Cambridge, Mass.: Harvard University Press, 1987). For a more general discussion of technique and design, see Cyril Stanley Smith, *A Search for Structure* (Cambridge, Mass.: MIT Press, 1981), especially chapters 8 and 9.

2. No proper excavation report has ever been published; for references to a few preliminary reports, see the article by Keyser cited in note 3. The Houma foundry was active in the late sixth and early fifth centuries B.C. On the evidence of bronzes unearthed from a mid-sixth-century tomb at Henan Xichuan Xiasi, which seem to have been cast using pattern blocks but which I

have not been able to examine closely, the technique described here in connection with fifth-century vessels must have been in use at least a century earlier.

3. Keyser examined a famous pair of fifth-century *jian* vessels now divided between the Freer Gallery and the Minneapolis Institute of Arts ("Decor Replication in Two Late Chou Bronze *Chien*," *Ars Orientalis* 11 [1979], 127–62). I have recently been studying other bronzes likely to have been cast at Houma, notably the Freer *hu*, a vessel which shows interesting variations on the technique Keyser describes.

4. In his senior thesis (Princeton University, 1989) my student Raul Gutierrez, to whom I am indebted for these observations about the main register of the Freer *hu*, showed also that the Freer *hu* and the British Museum *hu*, though not made as members of a matched set, were made with the same pattern blocks (to be precise, most though not all of the blocks used to make the Freer *hu* were reused to make corresponding registers on the British Museum *hu*). Unmatched bronzes have not previously been connected in this way, and the discovery has a number of interesting consequences. Among other things it supplies a date for the Freer *hu*: The British Museum *hu* carries an inscription which suggests that it was made in or shortly after 482 B.C., and the date of the Freer *hu* should not be earlier by more than the lifetime of a pattern block—whatever that was.

5. A bronze quadruped likely to be from Houma now in the Freer Gallery (Thomas Lawton, *Chinese Art of the Warring States Period*, catalogue no. 35, Washington, D.C.: Smithsonian Institution Press, 1982) is one of four or five castings that were almost certainly made from a single decorated model (the other two I have been able to examine at first hand, in the British Museum and the Brundage Collection, match the Freer bronze to the last detail).

6. See Ursula Franklin, "On Bronze and Other Metals in Early China," in *The Origins of Chinese Civilization*, ed. David Keightley, 279–296 (Berkeley: University of California Press, 1983).

7. Chapter 1 of Adam Smith's *The Wealth of Nations* (1776) is the classic description of the efficiency obtainable through division of labor (efficiency long since achieved in the Chinese imperial porcelain kilns at Jingdezhen, to judge by descriptions written in 1712 and 1725 by the French Jesuit Père d'Entrecolles). Henry Ford's article on mass production in the 1947 edition of the *Encyclopaedia Britannica* is equally vivid, though his definition of the term adds an emphasis on interchangeable parts and mechanization.

8. I follow with minor changes the translation given by William Watson in "Chinese Lacquered Wine Cups," *British Museum Quarterly* 21 (1957), 21–25. Similar inscriptions are discussed in chapters 4 and 5 of Wang Zhongshu's *Han Civilization* (New Haven, Conn.: Yale University Press, 1982).

Technological Styles: Transforming a Natural Material into a Cultural Object

Rita P. Wright

This essay differs from most of the others in this volume in that the materials discussed are from a prehistoric context, when there is no recourse to written documents. In it I first discuss some points of similarity and dissimilarity among orientations to the study of "things" from the point of view of an anthropological archaeologist. This section is followed by a discussion of conceptual and physical contexts, which are introduced as potential points of common ground in the study of material culture. As an illustration of their utility, I elaborate on these concepts through a discussion of pottery from the Harappan civilization. This civilization, the material culture of which has been found in present-day Pakistan and parts of India and Afghanistan, reached its classic phase during the second half of the third millennium B.C. Although the civilization possessed a written script, the signs of which are present on small seals used for marking property and occasionally as graffiti on some ceramic objects, it is as yet undeciphered. Consequently, material remains are the first and last resort in understanding the civilization.

It is useful, in the context of the interdisciplinary symposium "History from Things" to discuss at least briefly some of the similarities and differences in research perspectives that were brought to it (for example, in folklore, art history, geography, and so forth), in contrast to my own as an archaeologist trained within the discipline of anthropology. Perhaps most encouraging was that the disciplinary lines that once would have made such a symposium impractical had grown fuzzy. Also striking and indeed one of the objectives of the conference was a common consent to place objects or artifacts at the center of discussions, rather than relying exclusively on oral and written sources. And finally, objects were discussed in their cultural context rather than viewed for their universal or purely aesthetic qualities. These three threads drew the participants together.

Another common theme among the conference participants was a reliance by many on concepts derived from anthropology, but ironically this apparently common ground turned out to be a point of divergence. Although participants apparently were speaking the same language, communication was hampered by a lack of consensus about the meaning of some concepts discussed. A better or more commonly agreed upon understanding of these differences potentially could smooth the way for a more fruitful dialogue in the future, and the following comments are offered in that spirit.

First, the definition of anthropology was restricted to a form of analysis drawn from cognitive anthropology and structuralism. Thus "things," as objects of study, were viewed exclusively as reflections of underlying mental constructs. Moreover, the definition of anthropology was overly circumscribed to include only the attempt to discover a culture's beliefs, values, and attitudes. Although this definition is correct as far as it goes, the analytical parameters of anthropological models are much broader when other models and even the structuralist approach are viewed from the vantage point of archaeologists trained within the discipline of anthropology. In fact, although anthropological archaeologists do seek to discover societies, beliefs, values, and attitudes, the focus of many (if not most) is to move from ideological considerations to an understanding of social relations—that is, the logic and coherence of the rules or order that govern the conduct and social organization of a particular society. Second, although some archaeologists do use the structuralist model in their analysis, many do not, and a further difference emerges if one considers the goals of archaeologists who use other models of anthropological analysis. In them objects (material culture) are viewed in the context of other factors—for example, adaptations to ecological circumstances such as in cultural ecology and systems theory or as keys to sociopolitical organization (Trigger 1989:28), as is the case in settlement pattern studies.

The use of these different models in archaeology may be a reflection of the different circumstances under which archaeologists encounter the objects they study. My third point, then, is that the tools of the archaeological trade differ significantly from those of the other disciplines. Most archaeologists see their materials for the first time within the context of field excavations (essentially a world of dirt and mundane things—for example, remnants of walls of buildings, house floors, hearths, things left where used or discarded) rather than as single objects in a museum context. Working within a field context, they naturally gravitate to questions about the various groups that inhabited the sites they excavate. In encountering objects in the context of a craft-producing area, their questions may relate to social relationships in the workplace, the home, the wider world of commerce, and the exchange of ideas and products, as well as particular aspects of social relations: What impact did the artisan and the artifact have on society? What place (with respect to status or wealth) did the artisan occupy in the society? How were the products distributed or exchanged within the society? And how did distribution systems affect societal developments? In other words, the artifact more often than not stands in a relationship to other associated artifacts found within a specific context (a room within a household or administrative storage center, for example).

Finally, because many archaeologists work in societies for which there are no written documents, they must rely on concepts and analogies derived from the study of living cultures to interpret the archaeological evidence. This orientation to materials is comparative in that inferences about prehistoric societies rely on analogies either as representative of a type of social organization (a band, a tribe, or a chiefdom, for example), as a direct analogy thought to be descendant of the archaeological group being studied, or as a cross-cultural analogy based on the similarity of the environmental-ecological setting or some other factor. Hence, the dialogue between the artifact and the archaeologist does not involve a world of words. This is a significant difference from other conference participants, since many of their analyses rely, in the end, on oral or written histories to boost their conclusions.

That said, I would like to turn to two arenas that constitute potential points of common ground. First, I discuss and redefine two concepts— conceptual context and physical context—drawn from the works of Henry Glassie. Second, I review the use of structuralism by some prehistoric archaeologists and historians and demonstrate its utility in the Harappan context. Its principal aim is to demonstrate how structuralism, when combined with other lines of evidence, can provide an important tool in drawing out social factors.

CONTEXTUAL AND STRUCTURAL ANALYSIS

The contextual analysis of materials is, in general, associated with cognitive anthropology and structuralism. In a paper he provided before the conference, Glassie outlined a program of contextual analysis in which eight contexts were defined.[1] I want to discuss just two of these contexts— the conceptual and the physical—and redefine them for use with objects found in prehistoric settings. A conceptual context, as defined by Glassie, refers to the creator's mind. Because my own interests are in prehistoric technologies, I have narrowed the conceptual context to refer specifically to the act of production by the artisan and the technological manipulation of materials. Specifically, my use of the terms refers to the production choices made by an artisan in transforming a natural material into a human creation. The second context, the physical, refers here to the association of the object out of its original, conceptual context as it moves from producer to consumer, out of the workshop and into its use context. In other words, after an object is created it moves into a new realm, both spatial and temporal, as it becomes associated with other objects and a social world of individuals who possess the object. In that sense the focus is not on the thing, the artifact, but on its makers and users as a window into social relations. It is as "things-in-motion" (Appadurai 1986) within the context of the social place of the artisans and users that the analysis derives its meaning. Thus the artifact is less a text to be read than a story to be told or unfolded about the social impact of the actions of people and their manipulation of objects through space and time. In asking such questions as where the creators and users of the products fit into the social structure of the society, the object is a prop for discerning these relations.

These definitions are more in line with my previous comments on the broader goals of anthropological archaeology—that is, to move from attitudes and values to an understanding of the social dynamics of the groups being studied.

As I indicated earlier, archaeologists do use models from cognitive anthropology and structuralism in their analyses of prehistoric materials.[2] However, unlike the definitions of conference participants, these archaeologists define the goals of structuralism to conform more closely to the discipline of anthropology as a whole. In that sense, although influenced by cognitive anthropology, an American and British invention, and structuralism from the works of Claude Lévi-Strauss, a French anthropologist, their studies represent a significant modification of these other models.

Archaeologists who use structural analysis in prehistoric contexts attempt to infer aspects of social organization. One field in which research has been directed toward this goal is the study of Paleolithic art, where the approach dates to the early work of Leroi-Gourhan, although originally it had more limited goals than as currently practiced. Leroi-Gourhan was interested in "the underlying structural or generative principles for the making and placing of specific images on cave walls" (Conkey 1989:135). Later, other archaeologists used structuralist principles in the study of mobile artifacts, such as bone and antler implements and figurines.

These archaeologists brought two new elements to their studies. One element was the archaeological context (chronology, site stratification, and so forth), which had been missing from Leroi-Gourhan's work. The second element, more directly relevant to this paper, was social action. As Conkey has shown in an extensive and perceptive review of the structural analysis of Paleolithic art, in Leroi-Gourhan's attempts to evaluate the place of cave art in a socioecological context he stopped at imagery and did not provide, in Davis's words, a " 'genuinely social analysis of particular cultural products/artifacts' " (Conkey 1989:151). A major shortcoming was its lack of a "referential context of social action, no actors, intentions, reasons, or query into why this particular kind of structural mythogram might have been meaningful to these particular makers-users-viewers" (Conkey 1989:145).

In partial response to these omissions, some archaeologists working in the Upper Paleolithic—for example, Conkey—have used cognitive and structural analysis as a more direct reflection of the social relations within a society. Here the principal goal has been to define the stylistic attributes of a group of objects, a type of analysis discussed by several of the conference participants but again with significantly different (in my sense, more limited) goals. Defining stylistic traits, or the formal characteristics of particular objects, is a staple in archaeology in that artifact typologies are routinely used to define the spatial limits of a particular type of material. These spatial divisions define the object within the context of a particular "archaeological" culture. A corollary to this is delimiting the boundaries of cultures on maps.[3] Archaeologists who follow Lévi-Strauss draw on principles from structural linguistics to elucidate the structural principles under which an artifact comes into existence. These derived principles are their entry point into elaborating on the way in which style works to maintain boundaries of inclusion and exclusion. Thus it is a primary mechanism in the identification and membership in a particular social group and the exclusion from others. As Conkey (1989:148) puts it, "If artifact style were rooted in the deep semantic structure of a cultural system . . . then there is a more substantive basis for the pursuit of style as a part of the processes of (social) boundary formation, mediation, and maintenance."

My principal point in reviewing the structuralist model in Paleolithic analyses is to widen the more limited perspective that views anthropology as an attempt solely to discover a culture's beliefs, values, and attitudes so that it includes one that takes as its central aims a social analysis. The Paleolithic examples suggest that the process of production and use of an object represent "generative principles" that are cognitive maps not only of ideological conceptions but also of social action. In archaeology these maps of social action are suggestive of strategies (whether conscious or unconscious) of social identity around which boundaries among different groups are structured. In that sense material culture is not neutral but plays "a central role in the ideological representation of social relations" (Conkey 1989:151).

One other example of a cognitive-structural analysis is the research of Keightley (1987), a historian working on pre-Shang China. His analysis is of particular relevance to this discussion because it deals with a prehistoric complex society that more closely matches the Harappan context than the less complex hunter-gatherer societies of the Upper Paleolithic. Moreover, it explicitly attempts to infer elements of social structure present in the pre-Shang through an analysis of its material culture. His discussion of Chinese Neolithic pottery has provided me with the inspiration to work through a similar scheme for Harappan pottery.

A central premise of Keightley's approach is that the technology a people practice and the forms they create are a reflection of the social structure of the society in which the objects are produced. He develops this premise in the context of prehistoric China, in which a series of stylistic and technical traits are linked to the thought and behavior of inhabitants directly antecedent to the Shang state.[4] Specifically, he assumes that the relatively more complex social structure of Neolithic groups on the East Coast, rather than those from the Northwest, provided a direct impulse for a general pattern of stratification in the Shang civilization.

A second assumption is that between material and social life there is what might be termed a transference of principle from acts and habits that are manifest in one area of life to another area, even though this transfer may be unconscious. Keightley states: "The way people act influences the way people think and . . . habits of thought manifested in one area of life encourage similar mental approaches in others" (1987:93). The technology or way in which people manipulate materials, for example, can be linked to social process; thus pottery and other artifacts can reflect "*social structure* [italics added] and cultural expectations" (1987:93).[5]

Keightley develops his analysis in the context of a variety of factors, but here I emphasize the technical aspects of pottery, especially those related to manufacture and use. Of particular interest are inferences based on the artisans' manipulation of materials—that is, the conceptual context. For example, East Coast potters created a diversity of forms—dishes, bowls, jars, dishes and bowls on tall stands, tall stemmed goblets (*bei*), and bowls built on tripods (*ding*), to name a few—by joining segments of pots together and imposing a number of design elements that extended clays beyond their workability range. Creating these forms involved the separation and assembling of parts of objects, experimentation, and a complex technology. These factors reflect a set of social relations in that production involved coordination and scheduling, a cooperative work force, and communication among producers. In contrast, Northwest potters produced a restricted range of forms—elaborate bowls, dishes, and jars—and although some of these vessels were made by joining segments together, potters made every effort to conceal their joins. Here, the emphasis appears to be on harmony and unified shapes in contrast to the discontinuities accentuated on the East Coast, where, according to Keightley, "pots explicitly revealed the process by which they were made" (1987:99).

The differences outlined are the result of technical manipulations in production but reflect intellectual orientations to materials. Although to some degree these differences may be the result of differing levels of technical expertise or available resources, they go deeper than this. According to Keightley, they reflect basic, deeply embedded concepts of social structure. On the East Coast they suggest a technical, bureaucratic impulse that is componential and prescriptive and in which experimentation was highly valued. In contrast, the Northwest orientation is more holistic; it reflects a less radical impulse to change and a greater acceptance of natural clay qualities. Whereas on the East Coast work groups were composed of cooperative units, in the Northwest they were personal and perhaps isolated.

Keightley also considers the physical context. Here, the primary difference between the East Coast and Northwest is specificity of function in contrast to a generalized, all-purpose quality of the pottery. Specificity of purpose reflects a general requirement of accuracy and specialization. Keightley reasons that if pots were designed for specialized purposes, then ". . . greater differentiation in pottery would have resulted from a more socially differentiated society" (1987:108). For the East Coast the wide variety of forms implies not only specific purpose but also a concern with fit, constraint on use, and thus a right and wrong use for objects to which only some people had access. For the Northwest, in contrast, the more limited number of forms implies vessels of general purpose, manipulated in the context of less constrained and more generalized use and access.

Finally, Keightley links both the conceptual and physical context to "mentality." Although he admits he is on "disputed ground" in doing so, this final step is consistent with his central premise that a transference of principle from conceptual and physical contexts reflects a shift from a relatively undifferentiated set of customs to differentiated ones. By enhancing those signs of differentiation in the objects themselves and also in the "mental realm" (1987:94), they ultimately reveal for the East Coast

> a world view that was fundamentally controlled, precise, measured, standardized, mathematical, componential, articulated and differentiated. And the special, fragile quality of some of the East Coast vessels, together with the impressive amounts of labor required to produce the jades, further suggests a world that was more hierarchical, a world in which certain finely made objects were reserved for special functions and, presumably, for special people. Craftsmen were not only working to prescribed plan. They were working for others. (Keightley 1987:112)

As a prescription for life they translate into a more egalitarian ethic in the Northwest in contrast to the strong, intellectual pressure to expand and build evident among the incipiently stratified communities on the East Coast.

This review of Keightley's work provides the basic framework for my attempts to examine Harappan pottery as a reflection of more general attitudes in Harappan society. These efforts, which frankly are experimental, I hope will provide a window into Harappan social structure and also a critique on where the method fails and where it is useful in the Harappan case.

I devote the remainder of this paper to the development of some examples of contextual and physical contexts, using ceramic artifacts from the Harappan civilization, a civilization that coexisted with ancient Mesopotamia and pharonic Egypt in the last half of the third millennium B.C. The Harappan civilization is best known from its two major cities, Harappa and Mohenjo-daro, but in addition to these large settlements there were numerous towns and villages, principally along the Indus river and its tributaries but also in contiguous as well as distant regions. Its vast geographical spread beyond the Indus River in Pakistan and into parts of Afghanistan and India make it the largest early civilization and one that rivaled its contemporaries in geographical extent.[6]

CONCEPTUAL AND PHYSICAL CONTEXTS OF HARAPPAN POTTERY

One central issue in Harappan studies (Harappan civilization is synonymous with the Indus Valley civilization) today is understanding the transformations occurring in Harappan society as a result of the change from village to city life. This transformation occurred at approximately 2500 B.C. in the Indus Valley. Three factors frequently cited as central to this process are the production, distribution, and exchange of products. Large-scale pottery production, as well as other crafts, and evidence of the trade or exchange of pottery, for example, are cited as manifestations of these changes, although we are only just beginning to understand how they affected social life.

My entry point into the discussion is the technology of prehistoric pottery. In my own work with pottery I have tried to consider both its stylistic and technological dimensions, since stylistic factors are affected by technological constraints. However, having defined an artifact's style, I find it useful to separate it from its technological style. By technological style I refer to the production techniques that transform natural materials into cultural objects and the production sequences carried out in producing them—that is, the conceptual context.[7] In ceramic studies technological styles are grouped according to the specific technical choices potters make in the production process. These sequences and choices can be combined in a variety of ways, depending on the overall morphology and design elements desired in the final product.

The reconstruction of ancient technologies is carried out in a kind of miniexcavation in which pots are first examined macroscopically for morphological characteristics, such as shape and form, and for indications of manufacture, such as tool marks and so forth. Later, they are examined microscopically, and samples of pottery are subjected to more detailed analysis of factors not visible with the naked eye—for example, chemistry of pigments used in decorative paints, temperatures reached in kilns, and so forth. The result is an articulation of both the object's physical attributes as a final product and the creative process, beginning with the collection of raw materials to the final stages of manufacture.[8] In this sense I find the separation of conceptual and physical contexts useful.

The Harappans produced a variety of pottery types (more than one hundred types are known during the urban phase of the Harappan civilization), which range from miniature jars to forms that had an external height of 90 centimeters and a maximum body diameter of the same dimension (Dales and Kenoyer 1986). The techniques used in producing pottery vary; some pottery was produced on a potter's wheel using a method in which a large amount of wedged clay was placed on the wheel and pots were thrown "on the hump." The method was extremely efficient in that a single piece of wedged clay could be used to produce several vessels (see fig. 1 for examples). Other vessels produced by the Harappans involved a more elaborate technology with respect to production sequences. These vessels were produced in sections, sometimes in two or three parts and then joined together (see fig. 2, for example). Sections were made either in molds or directly on the potter's wheel. Because individual pieces could not be moved while the clay was plastic and because clay shrinks as it dries and there were optimum dry and wet times in which to join segments, Harappan potters exercised considerable scheduling, planning, and control in producing these objects. How these methods provide insights into social relations will be discussed in more detail later.

Figure 1 illustrates several typical Harappan cylindrical forms that

Fig. 1. Harappan cylindrical forms. Photograph by Charlotte Schmid-Meybach.

*Fig. 2. Harappan ledge-shouldered and small and medium jars. Photograph
by Charlotte Schmid-Meybach.*

potters produced in a range of sizes (with respect to ratio of height to
maximum body diameter), indicating a considerable variation in volume
capacity. Perhaps as a result of the repeated throwing of the same vessel,
in which a rhythm of work and movement was established, the vessels
were standardized in their shapes. The production sequence was simple
and efficient. Small and taller cylinders were raised "on the hump" and
simply lifted from the wheel, dried, and later kiln fired. No adding of
handles or surface texture or finishing occurred. Traces of the actual
process of manufacture, however, are still present. Especially evident are
thumb and other finger marks; no effort was made to conceal these imprints, just as the visible mark of the string with which they were removed
from the wheel was not smoothed over or trimmed.

The surfaces of vessels are plain, and the basic form is unmodified.
The only elements that might be considered decorative, with the exception
of the form itself, are specks of mica that reflect off the surface of the
vessel. In fact, mica is present in the pastes of practically all Harappan
vessels, although it may be partially concealed when slips or decorative

motifs are applied to their surfaces. Although the presence of mica no doubt reflects the available clays (it may have been added to clays, but many clays in the area already contain micas), potters clearly would have noticed its reflective qualities on the surfaces of the final products.

Other common shapes are the two forms shown in figure 2. These vessels ranged from miniatures to 14 centimeters in height. Again, the same shapes were made, but the ratio of height to width varied. The shapes are drawn on the wheel into a basic cylinder, after which the tops of jars are collared and necks and rims turned. When the pots were leather hard (hard enough not to be deformed by handling but pliable enough to scrape the surface), the pot was inverted on the wheel, its base as well as its sides trimmed to its maximum body diameter. Above this point it was smoothed to the neck, leaving a velvety surface. Between the maximum body diameter and the base the surface was scratched, and diagonal lines were made in preparation for the application of a cream slip, or wash. The pot was dipped into the slip up to (or just above) its maximum body diameter; in some cases the slip was scraped away, revealing the clay body in raised areas and slip in depressed ones; in others the slipped vessel was left as it was.

The result is a surface that fires to a rose paste, contrasting with a lighter surface superimposed upon it. Thus a simple shape was created in a variety of sizes, and then color and textural contrasts were applied to its exterior. In both cases the rose color and cream slip applied over roughened surfaces contrast and call attention to manipulation of the surface. Combining changes in color and texture enhances visualization of the production process and highlights the deep permanent marks made on the clay in their creation.

The jar illustrated in figure 3 is one example or variant of large, painted jars produced by Harappan potters. They differ in size (some may be as tall as 90 centimeters with the same maximum body diameter), but what they have in common are their componential construction, the elaborate decorations on their exteriors, and the quality of their fine and detailed painting. Smaller versions of the type were produced on the potter's wheel but were modified, either through the use of the paddle-and-anvil technique or through the joining of whole components. Some large vessels were constructed in molds or on the potter's wheel and consisted of two or three components joined together. These vessels represent exceptional achievements in that they required pushing clays beyond

Fig. 3. Harappan painted jar. Photograph by Charlotte Schmid-Meybach.

their normal limits, both in conceiving the shapes to be produced and in the planning, scheduling, and coordination required to achieve the ideal envisioned. Sections had to be dried and rejoined with precision and at optimal times. Great care was taken to smooth over the surface joins on the exposed exterior, but only just to the inside of the vessel opening on the interior, as far as can be seen at eye level. As anyone who has tried to move one of these vessels can attest and as the multiple steps in the production sequence suggest, it seems reasonable to assume that several individuals were involved in producing them.

The forms were decorated with a red slip prepared from hematite or highly ferruginous clays and applied to the entire surface. A second mixture of paint-slip to achieve a different color was prepared from iron oxide or manganese oxide, and some simple lines and forms were applied with the pot on the wheel as it was turned. More detailed designs were applied after this initial painting. They were developed in registers, using a combination of geometric and natural motifs. The fish-scale motif seen in figure 3 shows how the Harappans accommodated a natural motif to the created form. Motifs of this kind were applied to contoured surfaces, in this case enhancing the three-dimensional illusion. Other motifs applied in registers typically were natural designs derived from flowers, leaves, and so forth, as shown in figure 3. There is clear evidence of considerable precision in assembling the parts of these vessels and an explicit intention to transform shapes and motifs taken from nature into a human vision.

Figure 4 illustrates what might be called the ultimate Harappan clay form, the dish-on-stand. Of all Harappan pottery these stands probably required the most deliberate handling and preplanning to allow for the clay's shrinkage properties. They were constructed in two pieces, the lower half on the potter's wheel in one operation and left to dry, and the dish or bowl formed and joined to the base in separate operations. Success in producing the form is totally dependent on centering the object throughout the different parts of the process of building and rebuilding, again stretching the limits of materials and what can be accomplished on a potter's wheel. They reveal a shaping of clay in new ways, extraordinary technical skill, great care in clay preparation, and significant experimentation.

INTELLECTUAL TRENDS AND SOCIAL STRUCTURE

As I indicated in my introduction, cognitive and structural analyses are dependent on patterns in material culture, and it is possible to detect several clearly discernible patterns from this analysis of Harappan pottery. First, the forms created emphasize the restructuring of materials and juxtaposing of shapes, textures, and colors. Examples are the many forms that required building segments of pots in components and fitting those components together. This production sequence effectively imposed a new

Fig. 4. Harappan dish-on-stand. Photograph by Charlotte Schmid-Meybach.

structure on the natural clays and pushed them beyond their normal workability range. Second, the forms required substantial vision in their conception and planning and a drive (perhaps a need) to experiment with known techniques. In doing so the potters transformed a limited number of known forms to ones beyond what was previously known. In other words, in conceiving new forms potters seem not to have been restricted by the limits of the known techniques; instead they conceived of ways to combine techniques to realize their new vision. And third, this new vision required and demanded precision and control that challenged the skills they possessed.

This ability or need to impose change and control natural materials is apparent also in decorative motifs. Examples are the recreation of natural forms known from their environment to ones that bear the clear stamp of a human conception. The fish motif referred to earlier, which was not applied to flat, two-dimensional surfaces such as on the interior of dish forms and thus was not rendered as static and a mere representation of its original form, was instead recreated on a shape that replicates the three-dimensional qualities of the original. It was a totally new, human creation in that its body was restructured from clay. This same imposition of order is evident in other representations of animal forms by enclosing them within registers. Other natural forms, such as geometrics, were recombined and woven together in interlocking but still naturally orderly designs. Perhaps the ultimate transformation, which was in fact a technical skill developed several millennia earlier, is the use of natural pigments to achieve color effects. Natural pigments were transformed and exploited by the control of temperatures and atmospheres in kilns; here is a direct and clear imposition of the human hand and mind, a sort of taming by humans of nature and mastery of their natural environment.

Potters drew attention to this transformation by roughing up surfaces (as in figure 2), by burnishing exteriors, thereby giving them a lustrous quality (as in figure 3), and by painting exquisite designs that drew attention to them. Although less straightforward (or perhaps I should say more speculative) is the use of micaceous pastes, which I believe effectively conveyed the same message (drawing attention to transformations) and emphasized the mastery of potters of the clay system.

These same qualities can be found in their physical context. First, common to many Harappan pots is production of a single form in a wide range of sizes, implying that they were used for different purposes. Obviously, the production of a single shape in a variety of forms indicates specialized function not only of the form itself but also of the variation of size in which it is produced, even if only to suggest different quantities of the same product. The forms also vary in their archaeological context, but some are made for funerary purposes; many (but not all) examples such as that shown in figure 1 lack evidence of wear and are found in burial contexts. Most likely, they contained liquids or other substances before they were placed in graves, although no one has as yet attempted an analysis of the function of the forms illustrated (or any other Harappan form for that matter). We do know that they often are present in graves, that some are found great distances from the Harappan heartland, and that when they are found at Harappan and even at non-Harappan sites they are remarkably standardized in size and design. The Harappan dish-on-stand is found in a variety of contexts, including graves; there is no indication of how they were used, but clearly whatever was placed on them was meant to be elevated, set off the ground, and made clearly visible. Thus the variation of vessels, shapes, and forms clearly implies different functions, even if we do not know what those functions were. The kinds of restrictions on handling and use that Keightley had discussed for the East Coast pre-Shang are present here. And again, like the pre-Shang, they imply an enriched vocabulary to name them and handle them in different ways, because they needed to be lifted in specific ways to avoid breakage or spillage and damage to their contents. Extraordinary care and precision are necessary in handling the dish-on-stand to avoid the disassembling of its parts. Implied here are the same "channels of constraint," in which seemingly insignificant differences (height, presence or absence of carination, and textured surface) constrain the way a pot is used and imply a right and wrong use and handling.

These conceptual and physical examples of Harappan pottery closely fit although they do not conform exactly to an orientation to the natural and material suggestive of the kind of "intellectual pressure" that Keightley (1987:113) found in the pre-Shang East Coast, an interpretation that does not stretch beyond what is evident in the production and use of the vessels themselves. The only assumption here is that potters knew what they were doing and were in control of their final product.

Can we move from our examples of potters, who transform earthly things beyond what had been conceived before by breaking down natural elements and restructuring them, to social life? Was this impulse to transform and control nature evident in other walks of life?

If we are to move from these generalizations to mental constructs or speculations about social structure, it is useful to examine other crafts and the archaeological context of production to assess whether these same orientations were present in other arenas. It might be argued, for example, that the transformations described are always the case when working with clay. At the minimum we can look briefly at the logic of the production of other crafts and go beyond the objects themselves to the archaeological contexts in which they have been found.

OTHER CRAFTS AND ARCHAEOLOGICAL CONTEXTS

There are many illustrations of the same impulse to break down and recreate and transform materials in other ceramic products and in stone work (Vidale 1989:180). With respect to ceramics we have two examples. Stoneware bangles were made in a complex process in which clays were selectively refined and fired at extremely high temperatures in enclosed jars (Halim and Vidale 1983). The product is a hard, uniformly textured surface; when broken, some have a "glass-like fracture." Similarly, faience production required breaking down and rebuilding materials—crushing and grinding quartz pebbles, mixing them with other substances, shaping them by hand or in molds, and then firing them[9] (Kingery and Vandiver [1986:9] discuss faience manufacturing process). Stone working also provides examples of the restructuring of the natural stone into a totally new form. Steatite beads were produced by grinding the soft stone into powder, reshaping the paste into microbeads, and firing them to restore hardness (Vidale 1989:178). This process contrasts with the less complex and less transformative method, also practiced, of sawing fragments of steatite to produce beads. The production of ornaments from carnelian also involved a reconstructive process in which chalcedony was transformed to a uniformly reddish color by refiring the stone in a reducing atmosphere. In each instance—faience, stone bangle, microbead, and carnelian production—there is a clear intent to reconstruct the natural into the human product beyond what might have been expected. As Vidale has put it:

> In all Harappan craft production, a major emphasis is placed on the creation of artificial substances more than the employment of precious, well recognizable raw materials. Even gold in some of the richest hoards is present no more frequently than silver and electrum, and it is often mixed with other metals. Chalcedony was fired red and chemically colored; clays and minerals were transformed into beautiful ceramics and glazes; steatite was the technological pivot of an extremely wide range of complex pyrotechnological treatments, the result of a hybridization of lithic and ceramic technologies. (1989:180)

These examples reinforce my argument about pottery production in that here we find the same impulse to transform natural products into a humanly altered material. Moreover, each craft suggests the same need for scheduling and planning, precision, and intimate knowledge of materials described for Harappan pottery production. Stone that is worked and chipped can be set aside, for example, but the restructuring of steatite and chemical alterations in firing stone require more sustained attention and coordination to accomplish the several steps in the manufacturing process.

Another dimension that should be considered is the archaeological context of production because it provides additional insights into social relations. In this discussion I have assumed that the mere handling of the vessels, not to mention the multiple steps required in their creation, required more than one producer and thus cooperative units of producers. This interpretation conforms to the archaeological evidence in at least three Harappan urban contexts—Chanhu-daro, Mohenjo-daro, and Harappa—where we have been able to identify a number of craft-producing workshops.

Although our current understanding of how such workshops were organized is poorly developed, production contexts known from the archaeological record suggest five possible systems of organization. One type of workshop consists of small-scale workshops located on the margins of urban sites, such as Mohenjo-daro, where rows of separate workshops for the production of various crafts, possibly a craft quarter (Bondioli et al. 1983:9ff.), have been found. Most of these workshops were successively replaced by different crafts over time, and there is no evidence of administrative control, suggesting groups of independent producers. A second type of separate workshop at Mohenjo-daro, however, does show evidence of bureaucratic control. This evidence is in the form of seal impressions embedded on the saggars in which stone bangles were fired (Halim and Vidale 1983). A third type of workshop, also found at Mohenjo-daro, is isolated kilns and other craft-producing debris within dwelling areas, again suggestive of small, independent units of producers (Vidale 1989:178). A fourth type is represented by a specialized pottery production area at the site of Harappa not directly associated with dwelling areas. Production in this area is restricted to a limited number of forms, and there is consistency in the production technologies used, suggesting sustained and continuous transmission of prescribed patterns of manufacture over a substantial period and thus a stable group of producers (Wright 1991). A fifth type known from the early excavations at Harappa by Vats (1940:58) consists of the remains of a metal-working area found in association with "workmen's quarters." This association is similar to the architectural units at the center of the site of Chanhu-daro that have been described as a series of "warehouse-cum-workshops" in which a variety of crafts, but not pottery, was produced. These production areas also suggest "economic or administrative control" (Vidale 1989:180).

This reconstruction of the archaeological context and the organization of production is wholly in keeping with the complex social structure inferred from the structural analysis of pottery, since it implies a degree of social differentiation among producers. Our current understanding of these workshops indicates that some crafts were administratively controlled while others were not. The principal point is that different crafts were absorbed into the urban environment in different ways if we compare the metal-working area at Harappa with the pottery workshops or the stone bangle–producing workshops at Mohenjo-daro with the pottery production at Harappa or Mohenjo-daro. Thus in urban contexts producers were artisans who were independent producers as well as directly controlled by a centralized administration.

HOMOLOGIES AND ANALOGIES

Where, then, does this leave us in our understanding of the Harappans? It is generally agreed that studies in which archaeologists are dependent on material culture alone (as in the Harappan case) will require research methodologies that differ from those for which there are written documents, ethnohistorical or direct historical analogies. Here, I have attempted to broaden the basis on which to infer aspects of social organization by combining a structural analysis with the archaeological contextual evidence.

A major problem in resolving questions about social organization in Harappan studies is the lack of written documents[10] or any other direct evidence (for example, ethnohistorical accounts or direct historical analogies with living peoples in the region) to support or refute our interpretations. Although in Harappan studies there is a long tradition of using direct analogies and more recent attempts by Kenoyer (1989) in working with craft producers have provided an important new direction in the study of production processes, inferences based on direct analogies of social organization can be only speculative in view of the long time span between the collapse of the Harappan civilization (ca. 1800 B.C.) and the present.

These questions lead us back to Keightley's interpretations of pre-Shang social structure, for his interpretations are apparently derived solely from the analysis of material culture, although they show a fit with other archaeological evidence. Chang (1986:295), for example, has described the same period as one in which "increasing differentiation among the populace in economic wealth and political power" occurred. The fit, then, between Keightley's structural analysis of the ceramic evidence and Chang's based on other lines of evidence suggests that the approach has validity and that to some extent the materials speak for themselves.

One significant caveat, however, is that to a large extent Keightley's (and Chang's) analysis is based on a direct analogy. Although in the pre-Shang periods written accounts are absent, reliable textual sources exist for the later Shang (Chang 1986:296). Both Keightley and Chang use these later sources as a general framework for understanding the material culture of antecedent periods; in other words, they assume a homologous relationship between the Shang and the pre-Shang. The later Shang sources thus provide a basis on which to propose tendencies to thought systems, meanings, values, and beliefs and the kind of stratification that he imputes to the pre-Shang.

The research methods for material culture studies in the Harappan context must accommodate themselves to a more severely limited set of evidence. My own limited and incomplete attempt at structural analysis here does show a fit between the formal properties outlined and other interpretations based on the archaeological evidence. I have tried to show by developing multiple lines of evidence to complement the structural analysis that the method is useful in studies of early civilizations such as the Harappans. First, as Conkey has pointed out, we can safely state that material culture is not "neutral" in that it is a product of human categorization (1989:151). Second, if we accept that artifacts are "meaningfully constituted cultural products," then it may be possible to access their social referents using Keightley's methodology but without the more direct documentation used in the Shang case. Third, the inclusion of other archaeological evidence provides an independent and in this case a converging line of evidence from which to assess the results.

Scholars have developed their studies of material culture in a variety of contexts, but major divisions exist in their methods depending on the range of evidence available for study and their theoretical orientations. In this paper I have emphasized the division between scholars who have recourse to written sources and those who do not, and I have introduced different models from anthropological archaeology. One aim of the paper has been to outline the specific problems in studies in which material culture alone is the primary source of evidence and develop a common set of concepts. I have illustrated these points through a study of the technological style of Harappan pottery.

A large portion of the paper was drawn from the work of Keightley (1987); in drawing on Keightley, my goal has been to investigate the utility of structural analyses of materials as a window into social relations in contexts in which written documents are absent. Although I am fully aware of the numerous problems[11] with the analysis presented here and its need for considerable refinement, I have suggested that the structural analysis of materials combined with other lines of evidence, such as a discussion of a range of objects and their archaeological context, could provide archaeologists with a potent new line of evidence against which to test their interpretations. It is a suggestion presented in the spirit of the ideas discussed at the "History from Things" symposium and in the essays contained in this volume.

NOTES

Fieldwork and analysis were conducted as part of the University of California, Berkeley, project at Harappa, funded in part by the Smithsonian Institution Foreign Currency Program and the National Geographic Society. Three leaves of absence, one supported by The College of William and Mary while I was a member of the faculty there and two others by a fellowship granted by the John D. and Catherine T. MacArthur Foundation while I was on the faculty at New York University, made it possible to conduct fieldwork at Harappa. I am indebted to these institutions for making this research possible. I owe special thanks to George Dales, director of the Harappa project, J. Mark Kenoyer, co-director, and Richard Meadow, acting director, for inviting me to participate at

Harappa and for facilitating my work there. Finally, I thank Dr. Ahmad Nabi Khan, director general, the Department of Archaeology, Government of Pakistan, for the privilege of working at this very important site. I am most indebted to Ivan Karp for introducing me to David Keightley's work and to Keightley for the inspiration provided by his splendid paper and comments on an earlier draft of this paper.

1. These concepts were outlined in a preconference paper provided by Glassie, which was not discussed at the conference itself. Instead, he provided us with a richly textured ethnography of Turkish artisans with whom he is currently working. For that reason I have not gone into detail about the several different contexts he outlined. My own interest here is in redefining two of them for use with archaeological materials. I found that the conceptual and physical contexts stimulated my own thoughts on material culture, although the terms took on meanings different from Glassie's original formulations.

2. Archaeologists working in historical archaeology—for example, Leone (1977), Deetz (1977), and Fritz (1978)—also use these models; I have concentrated here on prehistoric contexts in that I have tried to emphasize major differences in working with cultures for which written records do not exist.

3. There is an extensive literature on this topic; for examples, see Conkey (1978), Plog (1980), and Wobst (1977).

4. I sincerely hope that David Keightley will not be offended by this brief summary of his article. In the original article he synthesizes a great deal of evidence from the Chinese sequence and presents an elegant argument— elaborate, detailed, and complex—which is presented in summary form here.

5. In addition to the works of cognitive anthropology, Keightley's analysis follows that of other archaeologists who study technological styles. They take a related point of view, the best examples of which are from the works of Lechtman (1977). In an early paper on this topic she and Steinberg drew an analogy between technologies and the visual and musical arts, stating that technological styles, as did other arts, reflected cultural preoccupations that were expressed in " 'the very style of the technology itself' " (quoted in Lechtman 1977:4). Later, Lechtman expanded on the concept through a more detailed definition and through illustrations from her own work on ancient Peruvian metals. If a technological style represents manifestation of a pattern and if a variety of techniques is available in a manufacturing process, the process selected—assuming that a variety of techniques is known, appropriate raw materials are available, and so forth—to the exclusion of others, the technological style ("the formal integration" of a set of "behavioral events" [1977:7]), might not the technology, as Leone had suggested (1973), but an expression of underly-

ing cultural patterns that transmits principles integral to the cognitive map of that society. She states:

> . . . what lay behind the technological style were attitudes of artisans towards the materials they used, attitudes of cultural communities towards the nature of the technological events themselves, and the objects resulting from them. The basis of Andean surface enrichment systems lies in the incorporation of the essential ingredient into the very body of the object. (Lechtman 1977:10)

There are many similarities between Lechtman's orientation to materials and Keightley's approach to Chinese ceramics, although his work is more specifically focused on the translation of actions and conceptions of the artist to formal qualities of social structure. Lechtman's work moves directly to ideological conceptions of order rooted in religious concepts, apparently bypassing social structural phenomena, although this may reflect more the materials and nature of the civilization she studies than any difference between her work and Keightley's.

6. For an overview of the development and collapse of the Harappan civilization, see Allchin and Allchin (1982).

7. The term "technological style" is used in other ways in the anthropological literature. Lechtman (1977), for example, defines technological styles as the reflection of a kind of cognitive map shared by the artisan and his or her culture. The act of production is a kind of "technological performance" and represents something that is "not communicable verbally" (1977:13).

8. For discussions of the approach, see Arnold (1988), Kingery and Vandiver (1986), Olin and Franklin (1982), Rice (1987), Rye (1981), Shepard (1965), and Wright (1989).

9. Faience beads were noted for the Indus civilization in the first reports of excavations at Mohenjo-daro (Marshall 1931).

10. There have been many attempts, past and ongoing, to decipher the Harappan script. Today, there are numerous claims to decipherment but no consensus. Even when the text is deciphered, however, it is not likely to provide us with the kind of rich details known from Mesopotamian or Egyptian textual evidence. The writing that has come down to us is on seals that contain only a few signs; this reflects either the extent of the messages that the Harappans wished to convey or possibly that the writing of more complex messages is recorded on other media with poor preservation qualities and is now lost to us.

11. I am not implying that there is a simplistic link between orientations to materials and general thought processes within a society; I have proposed that

structural analysis may provide an additional line among multiple other lines of evidence. Many problems exist with this suggestion: For example, it is obvious that materials crosscut different social groups and therefore may represent ideologies of specific groups; that particular materials may be produced for quite specific social or ritual functions and therefore may not be universally used within a society; and ultimately that delineating formal properties and interpreting their meaning can never be conducted as a scientific enterprise but rather must remain a humanistic endeavor.

REFERENCES

Allchin, Bridget, and Raymond Allchin. 1982. *The Rise of Civilization in India and Pakistan*. Cambridge, England: Cambridge University Press.

Appadurai, Arjun. 1986. *The Social Life of Things*. Cambridge, England: Cambridge University Press.

Arnold, Dean E. 1988. *Ceramic Theory and Cultural Process*. Cambridge, England: Cambridge University Press.

Bondioli, Luca, Maurizio Tosi, and Massimo Vidale. 1983. "Craft Activity Areas and Surface Survey at Moenjodaro." In *Interim Reports, Vol. 1*, edited by M. Jansen and G. Urban, 9–38. Aachen, Germany: Forschunsprojekt Moenjodaro.

Chang, K. C. 1986. *The Archaeology of Ancient China*. New Haven, Conn.: Yale University Press.

Conkey, Margaret. 1978. "Style and Information in Cultural Evolution: Toward a Predictive Model for the Paleolithic." In *Social Archaeology*, edited by C. L. Redman et al., 61–85. New York: Academic Press.

———. 1989. "The Structural Analysis of Paleolithic Art." In *Archaeological Thought in America*, edited by C. C. Lamberg-Karlovsky, 135–52. Cambridge, England: Cambridge University Press.

Dales, George F., and Jonathan Mark Kenoyer. 1986. *Excavations at Mohenjo Daro, Pakistan: The Pottery*. Philadelphia: University of Pennsylvania Museum.

Deetz, James. 1977. *In Small Things Forgotten*. Garden City, N.Y.: Anchor Press, Doubleday.

Fritz, John M. 1978. "Paleopsychology Today: Ideational Systems and Human Adaptation in Prehistory." In *Social Archaeology*, edited by C. L. Redman et al., 37–60. New York: Academic Press.

Glassie, Henry. 1975. *Folk Housing in Middle Virginia*. Knoxville: University of Tennessee Press.

———. 1982. *Passing the Time in Ballymenone: Culture and History of an Ulster Community*. Philadelphia: University of Pennsylvania Press.

Halim, M. A., and Massimo Vidale. 1983. "Kilns, Bangles and Coated Vessels: Ceramic Production in Closed Containers at Moenjodaro." In *Interim Reports, Vol. 1*, edited by M. Jansen and G. Urban, 63–98. Aachen, Germany: Forschunsprojekt Moenjodaro.

Keightley, David. 1987. "Archaeology and Mentality: The Making of China." *Representations*, no. 18 (Spring): 91–128.

Kenoyer, Jonathan Mark. 1989. "Harappan Craft Specialization and the Question of Urban Segregation and Stratification." Paper delivered at the annual meeting of the Society for American Archaeology, Atlanta, Georgia.

Kingery, W. David, and Pamela B. Vandiver. 1986. *Ceramic Masterpieces*. New York: The Free Press.

Lechtman, Heather. 1977. "Style in Technology: Some Early Thoughts." In *Material Culture: Styles, Organization and Dynamics of Technology*, edited by H. Lechtman and R. Merrill, 3–20. St. Paul, Minn.: West Publishing Company.

Leone, Mark P. 1973. "Archaeology as the Science of Technology: Mormon Town Plans and Fences." In *Research and Theory in Current Archaeology*, edited by C. L. Redman, 125–150. New York: John Wiley.

———. 1977. "The New Mormon Temple in Washington, D.C." In *Historical Archaeology and the Importance of Material Things*, edited by L. Ferguson, 43–61. Special Publication Series no. 2. Society for Historical Archaeology.

Marshall, Sir John. 1931. *Mohenjo-daro and the Indus Civilization*. London: Arthur Probsthain.

Olin, Jacqueline, and Alan D. Franklin. 1982. *Archaeological Ceramics*. Washington, D.C.: Smithsonian Institution Press.

Plog, Stephen. 1980. *Stylistic Variation in Prehistoric Ceramics: Design Analysis in the American Southwest*. Cambridge, England: Cambridge University Press.

Rice, Prudence M. 1987. *Pottery Analysis. A Sourcebook*. Chicago: The University of Chicago Press.

Rye, Owen S. 1981. *Pottery Technology*. Washington, D.C.: Taraxacum Press.

Shepard, Anna O. 1965. *Ceramics for the Archaeologist*. Publication no. 609. Washington, D.C.: Carnegie Institution of Washington.

Trigger, Bruce G. 1989. "History and Contemporary American Archaeology: A Critical Analysis." In *Archaeological Thought in America*, edited by Clifford C. Lamberg-Karlovsky, 19–34. Cambridge, England: Cambridge University Press.

Vats, M. S. 1940. *Excavations at Harappa*. Bombay, India: Bharatiya Publishing House.

Vidale, Massimo. 1989. "Specialized Producers and Urban Elites: On the Role of Craft Industries in Mature Harappan Urban Contexts." In *Old Problems and New Perspectives in the Archaeology of South Asia*. Wisconsin Archaeological Reports, vol. 2, 171–182. Madison: Department of Anthropology, University of Wisconsin.

Wobst, H. Martin. 1977. "Stylistic Behavior and Information Exchange." In *Papers for the Director: Research Essays in Honor of James B. Griffin*, edited by C. E. Cleland, 317–342. Ann Arbor, Mich.: Anthropological Papers.

Wright, Rita P. 1989. "New Tracks on Ancient Frontiers: Ceramic Technology on the Indo-Iranian Borderlands." In *Archaeological Thought in America*, edited by C. C. Lamberg-Karlovsky, 268–279. Cambridge, England: Cambridge University Press.

———. 1991. "Patterns of Technology and the Organization of Production at Harappa." In *Harappa Excavations 1986–1990: A Multidisciplinary Approach to Third Millennium Urbanism*, edited by Richard H. Meadow, 71–88. Madison, Wis.: Prehistoric Press.

The Biography of an Object: The Intercultural Style Vessels of the Third Millennium B.C.

C. C. Lamberg-Karlovsky

Specific classes of artifacts within the ancient Near East play an inordinately important role in reconstructing past cultural processes. Among these the inscribed tablets are most significant, indicating the privileged position held by written documentary evidence. Perhaps second to tablets for reconstructing patterns of time, space, and technological development has been pottery. Cylinder seals, metals, glass, seeds, and bones, to mention but a few others, have devoted advocates emphasizing their centrality toward an understanding of the ancient Near East. In recent years the entire archaeological site has become a class of artifact enabling a reconstruction of settlement and demographic patterns (Adams 1981). Indeed, to some scholars the classes of artifacts to be analyzed are entire civilizations (Saggs 1989).

Fig. 1. Representative examples of carved intercultural style vessels, ca. 2200 B.C., from Tepe Yahya. Peabody Museum, Harvard University. Photograph by Stephen Burger.

In this essay I take a simple class of artifact, the intercultural style of carved chlorite vessels, and trace the various historical-cultural interpretations given to this corpus over the past three-quarters of a century. The intercultural style vessels are stone bowls with elaborately incised decorative motifs (fig. 1). The stone selected for the production of these bowls is typically a talclike mineral, variously referred to in the literature as soapstone, steatite, or chlorite. The outer surface of the vessel is deeply incised, resulting in a complex variety of motifs in raised relief on the bowl's outer surface. Specific motifs of the intercultural style are illustrated on the maps. This class of artifact has received considerable attention in the archaeological literature dealing with the ancient Near East for more than seventy-five years. Invariably, all authors have concentrated on two aspects of this object: (1) its extraordinarily wide geographical distribution within distinctive archaeological cultures, from the Indus Valley and Central Asia to Mesopotamia and the Persian Gulf; and (2) its chronological occurrence, variously believed to range from 2800 to 2000 B.C. It is one of the most widely distributed single artifact types within the third millennium of the ancient Near East. The intercultural style vessels have been the subject of dissertations, book chapters, journal essays, and conference presentations over the past several decades. The artifact has lived through numerous interpretations, often of a conflicting nature, making its biography at times wholly schizophrenic.

Particular emphasis will be given in this paper to the importance assigned by various authors to the intercultural style carved vessels and the methods used (if any) to legitimize their interpretations. The study of a class of archaeological artifacts often takes on a role similar to the study of written texts. The archaeologist reads the object; the object itself is conceived of as a sign signifying specific meanings within the cultural context in which the sign is used. The totality of the signs (the full corpus) takes on the analogous form of a text, to be read as a signifier of a particular cultural behavior. A problem of considerable significance is to review the methods used in the study of any class of artifacts. In doing so one must ask what methods were used to permit the class of artifacts to speak for themselves—or, more realistically, be made to pretend to speak for themselves—and to what extent are the artifacts given a voice by the researcher to say what he or she wishes specifically to hear? This is by no means a new conundrum but one given greater epistemological significance in the post-modernist mode of thought (Shanks and Tilley 1987). Because of the emergence of particular schools of archaeology within the past two decades, one can virtually predict the outcome of a research design dependent on the affiliation of the researcher's paradigm, school, and so forth. Thus, it becomes increasingly clear that archaeological interpretations pertaining to identical problems differ according to one's affiliation to specific archaeological methods, whether traditional, "new," Marxist, structuralist, Marxist-structuralist, cognitive-symbolic, ecological-materialist, behavioral, conjunctive, or logicism. Each approach contours a distinctively perceived "reality," frequently juxtaposed against the "reality" perceived by another approach. One need only point to polar opposites, advanced in the interpreted past in the writings of Binford and Hodder, to realize that the epistemological approach dictates the narration of their understanding of that past.

In the 1960s Lewis R. Binford (1962, 1968 with Sally R. Binford) forcefully argued that archaeology must become explicitly scientific and eschew narrative expositions on the nature of the past. He believed such narratives were made credible only by the personal authority of the author. A scientific understanding of the past was believed possible by adopting an explicitly positivist philosophy, along the lines advocated by the philosopher of natural science Hempel (1966)—namely, the nomothetic deductive approach to scientific explanation. Within archaeology, under the leadership of Binford and his followers, this became a dominant paradigm of the 1960s and 1970s; it is referred to as the "new archaeology" or "processual archaeology." The emphasis of this "school" was explicitly materialist, neoevolutionary, and ecologically determinist (Binford 1962).

The rejection of the "new archaeology" is evident in the writing of numerous authors, but the focus of its negation is best articulated in the writings of Hodder (1982, 1986). Hodder has convincingly argued from ethnographically well-documented cases that material culture is not merely a reflection of ecological adaptations or sociopolitical organization but an active factor that can disguise as well as create elements of social organization and behavior. Hodder's emphasis on the symbolic contrasts with processual archaeologists' emphasis on the materialist and gives rise to renewed archaeological interests in the importance of art styles, religious beliefs, cultural traditions, and cosmology, topics that could not be readily integrated into the "new archaeology" emphasis on materialist-ecological concerns. Archaeology remains today balanced between two distinctive approaches: (1) the neoevolutionary perspective, which emphasizes a materialist-ecological directive in search of lawlike processes that pretend to offer explanations for the complexities of cultural evolution, and (2) those archaeologists who emphasize the cognitive, symbolic context of human behavior, underscoring in their approach a hermeneutic quest in which the past will forever be a foreign country. I will attempt in this paper to trace the history of research on the carved steatite-chlorite vessels. In recent years this corpus has come to be known as the intercultural style carved chlorite vessels (Kohl 1978).

The importance and great variety of carved stone vessels in Mesopotamia was first explicitly realized by Edgar Banks in his excavations at Bismya, ancient Adab (Banks 1912). In his 1905 excavations on Mound V, a temple in which he reports various strata containing "bricks of Dungi (Shulgi) and Ur-Engur (Urnammu), the gold of Naram-Sin, and the bricks of Sargon," he found "a series of long, grooved bricks, fifteen in number, telling of at least that many kings who lived before Sargon's time and who took part in the temple's reconstruction" (Banks 1912:237). Within this temple Banks emphasizes the importance in his excavations of a temple dump, "where the priests threw away their broken and discarded vases and other objects no longer required for the temple service." The excavator reports the recovery from this dump of plain, engraved, and inscribed stone vessels of "every conceivable shape" (forty-five shapes are illustrated), made of alabaster, prophyry, onyx, sandstone, marble, and perhaps freestone. One inscription on a blue-green stone (probably steatite-chlorite) contained a reference to "Bar-ki [Mesilim], King of Kish," a contemporary of Urnanshe of Lagash and thus probably of the Early Dynastic IIIa period (ca. 2600 B.C.). This cache of stone vessels, however, is of little chronological value today because they range from Early Dynastic (2700 B.C.) to Ur III (2100 B.C.). Within this cache several vessels can be identified as of the intercultural style, including some with incised motifs containing architectural, animal, and human figures akin to those best documented recently from the island of Tarut, Saudi Arabia (Zarins 1978).

Banks focuses on three considerations that have occupied the interest of archaeologists and art historians to the present day: First, "Where did the inhabitants of the stoneless, alluvial plain obtain the great variety of beautiful material for their vases?" (Banks 1912:262). He points to the presence of the significant place-name Magan, which third millennium texts refer to as their source for obtaining copper and stone. He believed Magan to be the Sinaitic Peninsula; today we know it to have been Oman. Banks also points to Armenia and Persia as regions from which Mesopotamia obtained its stone sources. While recognizing that distant areas were of significance for Mesopotamia's resource base, he opts for the reasonably parsimonious view that "there is no reason why the ancients should have gone far from their own valley for their stone" (1912:263).

Second, "How did the ancients shape their vases?" (Banks 1912:263). There follows a rather minimalist discussion of his observations of chisel marks, lathe marks, polishing methods, and the use of copper cutting implements.

Third, although Banks recognizes that the cache of stone vessels was unlike anything previously found, his final opinion is unequivocal: "They are undoubtedly Sumerian of an early age." Although Banks is rarely referred to in the recent literature, he set the stage for the ongoing concerns relating to the dating of this class of material, its role in trade and exchange, and the cultural identity of the manufacturers. The earliest recognition of the importance of this corpus avoided the issue of its specific date and the mechanisms for its trade or exchange while providing the product with a definite Sumerian identity.

The next important step in the study of this corpus was reported in a letter to *The Times* (March 26, 1932) by Henri Frankfort and two short notes in *Antiquity,* one by Ernest Mackay (1932) and one by Henry Field (1933). Frankfort reported on the recovery of a cylinder seal from Tell Asmar of "Indian workmanship," which was recovered in a house dated to the Dynasty of Akkad, which he dated to 2500 B.C. Also in 1932 Mackay (1932:357) recovered from Mohenjo-daro in the Indus Valley "a fragment of a steatite vase bearing *exactly* the same intricate and very unusual pattern as a double vase of steatite found at Susa." Mackay, following the date offered by M. de Mecquenem for the level in which the Susa vessel was found, provided a date of 2800–2700 B.C. for the lowest level of Mohenjo-daro. More significantly he states: "That the vase of which the fragment from Mohenjo-daro formed a part was an importation from Elam is rendered the more certain by its being a greenish-grey steatite, of which it is the only piece that has been found in the Indus Valley excavations." The assumed similarity of stone type, based on a shared hue and Susa context, was sufficient for Mackay to suggest an Elamite origin, Susa being one of the principal capitals of the Elamite civilization. Banks's earlier Sumerian attribution was thus directly challenged. The Mesopotamian, specifically Sumerian, provenience was renewed within the following year by Field (1933), however. Reporting on three carved steatite vessel fragments recovered from Kish that "bear the same remarkable and intricate pattern as those figured from Mohenjo-daro and Susa," he confirmed a date of 2800 B.C. and stated that they "add yet another link in the chain of cultural evidence for the close interrelation between these early civilizations (Mesopotamia and the Indus) in the early part of the third millennium." The carved steatite vessels played an early and very significant role in cementing the chronological contemporaneity for at least a portion of the Mesopotamian and Indus civilizations. Trade was recognized as the vehicle that brought both civilizations into contact, and the chlorite corpus was contended as being either Sumerian or Elamite. With the recovery of an increasing number of items of this class from Mesopotamian sites, Frankfort's views came to prevail. It is worth quoting his observations on a vessel recovered from Khafaje in Mesopotamia:

> The vase . . . shows a more orderly arrangement. It contains a pair of humped bulls, of the Indian Zebu breed which is not native to Mesopotamia. *But the vase was not imported.* . . . Other elements of the decoration likewise recur on Mesopotamian vessels of steatite. The meaning

of the designs remains obscure. It seems certain that it is in some way concerned with the great natural forces which the *Mesopotamians worshipped.* . . . A long-nosed, long-haired Sumerian figure is seated upon two humped bulls [emphasis added]. (Frankfort 1955:19)

To Frankfort the vessels were clearly Mesopotamian products, manifesting Mesopotamian religious beliefs and depicting Sumerians. Chronologically he placed them within the Early Dynastic II to Akkadian periods, 2800–2300 B.C. This was the prevailing opinion until the 1960s.

In the 1960s four important contributions were made to the study of this corpus: Delougaz (1960), Khan (1964), Durrani (1964), and Herz (1966). Delougaz in his 1960 study undertook a specific review of the hut-pot motif, one of the most characteristic in the intercultural style repertoire (fig. 2). This study is, incidentally, an early example of experimental archaeology within the Near East. Delougaz constructed an architectural model to test his hypothesis on the method and building materials that he believed were used in constructing the dwelling depicted on the vessels and referred to as the hut-pot motif. He concluded that the carved vessels were of religious character, noting their temple context within the archaeological record; were constructed of wickerwork and mats; served as unroofed corrals or sheepfolds; functioned as sacred enclosures for herdsmen; and although found in Mesopotamia were of foreign origin.

In 1964 F. A. Khan, influenced by Sir Aurel Stein's (1937) discovery of this type of carved vessel at Katukan, Khurab, and Bampur in southeastern Iran, states: "It is generally believed that the incised stone ware with 'hut' design originated in the Bampur Valley" (1964:30). Khan takes issue with this "general belief," which was actually advanced by only one scholar, Piggott (1950), and places the origin of this artifact type once again as either Susa (Elam) or Mesopotamia (Sumeria). Perhaps the most useful study undertaken decades ago is that of Farzand Durrani (1964), published in the first volume of a rather inaccessible and poorly distributed journal, *Ancient Pakistan.* In this lengthy study Durrani provides the first catalogue (one with forty-one objects known to him from the literature), a discussion of their archaeological context, and a rudimentary typology of vessel shape and design motifs. This typology distinguished three major types: (1) curvilinear and geometric designs, (2) architectural scenes, and (3) human and animal figures. He indicated that these design motifs on single vessels were not mutually exclusive and accepted the then-common view that within Mesopotamia they date from 2800 to

Fig. 2. Hut-pot motif on incised plaque, ca. 2200 B.C., from Tepe Yahya. Peabody Museum, Harvard University. Photograph by Stephen Burger.

2300 B.C. Of particular interest is his attempt, the first of its kind, to distinguish different centers of production for his three types. Thus, he referred to the second and third groups as of Mesopotamian origin, whereas he speculated that the first group originated in Baluchistan (again following Piggott [1950]). It is clear that the greater numerical presence of the second and third groups recovered from Mesopotamia continued to sway authors to look to that area for their origin.

Discussions pertaining to this class of artifact changed abruptly with the excavations at Tepe Yahya in southeastern Iran. The excavations at Tepe Yahya in the early 1970s led to three specific perspectives.

CHLORITE WORKSHOPS

Excavations at Tepe Yahya recovered more than 150 fragments of carved chlorite bowls of the intercultural style in virtually every stage of manufacture. On certain surfaces of Period IV-2 (ca. 2400–2200 B.C.), hundreds of fragments of chlorite debittage were clustered several centimeters thick and scattered over several square meters. In addition, within 25 kilometers of Tepe Yahya a mine from which chlorite was being quarried was discovered. The presence of this workshop and quarry was first reported in Lamberg-Karlovsky (1970), and a complete catalogue of the intercultural style vessels from Tepe Yahya has been published in Lamberg-Karlovsky (1989).

PHYSICO-CHEMICAL ANALYSIS

With the discovery of a local workshop containing most of the known motifs and vessel shapes and the evidence for the local quarrying of the chlorite as well as the much discussed widespread distribution of the intercultural style, our approach at Tepe Yahya became rather self-evident. An attempt was made to "fingerprint" by X-ray diffraction the chlorite samples recovered from the local mine, the chlorite being manufactured at Yahya, and objects previously recovered from distant sites (Mesopotamia, Iran, Baluchistan, and the Persian Gulf) that were exhibited in different museums around the world. This analytic program was undertaken to establish whether the local mine provided the resource for Yahya's chlorite bowl production; whether the chlorite bowls found on distant sites (for example, Mesopotamia) were derived from production at Yahya; and whether analytical results would permit the full corpus to be clustered into distinctive production centers. This study was undertaken at Brookhaven National Laboratory by Kohl (1975) for his doctoral dissertation with the collaboration of Harbottle and Sayre (Kohl, Harbottle, and Sayre 1980).

The following important conclusions were derived from this study: First, the intercultural style found at Yahya is consistent with local production from the discovered local mines. Second, multiple resources were used to produce the vessels from Bismya (southern Mesopotamia), Mari (northern Mesopotamia), and Tarut and Failaka (both in the Persian Gulf). Alternatively, a single source of great physico-chemical variability was exploited for its production, an unlikely but possible circumstance. Third, chlorites analyzed from Mesopotamia (Nippur, Khafajeh, Kish, and Ur) show a remarkably similar composition but differ from that of the Yahya source. Fourth, chlorite artifacts from the Arabian peninsula fall into two highly distinctive groups, suggesting the exploitation of two different resources. Fifth, less conclusively, a resemblance between chlorites from Susa and Mari, on the one hand, and between those two sites and Yahya, on the other, may suggest an exchange in intercultural style vessels that bypassed southern Mesopotamia.

INTERACTION SPHERES

In 1973 Maurizio Tosi and I attempted to integrate the burgeoning data derived from numerous sites on the Iranian plateau, the Gulf, Baluchistan, and Central Asia by introducing the concept of interaction spheres. In the resulting paper (1973), by comparing similar ceramic types, the differential distribution of specific mineral resources, interdependent settlement, and subsistence patterns, we offered "in a preliminary fashion our view that sites on the distant Mesopotamian periphery— that is, the Iranian plateau—were not "dependent upon Mesopotamia through a process of diffusion but through an *internal* and *interdependent* urban process . . . an economic and social dialectic provided the feedback which contributed toward the integration of Mesopotamia *and* the sites of the Iranian Plateau." Further research in the Gulf, Central Asia, and northern Mesopotamia has expanded the geographical scale and cultural complexity of these interdependent interaction spheres.

In the same year in which this article was written de Miroschedji (1973) undertook an important study of the carved vases and objects of steatite (chlorite) in the Louvre Museum, Paris. In this study he differentiated a "series ancienne," consisting of what Kohl (1974) was later to term the "intercultural style" and dated to the Early Dynastic I/IIIA period, 2800–2500 B.C., and a later "series recente," of different shapes and design motifs, which Miroschedji dated to Old Akkadian–Isin Larsa times, 2500–2000 B.C. Zarins (1987) has recently suggested that the "series recente" represents objects produced from Arabian and Omani sources. Cleuziou (1981:279–294) has further added to these a third chlorite vessel type, the "series tradif," dated to after 2000 B.C., which like the "series recente" differs fundamentally, save for the use of the same type of stone, from the decorative motifs of the intercultural style.

Only within the last decade have various models using the intercultural style corpus been proposed to elucidate the economic networks uniting Mesopotamia to the distant reaches of the Iranian plateau and beyond.

Before these models the distribution of intercultural style vessels was simply posited as the by-product of trade. The nature and form this trade took was not explicitly addressed. Four major though not necessarily mutually exclusive views have been expressed.

The first, which I explicitly contoured, used the production of chlorite bowls at Tepe Yahya to suggest the existence of a market network operating within specifically defined interaction spheres. This market network expressed the existence of private entrepreneurial activity in which specialized production of such goods as chlorite vessels at Yahya, lapis lazuli production at the contemporary site of Shahr-i Sokhta in eastern Iran, and metal production at Tal-i Iblis in southern Iran conformed to mechanisms of supply and demand in the distribution of these specialized commodities on the Iranian plateau. Second, I suggested that the existence of such a market network resulted in the presence of an unbalanced exploitation in which Mesopotamia used its known agriculture surplus to obtain mineral wealth from the Iranian plateau. Third, I made an analogy to the third-millennium written epic "Enmerkar and the Lord of Aratta" as a textual echo for the existence of long-distance trade being documented in the emergent archaeological record (Lamberg-Karlovsky 1972, 1975; Lamberg-Karlovsky and Tosi 1973). Supplementing this perspective was a series of essays by Kohl (1978, 1979, 1989). Influenced by the views of Wallerstein (1974, 1980) and economic dependency theorists, such as Frank (1967), Kohl introduced the concept of core-periphery relations between Mesopotamia and the distant regions of the Iranian plateau and Central Asia. Kohl, while cautiously examining the core-periphery thesis, also viewed the context of trade within a market network but one in which the "highland settlements or other peripheral zones occasionally became locked into unequal exchange relationships (with Mesopotamia and Khuzistan) for both internal and external reasons," which are further detailed in his essay (Kohl 1989:228).

The recognition of the importance of trade and the interaction that united resource-poor Mesopotamia with the resource-rich highlands is at least as old as the writings of Sir Leonard Woolley (1934). His insights, derived from his excavations at the royal cemetery of Ur, where he recovered vessels of the intercultural style, are worth recounting:

> The raw material of nearly everything found in the graves is foreign
> to the Mesopotamian delta and had to be imported. The pottery of
> course is local, made in the kilns of Ur from the clay of the river-

banks, the dresses would have been of local cloth, but the gold came
from abroad, probably from the gold-bearing rivers of many lands,
the silver from southern Persia and from the mountains of the North,
the bronze from Oman, copper necessarily from foreign mines wher-
ever they might be, lapis-lazuli from the Pamirs, conch-shells from the
Persian Gulf, and from the Gulf also the fine white calcite of which so
many vases were made, and the carnelian for their beads; malachite
for eye-paint, hardwood for inlay, diorite for cups, and steatite for
cylinder seals, all had to be brought from afar, and though some of
these things might be spoil won in war and some tribute paid by con-
quered neighbours, most of it must have come by way of trade and for
what the merchants of Ur had to pay.

A people whose natural wealth was in flocks and herds, in grain
and dates, could not by the barter of these carry on so widespread
and wholesale a trade as would account for the material riches which
the offerings in their graves attest: wonderfully fertile though their
soil might be, grain is too bulky a thing for its distant export to have
paid very high profits, and as for cattle and sheep and goats, the
whole Valley of the Two Rivers was as rich in these as Ur, and even
the upland pastures right across to northern Syria were more than
self-sufficing, and only in the East could there be any market. The
explanation of the whole matter is this: that while the raw materials of
the things we find is of foreign origin, the things themselves are unquestionably of Sumerian make. Already in the fourth millennium Ur
was a great manufacturing city; for all these imported goods she paid
in manufactured articles, and the wealth of her citizens is the measure
of the skill of her craftsmen. Of that skill we are now in a position to
judge, and it is not difficult to believe that the products of Sumerian
workshops would find ready customers amongst the semi-barbarous
peoples of the outer world.

It is clear, then, that in order to pay for the gold and the lapis
and all the things that the Sumerian worker required for his craft the
Sumerian export trade went far afield and had to be well organized.
(Woolley 1934:394–395)

A challenge to the view of a market network and private entrepreneurial
activities as responsible for the trade of intercultural style vessels has
been recently advanced by Possehl (1986:75–80). Possehl issues his challenge on two grounds: (1) "good evidence for demand for these exotic
materials within eastern Iran" (thus, "it is unnecessary to even consider
Mesopotamia and Elam"); and (2) his belief in a model of "complimentary

reciprocity" as operating within a "closed, localized phenomenon," in which the intercultural style vessels were "consumed within an idiom of local ritual behavior." While Possehl challenges the formalist position for the existence of a market network, he also rejects the substantivists' position for the existence of "a fully developed redistributional system." In rejecting both formalist and substantivist models for economic behavior (see Polanyi et al. 1957), Possehl states, "It is this organic, undifferentiated nature of some economic behavior which appears to be revealed by the Iranian data. These were economic arrangements firmly integrated within more social configurations" (1986:79). Possehl's reflections on Marshall Sahlin's distinctions between trade and exchange, New Guinea commodity networks, the *kula* ring, and "Enmerkar and the Lord of Aratta" add little to a deeper understanding of the trade-exchange mechanisms known to have economically united eastern Iran, Mesopotamia, the Indus Valley, the Persian Gulf, and Central Asia at the end of the third millennium. Possehl's argument led to the obvious fact that economic relations are merely a part of more complex social relationships. Certainly, there was regional exchange within eastern Iran, and just as certainly there was long-distance exchange between this area and Mesopotamia as well as Elam and the Persian Gulf. There is absolutely no reason to restrict the existence of market networks and private and state merchants, documented for contemporary Mesopotamia, and simply characterize the periphery—that is, the Iranian plateau—as a backward non-market mentality (Powell 1977).

In this context it is important to recall Steinkeller's important study on the cultural geography of Iran in the third millennium:

> The extant cuneiform documentation suggests that the land of Marhaši was a major political and economic power in 3rd millennium Western Asia, which controlled the eastern section of the Iranian plateau and acted as an intermediary between Mesopotamia and Elam in the west and Meluhha in the east. (Steinkeller 1982:263)

The "land of Marhaši" mentioned in the late third millennium B.C. texts is convincingly identified by Steinkeller as located in the region of southeastern Iran. Thus, the community of Tepe Yahya, with its production of chlorite bowls of the intercultural style, would be one town located in the "land of Marhaši." The region of Meluhha, mentioned by Steinkeller, is generally believed to refer to the Indus civilization. Thus, Marhaši, a "major political and economic power," acted as an intermediary in the economic relations that directly involved such distant civilizations as Mesopotamia and the Indus Valley. More specifically, there are two decorated chlorite bowls in the intercultural style bearing inscriptions commemorating the Mesopotamian King Rimus's victory over Elam and Marhaši. That some form of vague exchange, which Possehl characterizes as a "relatively undifferentiated economic system" (1986b:79), characterized eastern Iran is totally negated by numerous third-millennium texts contemporary with the intercultural style corpus. Marhaši—specifically, eastern Iran—was the Mesopotamian source for numerous gems and indeed the principal source for duh-ši-a (possibly agate), by the Mesopotamians' own textual reckoning one of the three most valued gems within Mesopotamia (the others were lapis lazuli and carnelian). Lastly, Steinkeller (1982) has even suggested that the mineral called markušu or markašu, a soft stone for the making of bowls, whose name is derived from the country of its origin (Marhaši), is to be identified with chlorite-steatite. Possehl (1986:78) is correct in viewing "these commodity networks . . . in a highly social context, tightly woven within a set of other relationships." Those other relationships included major warfare between the kings of Akkade and Marhaši, the marriage of Mesopotamian royal daughters to Marhaši kings, diplomatic gifts between the kings of Mesopotamia and Marhaši, and market exchange involving gems, animals, and plants (Steinkeller 1982).

Recently Amiet (1986, 1988), with his incomparable knowledge of Elam, has made several observations directly pertinent to the role of intercultural style in economic interaction. Amiet (1988:131) has suggested that the manufacture of chlorite bowls at Tepe Yahya was undertaken by "semi-nomadic artisans . . . at a time perceptibly contemporaneous with Agade," around 2400 B.C. He further states that "it is tempting to designate the art form which is manifested in the chlorite objects, and hence, the whole culture it illuminates, as *archaic* Marhaši art and culture. . . . We shall refer to this culture as *early trans-Elamite*" [italics in original]. Amiet is clearly unhappy about my designation for the chlorite bowls; "it has been haplessly defined as a simple 'intercultural style' whereas it is in fact outstanding evidence of the strong cultural personality of its promoters" (1988:131). Clearly Amiet (1988:134) may be correct that the manufacture of chlorite bowls "suggests the existence of an artisan type of nomadism"; this suggestion promotes yet another context for an understanding of the mechanisms of their trade-exchange. As for the later "series recente" square-based chlorite flasks, he promotes their function as involving the transport of perfumes, "thus providing indirect evidence of a commerce of which we are almost totally oblivious."

Amiet's belief that "the production of chlorite vessels, which we readily locate in eastern Iran, was in any case exported in two opposite directions, to Susa, and to Bactria (Central Asia), where some remarkably similar flasks have been found" (1988:131) is one that I fundamentally disagree with. This in turn takes us back to the "hapless" term "intercultural style." Amiet offers the very specific term "archaic Marhaši" of the "early trans-Elamite culture" for the origins of this class of object. Kohl's analyses (1980) quite clearly indicate the presence of numerous production centers, including ones beyond southeastern Iran (that is, beyond archaic Marhaši). Are we to believe that the intercultural style from Tarut Island in the Persian Gulf, whose analysis shows to be clearly derived from their own local production centers, are products of "archaic Marhaši" of the "early trans-Elamite culture"? How are we to explain that virtually none of the chlorite analyzed from Mesopotamia could be shown to come from the single production site known from "archaic Marhaši," namely, Tepe Yahya. Are "semi-nomadic artisans" from Marhaši responsible for the wide distribution of this type, from the recently discovered intercultural style object with a hut-pot motif from Gonur Tepe in Soviet Turkmenistan to Tarut in the Persian Gulf? This appears to be highly unlikely. The term "intercultural style" was adopted precisely to emphasize that this type of material was produced by and found within the context of several distinctive cultures. One of these cultures was most certainly Marhaši, but the extraordinary feature of the intercultural style is the fact that it was produced and used within several distinctive cultures over a very wide geographical expanse. The reason for its intercultural use has perhaps to do with its function, which has escaped notice by virtually all who have commented on this material, save for Amiet's suggestion that the later chlorite vessels of "series recente" type served to contain perfume.

In the early years publications addressing the significance of this corpus were restricted to observations noting its wide distribution and importance to trade yet offered neither a typology of shapes nor an iconographic study of its design motifs. Speculations on the functional use of these objects and the mechanisms of trade and exchange were conspicuously absent. With the discovery of the production site of Tepe Yahya attention quickly shifted, as we have noted, to models of trade and exchange mechanisms. A typology of shape, a study of designs, and the functional utility of the objects continued to be ignored until recently (Lamberg-Karlovsky 1989). In this study of 544 chlorite vessels I suggested that the intercultural style, given its frequent association with burials and temples, "has a highly charged symbolic content pertaining to religious attitudes of death and burial." One must ask whether such an artifact enters into trade-exchange networks in the same manner as grain, metal, or other utilitarian commodities. Can a context-specific object pertaining to death and burial, an object related to a major *rite de passage*, be used to support world systems or gift exchange in the same manner as the more mundane commodities of grain, metal, textiles, and so forth? I do not think so. I would suggest that this object type represented a shared ideological and ritual significance to peoples of different cultures over a very wide area united by the specific belief system that the vessels symbolize. Objects of ritual and symbolic significance circulate within an economy in a very different manner than do commodities of a more mundane nature. It is precisely because they are so symbolically charged that they have such a wide distribution and are used by people within different cultures united in a common belief that the objects convey. That there was a mosaic of religious and ritual ideology throughout the Near East, subject to changing configurations, is well known (Jacobsen 1987). We suggest that during the several hundred years that this material was used it acted as a signifier, uniting people within different cultures that shared a particular cultic belief system pertaining to death and burial. The use of this material to support formalist or substantivist models of trade-exchange must take into consideration its archaeological context and function (burial and temple offerings). Whether produced by seminomadic Marhaši artisans or placed in the tombs of Sumerian queens such as Puabi, the extraordinary significance of these objects rests in uniting various peoples who shared a particular ideology of death and burial. This alone justifies the use of the term "intercultural style" and cautions against its facile use to support particular models of economic behavior.

Further evidence suggesting the importance of these objects to rituals of death and burial has recently been found in Shahdad, in southeastern Iran, and pertains to one of the most frequent motifs carved on the vessels, the hut-pot motif. At Shahdad numerous intercultural style vessels were recovered from elaborately appointed tombs (Hakemi 1972). More significant, Hakemi (1987) has recently published the existence of mud-brick architectural units, standing 80 centimeters to 1 meter in height, which served as headstones for the tombs. The headstones had carved or painted on their surface the typical hut-pot motif, consisting of three recessed doorjambs with down-curved lintels, identical to the designs carved on the chlorite vessels. This discovery unequivocally associates the motif with a burial context.

Over the decades surprisingly little attention was given to the nature of the design motifs carved on the surface of the intercultural style vessels. Frankfort, in the passage quoted earlier, thought the "meaning of the designs . . . obscure." As did all authors wrestling with the meaning of this corpus, he simply assumed that the designs referred to aspects of a cosmic theology fundamental to their religious beliefs. Emberling (1987) has attempted to unravel the meaning of these incised motifs by charting the incidence of specific motifs that occur in combination with different motifs. He attempted to unravel the "grammar" of meaning in the combining of distinctive motifs to determine the extent of randomness versus formalism in the iconography. The results of the analysis indicate the presence of two dominant motif clusters, one involving motifs associated with the hut-pot and a second involving the snake motif. In Mesopotamia and Elam the snake was an ambiguous symbol, symbolizing both death and rebirth. It is thus not surprising that the snake should be a central motif on objects pertaining to rituals of death, burial, and perhaps rebirth. The presence of architectural headstones depicting the hut-pot, recovered from burials at Shahdad, has already been noted. Specifically what this architectural facade symbolizes remains enigmatic; perhaps it is a motif symbolizing the home of the dead or the palace of one's afterlife. Certainly the motifs incised on the intercultural style vessels represent a formalized design structure representing a complex belief system readily comprehended by the artisans who produced them and the people who consumed them in Mesopotamia, the Persian Gulf, and the Iranian plateau. It is perhaps not unreasonable to suggest that behind the wide distribution of this type of incised vessel rests the archaeological evidence for the theological mosaic that the written texts tell us characterized the third millennium of the Near East. Where the archaeologist recovers a vessel of the intercultural style there exists a person or group adhering to the tenets of the cultic belief that the vessels symbolize.

The biography of this class of object has had a long and rich interpretive existence. At various times these objects have served as support for the existence of private entrepreneurial markets, as objects for reciprocal exchange or gifts among related kinsmen, as products made by nomadic artisans, and as elite goods extracted from peripheral peasants by the clever Mesopotamians who dumped their surplus grain on the exploited periphery. To these we add yet another interpretation, which archaeological context can clearly support—their use for rituals of death and burial.

The biography of the intercultural style indicates that it has led a long and richly varied life. Above all, its biography indicates that science and knowledge are cumulative. All recent interpretations rest on what was said and known within an earlier context. In the early part of this century it was simply impossible to discuss market networks, trade, and exchange when the distribution of this class of artifact was so imperfectly understood. When its wide distribution was partially realized, about 1950, discussions immediately turned to mechanisms of its trade. Without the benefits of a developed material science approach in archaeology, one could not turn to techniques of X-ray diffraction, neutron activation, and so on to determine its regions of provenience. Similarly, the serendipitous discovery of a chlorite workshop at Tepe Yahya added a great deal that simply could not have been predicted without the excavation of the site. The compilation of a comprehensive catalogue undertaken by Lamberg-Karlovsky (1989) was similarly not new but an additive effort to that first undertaken by Durrani in 1964. What, then, have we added to the ongoing biography of the intercultural style? The following points I believe are of significance and enrich the biography of this class of artifact.

First, there can be little doubt that the intercultural style carved chlorite vessels were in use in the ancient Near East from at least 2600 B.C. to 2200 B.C. Earlier theories that attempted to restrict their occurrence to a narrower time frame are simply not supported by the archaeological record. The intercultural style vessels are found over a wide geographical area throughout this time period. Further research, however, is necessary to determine whether there was a chronological sequencing of its popularity within different geographical or culture areas.

Second, physical-chemical analyses provide a coherent story regarding their production; the intercultural style vessels were produced in numerous geographically and culturally distinctive areas. Within southeastern Iran the site of Tepe Yahya is clearly involved with their production, while the manufacture of intercultural style vessels in the Persian Gulf differs from the resource used for their production at Tepe Yahya. Equally significant is the fact that the geological resources used for the production of this type of vessel in Mesopotamia, though still of the soapstone variety, differs from that known from both Tepe Yahya and the Persian Gulf. It can be said with considerable conviction that numerous production centers were involved with the manufacture of this distinctive artifact.

Third, the intercultural style vessel has long been regarded as an artifact of special functional significance. The specific nature of that functional significance, however, has been elusive. Typically it has been referred to as a ceremonial or ritual object. Our compilation of a comprehensive catalogue of objects in the intercultural style (Lamberg-Karlovsky 1989) led to an obvious observation: The greatest majority of this type of artifact was recovered from an archaeological context involving burials and temples. Though a far more detailed contextual and statistical study is required, I do not hesitate, given the evidence, to suggest that the intercultural style vessel had a direct participatory involvement with rituals and beliefs pertaining to death and burial.

Fourth, the challenge to the "new archaeology," with its emphasis on materialist explanations, led to a new concern for the meaning of art styles and symbolism. In this respect Kohl's work (1979, 1989), which focused on resource procurement and production centers, emphasized the materialist approach. Little attention was given to archaeological context; thus, the results elucidated in my third point were entirely overlooked. Similarly, no attention was given to the importance of the meaning of the iconography. My own research has indicated that there is a degree of standardization and formalism in the reliefs carved on the vessels (Lamberg-Karlovsky 1989). Such standardization and formalism indicate that in the numerous centers of production, geographically separated by thousands of kilometers, a shared ideology of meaning was manifest in the identical production of complex design motifs. A study of their archaeological context—burials and temples—together with an analysis of their identical design motifs occurring within distinctive archaeological cultures spread over thousands of kilometers suggests to me the existence of a shared belief system involving rituals and beliefs pertaining to death and burial.

Fifth, there is the question involving the social context for the distribution of these vessels. Were these vessels distributed through the mechanisms of formal markets involving supply, demand, prices, and so on or through exchange systems involving redistribution, reciprocity, or the exchange of luxury goods as gifts among elites? All earlier arguments emphasized materialist concepts and polarized formalist and substantivist models for the working of an ancient economy (Polanyi et al. 1957; Possehl 1986). Within this materialist context virtually all authors ignored the specificity of this object's archaeological context and function—namely, its dominant presence in burials and temples and its role in rituals of death and burial. Given the specific symbolic significance of this artifact, its distribution need not conform either to formal models of economics or to mechanisms of exchange theory. Behavior dealing with one of the great *rites de passage* of human existence—specifically, death—suspends the rationality on which theories of market and exchange systems operate (van Gennep 1909; Hodder 1982).

These five points add to our appreciation of both a materialist conception and a symbolic appreciation of one of the most widely disseminated objects of the late third millennium in the ancient Near East. Most significant, perhaps, we learn that in deriving a history from things we can come to the appreciation that the messages encoded in things are multiple and complex and that an emphasis on a single attribute of the thing is but part of its biography. In this context the research that emphasized the materialist aspects, detailing resource procurement and the mechanisms of trade and exchange, unfolded an important element in the biography of this object. My own emphasis on the symbolic significance of the design motifs and their archaeological context and function has focused on a different side of its personality. The two distinctive approaches are not mutually exclusive nor in fact contradictory but entirely complementary. The results derived from both perspectives contour a richer biography and a deeper understanding of this class of object. Doubtless this is not an epitaph pertaining to the biography of the intercultural style, for much remains to be understood. This paper represents my own confrontation with a single class of object over the course of twenty years. We have come to appreciate and comprehend its biography in a far more complex manner. Still, important questions continue to elude us. Perhaps someday an archaeologist will recover one of these objects and answer one of the most elusive questions of all: What did these vessels contain?

REFERENCES

Adams, Robert McC. 1981. *The Heartland of Cities*. Chicago: University of Chicago Press.

Amiet, Pierre. 1986. *L'Age des échanges inter-iraniens, 3500–1700 B.C.* Editions de la Réunion des Musées nationaux. Paris: Ministère de la Culture et de la Communication Edition de la Réunion des Musées nationaux.

———. 1988. "Elam and Bactria." In *Bactria Oasis Civilization*, edited by G. Ligabue and S. Salvatori. Rome: Erizzo Editrice.

Banks, Edgar James. 1912. *Bismya or the Lost City of Adab*. New York, G. P. Putnam.

Binford, Lewis R. 1962. "Archaeology as Anthropology." *American Antiquity* 28:217–225.

Binford, Lewis R., and Sally R. Binford. 1968. *New Perspectives in Archaeology*. Chicago: Aldine.

Cleuziou, Serge. 1981. "Oman Peninsula in the Early Second Millennium B.C." In *South Asian Archaeology*, edited by Herbert Hartel. Berlin: Dietrich Reimer Verlag.

Delougaz, Pierre. 1960. "Architectural Representations on Steatite Vases." *Iraq* 22:90–95.

de Miroschedji, Pierre. "Vases et objets en stéatite susiens du musée du Louvre." *Cahiers de la Delegation Archéologique Française en Iran* 3:9–80. Paris: Association Paleorient.

Durrani, Farzand. 1964. "Stone Vases as Evidence of Connection Between Mesopotamia and the Indus Valley." *Pakistan Archaeology* 1:1–50.

Emberling, Geoffrey. 1987. "Trade and Ideology in Third Millennium Mesopotamia: A Reconsideration of the Intercultural Style." Bachelor's honors thesis, Department of Anthropology, Harvard University.

Field, Henry. 1933. "Steatite Vases from Kish." *Antiquity* 7, no. 25:84–85.

Frank, Alex Gunder. 1967. *Capitalism and Underdevelopment in Latin America: Historical Studies of Chile and Brazil*. New York: Monthly Review Press.

Frankfort, Henri. 1955. *The Art and Architecture of the Ancient Orient*. Baltimore: Penguin Books.

Hakemi, Ali. 1972. *Catalogue de l'exposition: Lut Xabis (Shahdad)*. Premier Symposium Annuel de la recherche Archeologique en Iran. Tehran: Iran-Bastan Museum.

———. 1987. " 'Les Marquettes de Shahdad': Modèles de bâtiments sacrés du troisième millénaire." In *Fragmenta Historiae Aelamicae*, edited by L. DeMeyer, H. Gasche, and F. Vallat. Paris: Editions Recherche sur les Civilisations A.D.P.F.

Hempel, Carl. 1966. *Philosophy of Natural Science*. Englewood Cliffs, N.J.: Prentice-Hall.

Herz, Alexandra. 1966. "A Study of Steatite Vases of the Early Dynastic Period in Mesopotamia." Master's thesis, Institute of Fine Arts, New York University.

Hodder, Ian. 1982. *Symbols in Action: Ethnoarchaeological Studies of Material Culture*. Cambridge, England: Cambridge University Press.

———. 1986. *Reading the Past*. Cambridge, England: Cambridge University Press.

Jacobsen, Thorkild. 1987. *The Harps That Once . . . : Sumerian Poetry in Translation*. New Haven, Conn.: Yale University Press.

Khan, Farid A. 1964. *The Indus Valley and Early Iran*. Memoir 4. Karachi, Pakistan: Department of Archaeology and Museums.

Kohl, Philip L. 1975. "Seeds of Upheaval: The Production of Chlorite at Tepe Yahya and an Analysis of Commodity Production and Trade in Southwest Asia in the Mid-Third Millenium." Ph.D. diss., Harvard University.

―――. 1978. "The Balance of Trade in Southwestern Asia in the Third Millennium." *Current Anthropology* 19, no. 3:463–492.

―――. 1979. "The 'World Economy' of West Asia in the Third Millennium." In *South Asian Archaeology*, edited by M. Taddei, 55–85. Naples: Istituto Orientale.

―――. 1989. "The Use and Abuse of World Systems Theory: The Case of the 'Pristine' West Asian State." In *Archaeological Thought in America*, edited by C. C. Lamberg-Karlovsky, 218–240, Cambridge, England: Cambridge University Press.

Kohl, Philip L., Gar Harbottle, and Edward V. Sayre. 1980. "Physical and Chemical Analysis of Soft Stone Vessels from Southwest Asia." *Archaeometry* 21:131–159.

Lamberg-Karlovsky, C. C. 1970. *Excavations at Tepe Yahya, Iran, 1967–1970*. American School of Prehistoric Research, Bulletin no. 27. Cambridge, Mass.: Peabody Museum, Harvard University.

―――. 1972. "Trade Mechanisms in Indus-Mesopotamian Interrelationships." *Journal of the American Oriental Society* 92, no. 2:222–230.

―――. 1975. "Third Millennium Modes of Exchange and Modes of Production." In *Ancient Civilization and Trade*, edited by J. A. Sabloff and C. C. Lamberg-Karlovsky. Albuquerque: University of New Mexico Press.

―――. 1989. "The Inter-Cultural Style Carved Vessels." *Iranica Antiqua* 23:45–95.

Lamberg-Karlovsky, C. C., and Maurizio Tosi. 1973. "Shahr-i Sokhta and Tepe Yahya: Tracks on the Earliest History of the Iranian Plateau." *East and West* 23, nos. 1–2:21–53.

Mackay, Earnest. 1932. "An Important Link Between Ancient India and Elam." *Antiquity* 6, no. 23:356–357.

Piggott, Stuart. 1950. *Prehistoric India*. Harmondsworth, England: Pelican Books.

Polanyi, Karl, Conrad M. Arensberg, and Harry W. Pearson. 1957. *Trade and Market in the Early Empires in History and Theory*. New York: Free Press.

Possehl, Gregory L. 1986. *Kulli: An Exploration of an Ancient Civilization in South Asia*. Durham, N.C.: Carolina Academic Press.

Powell, Marvin A. 1977. "Sumerian Merchants and the Problem of Profit." In *Trade in the Ancient Near East*, edited by Jack Hawkins, 23–30. London: British School of Archaeology in Iraq.

Saggs, Harold E. W. 1989. *Civilization before Greece and Rome*. New Haven, Conn.: Yale University Press.

Shanks, Michael, and Christopher Tilley. 1987. *Re-constructing Archaeology*. Cambridge, England: Cambridge University Press.

Stein, M. Aurel. 1937. *Archaeological Reconnaissances in Northwestern India and Southeastern Iran*. London: Macmillan and Co.

Steinkeller, Piotr. 1982. "The Question of Marhaši: A Contribution to the Historical Geography of Iran in the Third Millennium." *Zeitschrift für Assyriologie* 72, no. 3:237–265.

Van Gennep, Arnold. 1909. *Les Rites de Passage*. Paris: Presses Universitaires de France.

Wallerstein, Immanuel. 1974. *The Modern World System: Capitalist Agriculture and the Origins of the European World Economy in the Sixteenth Century*. New York: Academic Press.

———. 1980. *The Modern World System: Mercantilism and the Consolidation of the European World Economy 1600–1750*, vol. 2. Cambridge, England: Cambridge University Press.

Woolley, Charles Leonard. 1934. *Ur Excavations: The Royal Cemetery*. Philadelphia: British Museum and the University Museum of the University of Pennsylvania.

Zarins, Juris. 1978. "Steatite Vessels in the Riyadh Museum." *Atlal Journal of Saudi Arabian Archaeology* 2:65–93.

The Sign of the Object

John Dixon Hunt

As participants in the "History from Things" conference, we were all interested in objects; what we did not share were assumptions and methods for studying them. This seemed to some a disappointment, as if material culture could be respectable only if it was monoperspectival, only if despite the far-flung disciplines from which we came we all stood together. But the huge variety of objects and the huge discrepancies in how they are contextualized—by themselves, by us as historians—mean that a plurality of approaches will be inevitable and, I believe, essential.

The tenses of my first paragraph (past, present, and future) suggest the dilemma of my trying to rehearse some of my original and direct responses to Jules Prown's elegant and provocative opening paper, to acknowledge some of the

papers and discussions that followed, and yet also to write for the anticipated life of these after the conference. Evidently, others did not see
"Cultural Truth: History or Fiction" as being as provocative as I did, at
least until we had proceeded some way into the sessions. By then, my
original narrow focus needed adjusting to register the larger territory that
was being opened out: What I had tried to question about Prown's approach and assumptions was subtly but significantly changed as we took
on more material.

One issue raised by Prown is a problem not only for material culturalists: Can we, as he seemed to wish, step outside our own cultural
givens, our own time and place, and "interpret the evidence of another
culture objectively"? This traditional ambition of all scholarship—to be
objective—seemed with us to take the form of evading verbal language
and eluding gradations, hierarchies, and differences. The two approaches
are connected, since an anxiety to find common ground always tends—
and we were no exception—toward the residual, the lowest common denominator of things, artifacts, or methods, and this meant trying to do
without any evidence other than objects, which effectively meant neglecting verbal documents.

At issue throughout our discussions was the primacy of objects over
other documents. This could be and generally was construed as a battle of
things against words, but in my view it need not always be so. This in turn
raised other issues related to the kind of history we wanted to write. The
problem with all new histories—the history of furniture, the history of
religion, the history of gardens—is that they tend to confirm what we
already know from other, more traditional approaches. That was, as I
realized afterwards, the thrust of my interrogation of Prown. What our
history from objects should be doing is making it new—as Ezra Pound's
modernist slogan had it, telling us things that we either did not know
already or did not know in that particular way. But here again what we
already know tends to derive or seek support from the language we already have at our disposal; so a new history must find a new discourse,
not just a new set of materials to work with.

The tendency of born-again material culturalists to premise their
approach on the dismissal of the word should cause disquiet. Since much
of our discourse was verbal (that is, we did not sit in silence and look at
slides), we were in no position to deny the mediation of words (just as, I
take it, none of us denied that a slide of a teapot was nothing like handling
the real thing). Perhaps the problem was that we were so aware of how
words structured thinking that we felt obliged to throw the baby (words)

out with the bath water (thinking). We were in danger of becoming apt citizens of Swift's republic in Book 3 of *Gulliver's Travels*, where verbal discourse is safely bypassed by the simple expedient of carrying around sufficient objects to "trade" in conversation! The issue could perhaps be better formulated as whether we could reuse language innocently—that is to say, language innocent of a priori structures.

The very language Prown used to describe his teapots was metaphorical *avant la lettre* (as one might say)—the teapot had a "body," one of its elements was a "*hand*le"—and also denoted mathematical precisions with its use of the adverb "exactly" and its dimensional analysis. This language therefore brought to his objects references that had their own substance and discourse, and of course his presentation was the richer for this verbal density. Hegel said that objects lose their naturalness, singularity and immediacy the more thought enters into them. But Prown, although he wanted us to share with him the objects as objects, by his very words about the teapots introduced linguistically-formed thought into them.

He brought to his analysis, in short, a whole congeries of professional, cultural, and psychological insights. These betrayed his own professional and personal culture at a particular point in time. The very themes he wished to extract from the card tables, for example, were very American (would I as an Englishman have viewed them exactly in the same way?) and very contemporary (the role of games in pre– and post–revolutionary America), as well as male (the now obligatory gesture toward gender relations). Further, despite his somewhat defensive remarks about connoisseurship, that skill brings with it all the professional and personal imput that has created his particular approach along those lines. In other words, our own personal, professional, and historical formation determines the kind of history—whether from objects or not—that we write. From this I would conclude that since we cannot dissociate ourselves from what we bring to the study of objects, we should not try to engage with them in a minimalist way. Let us welcome whatever other resources will help us read them fully.

Another concern I had with the analysis of both teapots and card tables was that what we were asked to accept as history derived from these objects was surely a priori knowledge from a wide cultural field. To announce topics of study that a description of the tables *tout pures* promoted was to know about such topics from other sources. Even the strategy of arriving via the study of objects at themes that had apparently not been foregrounded before (for example, breasts) was somewhat disingenuous. Indeed, quite a few people wrote about breasts, childbirth, and child rearing in the eighteenth century; Simon Schama's *Citizens* acknowledges just such a leitmotif. But the prior knowledge of such a body of literature and painting would not have much suited the claims for the study of objects that we were making.

It is hard not to be misunderstood. I welcome the way that the study of objects will reorientate us within cultural history, seeing already established themes (gender relations, games and play *topoi*, psychological responses to the everyday world) from new angles. For example, Tom Williamson rightly challenged the habitual assumptions of English garden history that privilege the elite garden and therefore produce a narrative of the cutting edge of new taste and design development at any particular period. He argued for a wider spread of research to take into account the maps and estate plans of lesser gentry who were more in the business of keeping up with the Lord Joneses than in promoting fresh ideas themselves. Thus Williamson could propose a different garden history, where a new selection of objects (maps, plans, field surveys, and so on) enforced new explanations of local developments. So far so good: Not only had he shown how gardens will serve as objects for study, but also his interest in local varieties—a much smaller segment of British garden history than is usually studied—restored an interest to what might otherwise have been considered a minor phenomenon. So we had evaded the double bind of being forced by old language to review new objects in traditional ways, and we had let the new objects determine the kind of history that they needed.

Yet did this new garden history really change the old? To have talked of the great estates—Stowe, Stourhead, Blenheim—and of the great designers—Kent, Brown, Repton—and to have neglected those who followed or did not follow their lead had not been to evade the historical events with which we were now confronted. It gave them different priorities. What, in fact, this pursuit of a new garden history ensured was that Williamson could explain the creation of Norfolk gardens in the late seventeenth and eighteenth centuries in terms of different social, political, and artistic assumptions. His objects—gardens—yielded a history of material culture that was fresh not simply because he focused on them as objects but because he chose to ask different questions of those historical phenomena. He wanted a history of social and political change, mapped by locality; garden history had previously been—in the tradition of art history from which it in part sprang—a history of changing design and taste in elite, often global or national examples.

There remains one crucial matter. I was impressed by Prown's suggestion of objects as fictions, analogous to dreams. That seemed to open up the study of objects, give them a vitality and energy (and, yes, a respectability) that they sometimes seemed to lack. Yet I was uneasy about his invocation of metaphor, a complex form that has a strikingly verbal structure. (Indeed, can one have visual metaphor?) Objects are, unlike metaphors, unchanged by virtue of being loaded with other significance (for example, teapots freighted with messages about breasts, Federal card tables with intellectual superiority, and so on). In a metaphor both vehicle and tenor subtly yet crucially modify each other, while teapots as objects stay irredeemably teapotish.

Is it not more useful to think of teapots and other objects as signs? And to study such signs in the same way that Terry Winograd studied discourse (fig. 1)?

The study of objects, like discourse, would then focus on a series of translations. And the questions would concern, first, how speakers (I use the discourse terms) encode their messages, with certain goals, within given linguistic and other cultural contexts, and while attending to traditions or conventions of production and, second, how hearers decode (in the case of objects this could be a user or a later historian) within different schemas, in fresh contexts that involve both pragmatic and intellectual control. In both encoding and decoding there is an act of translation, finding in one "language" adequate terms to give a reliable account of something in another. We may stress and strive for a clear, objective view of the original in its new form but should do so in full awareness of how each of us represents the world in his or her own way. Or we may register—which would be my own preference—the relativity of the exercise: Our history of this object now is different from that archivist or document-based historian over there or the view of the same object one hundred years ago (both involve different decoders). And just as there is reuse of objects in successive generations, there are successive interpretations that displace or accrete meanings.

Speech-act theory also has some useful bearing on this too. And to think of objects either as signs or as speech-acts is essentially to acknowledge their variety, including the variety of their means, effects, range (the importance of their surface being is as essential as what is less immediately palpable), and therefore the variety of our necessary approaches to them as objects. It is also to locate *mentalité* at the very center of our study of objects. Objects may be viewed as "performances" with elements of both

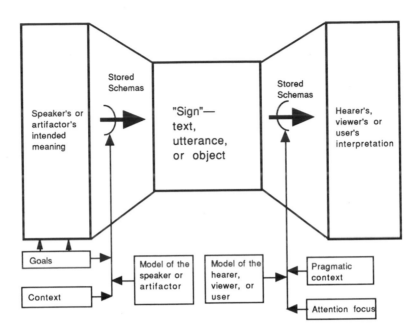

Fig. 1. Winograd's framework for understanding discourse. Based on a chart in Terry Winograd, "A Framework for Understanding Discourse," in Cognitive Processes in Comprehension, *edited by Michael A. Just and Patricia Carpenter (Hillsdale, N.J.: Lawrence Erlbaum Associates, 1977), p. 67.*

expression and communication. Such performances (translations into action, speech, gesture, or other shapes of emotions, beliefs, and ideas that exist independently of the new format) are more richly articulate than any subsequent gloss on them could possibly be: What they communicate by way of message is more translatable (because more simple) than what they convey by way of expression. This richness of expression that we find in objects is one reason that we surely want to foreground them, privilege their ontological status. Just as in the good old days nobody minded saying that they preferred a work of literature to criticism because the work was fuller, more compact, and more complex than the commentary, so with us the object appeals because within its sign is coded a richer range of meanings. It allows us more opportunities to perform as historians, for I agree wholeheartedly with Prown that the questions that objects pose are authentic ones.

Contributors

ROBERT W. BAGLEY is professor of art and archaeology, Princeton University, Princeton, New Jersey.

IAN W. BROWN is associate professor, University of Alabama, and curator of Gulf Coast archaeology, Alabama Museum of Natural History, Tuscaloosa.

MIHALY CSIKSZENTMIHALYI is professor of human development and education, department of psychology, University of Chicago.

ROBERT FRIEDEL is associate professor of history, University of Maryland, College Park.

ROBERT B. GORDON is professor of geophysics and applied mechanics, Yale University, New Haven, Connecticut.

JOHN DIXON HUNT is academic advisor to Oak Spring Garden Library, Upperville, Virginia.

MICHAEL OWEN JONES is professor of folklore and history, University of California, Los Angeles.

W. DAVID KINGERY is Regents Professor of Anthropology and Materials Science and Engineering, University of Arizona, Tucson.

C. C. LAMBERG-KARLOVSKY is Stephen Phillips Professor of Archaeology, Peabody Museum of Archaeology and Ethnology, Harvard University, Cambridge, Massachusetts.

MARK P. LEONE is professor of anthropology, University of Maryland, College Park.

PEIRCE LEWIS is professor of geography, Pennsylvania State University, University Park.

BARBARA J. LITTLE is an archaeologist with the National Park Service, National Capital Region, Washington, D.C.

STEVEN LUBAR is curator of engineering and industry, National Museum of American History, Smithsonian Institution, Washington, D.C.

JACQUES MAQUET is professor emeritus of anthropology, University of California, Los Angeles.

JULES DAVID PROWN is Paul Mellon Professor of the History of Art, Yale University, New Haven, Connecticut.

JESSICA RAWSON is keeper of oriental antiquities, the British Museum, London, England.

THOMAS WILLIAMSON is lecturer at the Center for East Anglia Studies, University of East Anglia, Norwich, England.

RITA P. WRIGHT is associate professor of anthropology, New York University, New York.